SO-DTQ-826

LITERACY ACROSS THE CURRICULUM

`A15045 483103`

Edited by

Carolyn Hedley

Dorothy Feldman

Patricia Antonacci

Fordham University

LC
151
. L47
1992
west

 ABLEX PUBLISHING CORPORATION
Norwood, New Jersey

Copyright © 1992 by Ablex Publishing Corporation

All rights reserved. No part of this publication may be reproduced, stored in a retrieval system, or transmitted, in any form or by any means, electronic, mechanical, photocopying, microfilming, recording, or otherwise, without permission of the publisher.

Printed in the United States of America

Library of Congress Cataloging-in-Publication Data

Literacy across the curriculum / edited by Carolyn Hedley, Dorothy
  Feldman, Patricia Antonacci.
     p.   cm.
    Includes bibliographical references and indexes.
    ISBN 0-89391-859-8.—ISBN 0-89391-915-2 (pbk.)
    1. Literacy—United States.   2. Interdisciplinary approach in
  education—United States.   3. Curriculum planning—United States.
  4. Literacy—United States—Evaluation.   I. Hedley, Carolyn N.
  II. Feldman, Dorothy.   III. Antonacci, Patricia.
  LC151.L47   1992
  375'.001—dc20   92-12459
                                        CIP

Ablex Publishing Corporation
355 Chestnut Street
Norwood, New Jersey 07648

With Love To Our Respective Husbands

Gene

Sam

Joe

Table of Contents

Preface

This volume is a culmination of a great deal of work that the three editors have done together at Fordham University: Dorothy Feldman has organized the Parents and Reading Conference at Fordham University for many years; Pat Antonacci, who teaches at Fordham, is President of the Westchester Reading Council and a program advisor to the annual conference of the New York State Reading Association; Carolyn Hedley has run the reading institute at Fordham University every summer for many years. Each of us has a current list of favorite speakers and topics we wanted to share around our reading theme, *Literacy Across the Curriculum*. *Literacy*, defined for our purposes here as thinking, talking, reading, and writing about classical works and more recently authored works of students useful in the subject areas, provided the basis for our collaboration.

Sponsoring an institute, or writing a book, should derive from a solid base of integrating and developing friendships; probably a foundation of long trust built on working together for many years fostered the Reading Institute, 1990. The conference seemed a pretty smooth operation—and a pleasure. The book that derived from our 2-week summer session was an equally delightful effort. Little temperament was displayed; editors and authors worked together agreeably and professionally toward task completion. We seem to be implementing what we're saying in this book, thus providing an authentic dimension to our collaboration.

ABOUT THE BOOK

Educators have become aware that classrooms must be interactive; that students must have models who speak well, write comfortably, and read transactionally, while working on tasks that are problem centered and relevant. Learning takes place during collaboration with knowledgeable adults and advanced peers, using considerate text structures that provide cultural and sociolinguistic relevance.

The goals of education are being changed to accommodate the development of higher level thought necessary to a technological society. If there is a lesson in the Gulf War, it is that we are in an era of unprecedented change. The assessment and evaluation procedures to look at this kind of technological and social change must be classroom based, ongoing, and appropriate to the objectives of global production and competition; the multiple choice or fill-in-the-blank test is no longer up to the task of evaluating what we really need to know to function in an electronic age. There is a growing sense that our management structures must alter along with our knowledge structures and strategic behaviors. Finally, we are truly in a new technical era, where we must understand other cultures and languages; data argue that our workforce populations will increasingly be urban, nonwhite, impoverished, and limited in English proficiency. Eighty-three percent of new workers will be a combination of women, minorities, and immigrants (Jones, Tinzmann, & Pierce, 1992). At the time of job entry, these populations will need a whole new set of abilities with which to function both socially and technically. Schools must change in a time when change itself is the only constant.

Policies and Practices for Literacy

The first section of the book deals with problems of schooling; the language policy and curriculum decisions that must be made for a multicultural, diverse, and changing society; and the literacy environment which promotes effective transmission of culture. What should the teacher be in classrooms of the 1990s? What is the nature of diversity and digression in these classrooms? These questions are discussed in the chapters that follow.

Charles Chew, head of the New York State Education Department, Language Arts Unit, writes in Chapter 1, "Policies for Literacy": "The direction for language arts instruction as a result of all this has been toward a process-oriented classroom, which focuses on all the language arts... The classroom which develops the creative language arts in students is one rich in language, rich in experience, and rich in adult as model." He elaborates his call to a life of the mind, including the aesthetic, literary, and cultural dimensions of humankind, in a style that can only be described as inspirational: the very person one would want to guide language learning policy at the state and national level. Thank heaven for Charlie.

In Chapter 2, "Learning Considered: A Model for Literacy Learning," Rita Brause deals with the crucial elements for establishing settings for learning. She states that learning is spontaneous, yet predictable, but not programmable. She describes the learner in the framework of motivation, attitudes, and commitment. Dr. Brause rounds out the chapter by setting the criteria for the evaluation of learning and the educator's responsibility for its occurrence.

Elizabeth LeBlanc and Carolyn Hedley work in the Fordham teacher preparation programs in quite different roles; but both have observed a fury of activity and busy-ness of teachers without an accompanying internal teacher response to their own professionalization. Chapter 3, "The Reflective Teacher," deals with the concerns of just what processes and strategies are involved in becoming more thoughtful, confident, and process-directed about what one is doing in classrooms. Classroom practice that derives from reflective problem-solving and decision-making processes of students and teachers is the focus of this chapter.

In Chapter 4, "The Virtues of Digression," Tom Newkirk tells us to abandon some of our habituated behaviors. He advises us to engage more in booktalk by students, to provide more opportunity for student participation, to become more open as teachers, and to appreciate and elaborate on student spontaneity, allowing children to deal with the "collective wisdom of mankind" in culturally sensitive, socially responsible ways. Being "totally on-task" may be inhibiting students' story making in our time. Dr. Newkirk more than makes the case for the "Virtue of Digression."

Strategies for Reading and Writing Across the Curriculum

In Part II, "Strategies for Reading and Writing Across the Curriculum," an implementation of ideas and policies discussed in the first section is our purpose; it's the "how to" of policy stated above. We need to learn how to set up and manage an interactive elementary classroom; we are provided methods and a model for the integration of reading and writing across the curriculum. There are various kinds of symbolism—language is but one. Visual thought, in the form of the children's art and the performing arts provide us graphic, visual, action models for thinking across the disciplines. In addition to visual thinking produced in art, we need specific language strategies for interactive reading and writing of text; a discussion of these factors and how they relate concludes the section on classroom practice.

Cora Five, in Chapter 5, "From Workbook to Workshop," claims as one product of her open, collaborative, literacy-oriented classroom: Her reading scores on standardized tests have greatly improved. No one has said that a literature-based classroom is less effective, but few persons have claimed that it is more efficacious in producing higher norm-referenced scores on multiple-choice tests. She describes her classroom; it's personalized, full of books, literacy events, and writing experiences. She has learned to listen, and she provides many student dialogues to make the point. The children know how to select books and have extended lists of books read to show their effort. Children are learning to think, to organize, and to produce. Finally, Ms. Five demonstrates how communication, evaluation, and research result from student process and production.

Ruth Nathan and Charles Temple in Chapter 6, "Classroom Environments for Reading and Writing Together," deal with demonstration in process writing and creative reading. Techniques for building trusting relationships with others, for sharing with students, for storycrafting, and for publishing are modelled. The authors deal with creating expository text, an often neglected genre. Proofreading and editing result; the authors demonstrate how these procedures are implemented across the curriculum areas. The classroom routines, presented toward the conclusion of their work, firm up the "how to" of teaching.

We debated on where to put Chapter 7, "Images: Partners with Words for Making Meaning," by Ruth Hubbard. It could have been a psychological treatise or a philosophical statement about the role of imagery in cognition. But the chapter was so full of common sense and wisdom, so replete with children's work and how to evaluate it, that we decided it could be used as a description of strategic behavior, and for assessment of children's thinking within the teaching framework. Pictures, graphic visual presentation of thought, or symbolism in pictured form are more basic to thought than the written word. Indeed, in other chapters, the point is made that the graphic presentation of information is closer to the way the mind works than the linear (written) presentation of thinking. Read on and see for yourself.

For the last chapter in this section, we culminate the discussion of strategic behaviors in reading and writing with Mary Ellen Vogt's work in Chapter 8, "Strategies for Leading Readers to Text." Dr. Vogt's strategies for approaching text and remembering it meet all the criteria for active reading—drawing on prior knowledge, becoming focused on the task, integrating new knowledge with old, working collaboratively with talented others, and integrating writing as part of reader response. The virtue of her work in Chapter 8 is that it is intended for the content area teacher, meeting the need for involving students in expository text.

Literacy Instruction and Assessment

Part III, "Literacy Instruction and Assessment," provides the teacher with one of the most needed dimensions of dynamic classrooms—how to evaluate student behavior, given the demise of extensive formal testing and a proposal of alternative assessment. The section begins with a sterling chapter on classroom-based and informal portfolio assessment, one of the best treatises on the subject yet, so have at it. Specific dynamics for story telling are presented in this section. Story retelling is one of the most powerful measures of comprehension and can be used as the basis for assessment, a model for the integration of learning and assessment of narrative knowledge results. Other evaluative models follow with the discussion of performance, projects, publications, and portfolios as sources for the evaluation of expository text.

Since we have already said that one must simply read Terry Salinger's chapter, "Classroom-Based and Portfolio Assessment for Elementary

Grades," in order to appreciate it, our best discussion of Chapter 9 is to underscore its high points: namely, Questions to Ask Before Beginning an Alternative Program, Entries for the Portfolio, Steps for Initiating and Evaluating a Portfolio Assessment, Rubric for Evaluation of Literacy Portfolios (a matrix), Checklists for Evaluation, Checklist for Monitoring Children's Strategies (children's reflective thinking), and others.

Dorothy Feldman and Pat Antonacci in Chapter 10, "Story Retelling: Combining Instruction and Assessment," provide a guide for narrative story retelling, one of the strongest strategies for evaluating comprehension. Graphic organizers for gathering and presenting information indicate specifically how evaluation of story occurs. A wealth of functional information exists here in a happy marriage of ideas and practice.

On the other hand, Denise Levine, using classroom-based assessment, evaluates comprehension of expository text balancing assessment of the understanding of story provided in the previous chapter. In Chapter 11, "The Four Ps of Context Based Assessment: Evaluating Literacy Across the Curriculum," Dr. Levine is interested in evaluation of multiple intelligences, including learner abilities in the performing arts, the humanities and the "hard" sciences. The Four Ps of alternative assessment are performance, presentations, publications, and portfolios, a nice mnemonic for remembering when you're doing evaluation. She uses the assessment of performance (drama, vocal and instrumental music, dance and storytelling as presented by artifacts—photos, slides, tapes, etc.), projects (and oral presentations), publications (perhaps simply logs or journals), and portfolios (the documentation and evidence of learning).

Stories and the Curriculum

Part IV of the book demonstrates our concern with the value of the many genres of story and poem in the curriculum. Literature can be integrated into all curriculum areas through the theme unit. In making the case for the inclusion of multicultural literacy across the curriculum, a lovely repertoire of techniques to teach science, math, or literature using the universal themes of ordinary life is presented in the first chapter of this section. How does the teacher move from story telling to its visual forms? In a felicitous chapter which begins with story, we are moved to discussion and dimensions of the performing arts in our work with children. Finally, a case for more common sense in allowing children to make choices for their own reading is made. Often we are too quick to close the options that may be essential to realistic problem solving.

Steven Tribus, who heads the New York City Board of Education Communications Arts Unit, has a legitimate interest in providing multicultural literacy experiences across the curriculum in a culture as diverse as that of the New York City metropolitan area. He runs teacher workshops of the most sensitive nature and applies his ideas for integrating literature, stories, poetry, drama, and the dance of many societies into the experiences of city school children. A refreshing application using some of the best world literature, stories, and poems in Chapter 12, "Multicultural Literature and the Curriculum," provides a demonstration of how to integrate the literature of many cultures into curricular subject matter, follows.

Bob Barton loves the story; he delights us with several stories and poems; then he shows us how children react to story and what a quick transition it is to move from their discussion to the dramatization of their interpretation of story. "Story Telling and the Drama Connection," Chapter 13 of our work, is a story in creation; the chapter shows us how to interpret children's discourse and help them create life stories and the many genres of drama.

We're running into censorship and the strict selection of reading matter for children in our society. Patricia Hermes, who has written many, many children's books, finds that she runs into objections when she deals with teen loss, suicide, and separation. Chapter 14, "If You Love Me, Read Me a Story," makes the case for allowing students to read books that may help them redefine and deal with their problems. Anecdotes and roles are used as demonstrations in a very convincing chapter.

Literacy Across the Curriculum

In Part V, we came to the conclusion that we should hear from the experts in the content areas. What are their views for integrating literacy practices throughout the subject areas? The section begins with a treatise for the introduction of multicultural experiences throughout the curriculum; it's a masterful presentation and a must-read. The authors in this section emphasize:

- that teachers must have grounding in the social sciences, geography as a case in point.
- that we must learn to make human stories of mathematical experience, eschew in rote learning. What makes for math problems that derive from life experiences, that are, at root, social experiences?
- that science teachers have developed a learning model, based on Piagetian constructs, for an interactive approach to science learning. Implications based on research of this model follow.

Our literary discussion on the case of literature across the curriculum for all populations includes the special learner; this chapter and bibliography for teachers of the special student is outstanding in its common-sense recommendations.

Clement London, in Chapter 15, "Curriculum as Transformation: A Case for the Inclusion of Multiculturality," nearly refutes the deconstructionists; he states a position for including diverse cultural thought and experience that is constructively integrative in a multicultural society. He does not eschew a moral posture. Human well-being and interest mandate that we make curriculum adjustments, that we engage in a curriculum transformation given the multicultural crucible that is our cultural heritage; minority needs have become majority concerns. We must be more creative in what has been called a new world order: fostering a curriculum of inclusion based on those very human and customary dynamics of argument, discussion, research, and intellectual and social agreement. He calls on the past, on reflective educators, to create the future.

"What Should a Teacher Know About the Social Studies?" asks Sam Natoli. In Chapter 16, Dr. Natoli demonstrates how little is known about the content of each of the social sciences (history, economics, governance, sociology, anthropology, and geography), using geography as a case in point. First, he explains that the social sciences need not be boring, nor a litany of facts and dates; the social studies should be useful and enriching and should foster a sense of stewardship regarding the planet earth. His discussion of the value, myths, thinking, and teaching of the social studies, particularly geography, follows.

In "Communicating in Mathematics," Drs. Driscoll and Powell (Chapter 17) state that the focus of mathematical teaching has changed. They are considering the urban at-risk student who, like many of us, is confused by the language of mathematics. These two math experts have worked out a system for doing and constructing (or reconstructing) math, defined as "the language and science of patterns." A Powell-created program for thinking and communicating in math follows, whereby students look for lifelike numerical experiences and operations, as a function of quantitative insight.

"The Learning Cycle" in science, described by Ed Marek in Chapter 18, includes a three-part paradigm: exploration, conceptual invention, and expansion, based on Piaget's mental model and is used as the basis of research in this discussion of measurement of conceptual understanding in science. Dr. Marek, in "Conceptualizing in Science," reports research on several exploratory studies: age/developmental research, teaching strategies, misconceptions of students, teaching practices, and misconceptions of teachers. Dr. Marek writes: "measuring concept understanding has occurred in many forms: multiple-choice questions, essay questions, clinical interviews, and combinations of these forms." It is becoming apparent that unobtrusive assessment is an approved method in science!

Nancy Ellsworth, in our final chapter (Chapter 19), "Literature for the Special Learner: The Urban At-Risk Student," discusses new dimensions of literacy in the United States, particularly as they influence the special learner. She draws upon her experience as an English teacher to suggest how children at risk can be taught effectively. She provides valuable references for the teacher of literature to the at-risk student, followed by an outstanding list of resources for teachers of the special learner.

ACKNOWLEDGMENTS

Special thanks must be given our authors. All of them are able collaborators; we appreciate the time they took to prepare their presentations, and later, their chapters. It's nice to know that you can work with a long roster of contributors, yet have not one distressing experience. Their names and achievements are listed in the section which follows. We also are grateful to a supportive administration within the School of Education—namely, Anthony Baratta, Regis Bernhardt, and Max Weiner. Fordham University has always underwritten our efforts to some extent we want to acknowledge the University's support of production and publication. Accolades to our students, who in many cases, have turned into the well-known colleagues who contribute to these volumes; their support and suggestions are invaluable. Heartfelt appreciation to Barbara Bernstein, editor at Ablex, who is a treasure in the publishing world. Would that every editor was as supportive! Thanks to Anne Goldstein, who does such a good job of typing these manuscripts. We have dedicated this book to our respective husbands, just because they are wonderful.

Carolyn Hedley
Dorothy Feldman
Patricia Antonacci
Winter 1991

REFERENCES

Jones, B.F., Tinzmann, M.B., & Pierce, J. (1992). How thoughts are made. In *Building the quality of thinking in and out of school in the twenty-first century.* Hillsdale, NJ: Erlbaum.

The Authors

Patricia Antonacci. Patricia Antonacci is president of the Westchester Reading Association and is very active in the International Reading Association and the New York State Reading Association. She teaches in the Westchester schools and at Fordham University at Lincoln Center and at Tarrytown. She has developed several reading programs and is active in the development of assessment techniques in the Yonkers public schools. Dr. Antonacci has authored chapters in the books *Whole Language and the Bilingual Learner* and *Reading and the Special Learner*; she is widely published in reading journals and is editor of *Natural Approaches to Reading and Writing*.

Bob Barton. Bob Barton believes that story telling and drama are among the most dynamic strategies available to teachers for nurturing imagination and fostering a love of reading and writing which is written about in his books, *Tell Me Another: Storytelling and Reading Aloud at Home and in the Community* and *Stories in the Classroom: Storytelling, Reading Aloud and Role Playing with Children* (coauthored with David Booth). Dr. Barton is a former teacher (elementary, secondary, postsecondary), Language Arts Consultant, and Coordinator of the Arts. In addition to being well known as a story teller, Dr. Barton has been an artist in residence at Artpark, Lewiston, New York, and has been a regular member of the story-telling programs at the Hans Christian Andersen Story Hour in New York's Central Park.

Rita Brause. Rita Brause is a professor at Fordham University Graduate School of Education. She is well known for her work on the teacher as researcher. Dr. Brause has published widely in language and reading journals, including the *English Journal, Language Arts,* and *Research in the Teaching of English*. Dr. Brause has written two books: *Search and Re-Search: What the Inquiring Teacher Needs to Know* (with J. Mayher), and *Enduring Schools: Expedience Replaces Excellence*.

Charles Chew. Charles Chew is director of language and reading programs for the New York State Education Department. He is widely respected for his integrity and wisdom regarding policy making at the New York State level. Dr. Chew has written and spoken widely at the New York

State Reading Association (NYSRA), the International Reading Association (IRA), and the National Council of the Teachers of English (NCTE). Dr. Chew has written two books: *Reflections by Teachers Who Write,* and *Reader Response in the Classroom*; he has several other books in press.

Mark Driscoll. Mark Driscoll is project director of the Mathematics Reform Project; additionally he is director of the Technical Assistance Project to the Urban Mathematics Collaboratives. His writings include *Stories of Excellence: Ten Case Studies from a Study of Exemplary Mathematics Programs, Teaching Mathematics: Strategies that Work,* and other books. His AB degree is from Boston College and his MA and PhD are from Washington University in St. Louis.

Nancy Ellsworth. Nancy J. Ellsworth, who is a professor at Fordham University's Graduate School of Education, has taught children as a reading specialist and special education teacher, and as an English and social studies teacher. She has published in *Exceptionality* and the *Journal of Reading, Writing and Learning Disabilities International.* Dr. Ellsworth received her BA and MA from Stanford University and her MEd and EdD from Columbia University, Teachers College.

Dorothy Feldman. Dorothy Feldman is a reading coordinator in the New York City schools, where she does teacher training; she is head of the STAR Program there. She is an adjunct professor at Fordham University and at Hunter College. For 10 years, she has been the Chairman of the annual Parents and Reading Conference at Fordham University, in addition to being a coordinator of the Reading Institute.

Cora Five. Cora Five has made a commitment to being a classroom teacher in Scarsdale, New York; she is highly active in professional organizations in Scarsdale. She has given workshops in the Lincoln Center Program for the Performing Arts; additionally she speaks widely at such conferences as NCTE, ASCD, NYSRA, IRA, and NYSEC. She has many articles and chapters in books, notably *Breaking Ground: Teachers Relate Reading and Writing in the Elementary School* edited by Newkirk and Graves. Her most recent book is *Special Voices.*

Carolyn Hedley. Carolyn Hedley, a co-director of the annual Reading Institute and professor of reading at Fordham University's Graduate School of Education, is active in the New York State Reading Association and is Vice President of the Westchester Reading Council. Dr. Hedley is co-editor and author of the books *Contexts of Reading, Home and School: Early Language* *and Reading, Reading and the Special Learner, Cognition Curriculum and Literacy, Whole Language and the Bilingual Learner,* and *Natural Approaches to Reading and Writing,* in addition to this volume. Dr. Hedley has published numerous articles in journals related to reading and writing instruction.

Patricia Hermes. Patricia Hermes is a children's author of numerous award-winning books for children and young adults. Some of her most recent titles include: *Heads, I Win; A Place for Jeremy;* and her first nonfiction book, *A Time to Listen (Preventing Youth Suicide).* Ms. Hermes is a recipient of the California Young Reader Medal, the Iowa Teen Award, the Pine Tree Book Award, the Hawaii Nene Award, and the Crabberry Award. One of her books was named an ALA Best Book of the Year. She speaks nationally and internationally on writing for children and the ethics of publication.

Ruth Hubbard. Ruth Hubbard received her BA from Colby College and her MA and PhD from the University of New Hampshire, working with Donald Graves, Thomas Newkirk, Jane Hansen, and others. Currently, she is an assistant professor in the Graduate School of Professional Studies at Lewis and Clark College in Oregon, working on teacher education programs related to early literacy, including graphic art as a dimension of literacy. She has written two books, *Authors of Pictures, Draughtsmen of Words;* and *Literacy in Process: Theory and Practice.*

Elizabeth LeBlanc. Elizabeth LeBlanc is professor in the Graduate School of Education, where she is in charge of teacher preparation programs. Formerly she was director of teacher education at Seton Hall. She received her doctorate from Rutgers University.

Denise Levine. Denise Levine is a teacher and reading coordinator in the New York City public schools and an adjunct professor at Fordham University. She recently received her doctorate from Fordham University in Language, Literacy, and Learning; she speaks widely and has run many teacher workshops on the writing process and on informal assessment; she has written many articles for the various NCTE journals.

Clement B.G. London. Clement London is a professor in the Division of Curriculum and Teaching in the Graduate School of Education at Lincoln Center. He coordinates the masters degree programs in curriculum studies and social studies education. He has published many books and articles on the Caribbean, having been brought up in Trinidad. His most recent publication is *Through Caribbean Eyes,* an oral history of the independence movement of Trinidad-Tobago. He has his doctorate from Columbia University, Teachers College.

Edmund Marek. Edmund Marek writes and teaches at the University of Oklahoma, where he is head of the Science Education Center. His articles, books, and grants are well known in science education, numbering into the hundreds. He receives many grants in science education and works in support of the local and national ecological systems. Dr. Marek is known for his teaching and has received the outstanding teacher award on at least two occasions, once from the Norman public schools and the other as a professor at the University of Oklahoma.

Ruth Nathan. Ruth Nathan is an Adjunct Professor at Oakland University, Rochester, Michigan, where she co-directs the Psychology Department's Reading Research Team. She is the director of several process-writing projects in the state; she is co-author of *The Beginnings of Writing* and *Classroom Strategies that Work: An Elementary Teachers Guide to Process Writing.* She is a contributor to such publications as *The Journal Book,* edited by Toby Fulwiler, and *Reading and Writing Environments,* edited by Timothy Shanahan, in addition to many journals in reading and writing education. Ruth speaks frequently at the NCTE. In addition to her many other contributions, she is a teacher in the Oakland public schools. She lives with her husband Larry and their three children.

Salvatore Natoli. Salvatore Natoli is Director of Publications and Editor of Social Education for the National Council of the Social Studies in Washington, DC. Prior to joining NDSS in 1987, Dr. Natoli was Deputy Director and Education Affairs Director for the Association of American Geographers. Dr. Natoli, an urban geographer, has taught at the junior and senior high school level and for many years at colleges and universities. He is author or editor of more than 60 publications in geography and he has recently authored or edited *Institutionalizing the Undergraduate Curriculum in Geography, Strengthening Geography in the Social Studies,* and *Social Studies and Social Sciences: A Fifty Year Perspective.* Most recently, he has written, "How a Geographer Views Globalism" in the *International Journal for the Social Studies.*

Thomas Newkirk. Thomas Newkirk is an associate professor of English and Director of Freshman English at the University of New Hampshire; additionally, he is director of the New Hampshire Writing Program since 1980 and the Writing Process Laboratory. He is a member of the Editorial Board of the National Council of Teachers of English. He has written *More than Stories: The Range of Children's Writing* and *Teachers Relate Reading and Writing in the Elementary School,* among others. Additionally, he is co-editor (with D. Graves and J. Hansen) of *Breaking Ground: Teachers Relate Reading and Writing in the Elementary School,* and editor of *To Compose: Teaching Writing in the High School.*

Arthur Powell. Arthur Powell is an associate professor at Rutgers University in Newark, where he teaches underachieving students in the Academic Foundations Department. He is a student of Freire and Cattegno, having written extensively on their contributions to mathematics education for underachieving students. He has published widely in such journals as: *Mathematics Education and Society, Science and Nature, Mathematics Teaching,* and *Mathematics in College.* Mr. Powell has taught in various mathematics projects, nationally and internationally, including Israel and France. He has received degrees from Hampshire College and the University of Michigan.

Terry Salinger. Terry Salinger is a researcher and test developer at Educational Testing Service; her special interests include alternative assessment of teachers and issues of equity in testing. She particularly focuses on teacher assessment alternatives to multiple-choice testing through the use of constructed responses, portfolios, and observations. Formerly she was a professor at the University of Texas and the University of Cincinnati. Dr. Salinger is author of *Language Arts and Literacy for Young Children;* she is widely published, focusing equally on reading and writing processes in young children, with particular interest in writing with computers, and on the teacher assessment alternatives noted above.

Charles Temple. Charles Temple teaches future teachers at Hobart and William Smith Colleges in Geneva, New York, where he chairs the Education Department. He writes songs for and with elementary students. He has done pioneer research on invented spelling with Edmund Henderson at the University of Virginia and is now investigating the ways children think about stories. He recently co-edited *Classroom Strategies that Work: An Elementary Teacher's Guide to Reading and Writing.* He has just completed the book, *Stories and Readers* with Patrick Collins. In addition he has written three other books on children's writing. Dr. Temple has been a Fulbright scholar in Portugal.

Steven Tribus. Steven Tribus is head of the Communications Arts Unit of the Board of Education of the New York City public schools. He is an authority on multicultural literacy and poetry and speaks at national and international conferences and workshops. He is the author of *Writing as a Tool for Learning.*

Mary Ellen Vogt. Mary Ellen Vogt is an assistant professor of education at California State University at Long Beach. She is former president of the California State Reading Association and holds high offices in the International Reading Association. She is author of *Responses to Literature: Grades K-8* and has articles in *Reading Today, School of Education Journal, The*

California Reader, and others. She is a favored speaker at the various language conventions, NCTE, IRA, and NYSRA, speaking to the topic of strategic reading behaviors. Dr. Vogt recently received her doctorate from the University of California, Berkeley.

PART I

POLICIES AND PRACTICES FOR LITERACY ACROSS THE CURRICULUM

Chapter 1

Policies for Literacy

Charles R. Chew

For my discussion of this topic, *policies for literacy*, I must first establish a basis of meaning for what follows—as my meaning may not be yours.

Policies suggest to me a definite course or method of action selected from among alternatives that, in light of given conditions, guide and determine present and future decisions. Literacy is competence in language arts— reading, writing, listening, and speaking. Although I know literacy can encompass any number of other areas of media, for the most part, I will not address these in what follows.

I want then to write about some of the courses of action that we need to take that will affect the development of language competence in our students.

For more than 10 years, there has been a revolution going on in the area of language arts. I trace the start of this revolution to a number of factors which came together at the same time. In the 1970s, there was a growing dissatisfaction with the product produced by our schools. Businesses, community, parents, and educators began to question the inability to read and write by those students graduating from our secondary schools.

At the same time research findings, particularly those of Donald Graves and his researchers in New Hampshire, began to suggest that there was a different way of approaching writing instruction, and that most of us had underestimated what students can actually do.

Many states, and New York led the way, began to move toward an assessment program which required students to write whole pieces of text and demanded that teachers rate what had been written. This approach was supported by curricular development that focused on process.

The direction for language arts instruction as a result of all this has been toward a process-oriented classroom which focuses on all of the language arts. I want to look at this process from the writing perspective and suggest that it has helped to integrate the language arts and provides the possibility for more literate students as well as teachers.

PROCESS

The recent discussion of, and implementation of, the writing process in our classrooms today provides the groundwork for developing an understanding of the connections among the language arts. Some of the most recent research strengthens these connections (see Calkins & Harwayne, 1990). However, before proceeding further, let us review, in a general way, the writing process as detailed and accepted in much of the professional discussion today.

We seem to agree that the writer goes through several stages in order to produce a finished product—prewriting (getting ready), drafting (getting it down), revising (changing and rearranging), editing (polishing for another's eye), and publishing (sharing). We know that a writer does not move through this process in a linear fashion but rather may be involved in the process in a recursive manner which permits movement back and forth between and among stages. The separation between reading, writing, listening, and speaking are not even as definite as they once were. Such action depends upon need, self-generated or required by an outside demand.

We have learned that individual authors do not move through the various stages in the same way and do not have the same needs or style; however, we have come to accept the idea that the stages are important as the writer moves toward an end product.

I now want to discuss these stages and suggest the similarities and connections to reading, speaking, listening, and to consider instructional implications.

Prewriting (Getting Ready)

The writer prepares for the task and can do so in a number of ways. These include but are not limited to: reading, note taking, questioning, interviewing, prewriting, reworking previous material, brainstorming, mapping and webbing, discussing, researching, thinking, dreaming, and drawing. The writer may begin to make some initial determinations about purpose, form, and audience, but at this point these may not be major determinants of what is yet to follow. Several researchers suggest that the mere act of writing will determine for the writer what is to be said (Elbow, 1981; Graves, 1983).

Whatever is included in this prewriting stage, we all agree that the majority of writers will do some of the above in order to move along in the process. For you, the teacher, the opportunity to integrate rests in the fact that the reader, listener, and speaker also pass through a similar "getting ready" stage, and such knowledge can be valuable information as you look at ways to enhance instruction.

The reader gets ready to read, and one should find ways to focus on this aspect of reading in order to produce more able readers. As readers, do we not capitalize on prior knowledge? Don't we raise questions about the forthcoming text? Preview materials? Make predictions? Begin to consider the purpose of the text and its meaning to us? Are these activities similar, and connected, to many of those just discussed in relation to prewriting?

Doesn't the listener/speaker go through a getting ready stage? Even with the most casual of conversations, the listener/speaker draws upon prior knowledge/familiarity of the context, manner of speech, mentally raises questions to be answered, or predicts directions in which the communication will go.

In more formal listening/speaking situations the parallels of this stage are more apparent. The listener commences with prior knowledge and questions to be answered. The listener begins to integrate what is heard with what is known or predicted would come, making some determination of the speaker's purpose and intent. For a more formal speaking situation, the speaker may well go through exactly the same type of preparation as does the author.

For instruction, the message is clear. The connections are there; we must take full advantage of them to strengthen the development of our students' language ability. A very practical suggestion would be to spend more time getting students ready for the task at hand by concentrating on some of the activities suggested above and by recognizing that getting ready time is vital in all the language arts areas.

Drafting and Revising (Getting It Down and Changing It)

These two stages are best discussed for the purpose of showing similarities among the various language arts segments in process.

The writer begins to write sustained discourse, letting the words flow unimpeded by a need for correctness as does the reader whose eyes begin to move quickly across the page. The notion of purpose, form, audience begins to emerge, and for the writer the product begins to take shape in its roughest form. At this stage, language is explored, words chosen, sentences formed. Meaning starts to emerge. No different for the reader, listener, speaker.

The listener tries to take in as much of the language as possible—connecting one thought to the next and mentally trying to link what is being said with what is known and what may be expected. Those preparing a formal speech may pass through the same process as the writer and even those who speak formally in an extemporaneous manner in all likelihood pass through similar steps.

In order to bring the piece to completion, the writer in most cases will revise what has been written during the drafting stage. Here the writer may eliminate, rearrange, elaborate, change what has been written. New words may be chosen, sentences reordered, or ideas joined and expanded as the piece takes on purpose, form, and consideration is given to the audience.

Is such a stage available to the reader, the listener? I believe it is. The reader certainly does not physically reorder the text, but mentally doesn't the reader revise? Predictions may be altered, new questions formulated. Sections of the text may be reread, paragraphs or sentences mentally eliminated, as the reader attempted to find meaning in the written words.

The listener may be engaged in the same process—reformulating what has been heard and making connections to prior knowledge or questions yet to be answered.

Instructional strategies therefore must consider and reflect the idea that all the language arts accommodate a drafting and revision stage.

Editing (Polishing It for Another's Eye)

At this stage the writer imposes the conventions of language on his or her product. Correct spelling, punctuation, capitalization, and acceptable usage are brought to bear on the written text. The speaker differs in the necessity of imposing these conventions as the speech is prepared or produced. The speaker has as aids intonation, body language, audience reaction (enabling perhaps on-the-spot revision), and the pause. The listener may not necessarily impose editing but is certainly assisted by the speaker's use of those listed above. Likewise the reader can more easily obtain meaning from the text through these conventions and may in fact impose mentally some of his or her own on the text.

Much of our time in the English classroom focuses on this stage of the process, and we have spent an inordinate amount of energy focusing on skills that need to be taught. We need to recognize that they are most sensibly taught at this stage of process, because it is at this stage that students can best be helped to see the relationships among the skills taught and the need for their use.

Publishing (Sharing)

The final stage of the process is publishing—making what has been relatively private, public. This stage does not necessarily have to be elaborate or formal and can range from pieces on the bulletin board to published books, but the idea is the sharing of what has been written with an audience—the act of communication.

Many of us in the profession have only now come to realize that this act is as necessary to insure the comprehensibility of text, and it has been stated that it takes two to read a book. Obviously the speaker is engaged in this final stage more often than not, but the case for similarities on the part of the listener are a little more difficult to discern. Perhaps that is because we do not often require the listener to share in much the same way that we are beginning to require of the reader.

Opportunities to connect the language arts through writing process are numerous. Any teacher who claims to have his or her class involved in this process, who is not involved in all of the language arts, is *not* engaged in writing process. In order for process to happen, students and teacher must be immersed in listening, speaking, and reading as well as writing, a course of action well worth considering.

This change of direction toward an integrated, process-oriented literacy development also holds the promise that all will recognize that language is central to all learning and is indeed a creative art.

The dictionary gives the definition of *creativity* as bringing into existence, making for the first time something from what appears to be nothing—bring into being—expressive of the maker.

Oliver Wendell Holmes said that every language is a temple in which the soul of those who speak it is enshrined. Another has claimed that language is the memory of the human race. It is a thread or nerve of life running through all ages, connecting them into one common, prolonged, and advancing existence.

Language indeed separates the humans from the animals. Language was created by man and woman and therefore embodies the elements of the definition of creativity given above. Even though language is not unique in the sense that it surrounds us in our daily lives, it is unique—created—each time a human being makes use of it. Even though the words which we use have a commonality of them, they are created anew each time used to meet the needs and purposes of the user.

And so the same thought can be expressed in many different ways. As from the *Iliad*:

> They die
>> An equal death—the idler and the man
>> Of mighty deeds.

Andrew Jackson puts it this way:

> When death comes, he respects neither age nor merit. He sweeps from earthly existence the sick and the strong, the rich and the poor.

Or Longfellow:

> There is a reaper whose name is Death
>> And with his sickle keen
>> He reaps the bearded grain at a breath
>> And the flowers that grow between.

Because we have not become the race of mutants that much of our science fiction literature depicts, in which we would be without creative thought and have little control of our language, we should recognize that, even when students are repeating the same words or groups of words, these students are creating.

Language is the essential ingredient of our discipline, and I have suggested that the use of language is creative even when more than one person is using the same language; therefore, it must follow that all strands of the English/language arts have the elements of creativity.

I would like to expand on this idea as it pertains particularly to reading and writing.

We do not usually think of the art of reading as creative and yet we know from the research in and discussion of the reading process that the reader creates from the written page. It is what the reader brings to the written work that creates meaning. It is from the vast resources of experience and knowledge (or lack of them) that the reader breathes meaning into what has been composed by the author. And just as we have seen in my previous examples, different approaches to the same idea by different writers, we each brought diverse meanings to the words read. And I have not touched upon the acts of rereading, reorganization, reinterpreting, and recreating that the reader does.

In composing, the creative act may not be as difficult to discern because the author must take the words and fashion them, invent an order and form to accomplish a purpose, to communicate a message. One such form immediately recognized as a creative art is poetry. It has been said that poetry is the eldest sister of all art and the parent of most. Another has described poetry as the queen of the arts. Another tells us that poetry is an art and chief of the fine arts: the easiest to dabble in, the hardest in which to reach true excellence.

I have said many times that I believe all writing is creative. Even the most banal business letter written for the RCT (Regent's Competency Test) has an element of creativity in it—perhaps not easily seen after rating 50 or so holistically, and perhaps not as easily appreciated as a line from Shakespeare or Faulkner. But each time we put pen to paper, there is invention; there is that expression of the maker or creator.

The same line of argument or reasoning can, I believe, be applied to the areas of listening and speaking, but I will not belabor the point.

Let me now spend just a few minutes looking at some similarities or crossovers between the language arts and the other recognized creative arts—music, dance, painting, sculpture, photography. In each case the artist, whether musician (performer or composer), dancer, painter, sculptor tries to communicate something to someone; and each is, to a certain extent, concerned with the effect of that piece of art on a reader, listener, viewer, etc. So there is a purpose for the piece.

Each art form is fashioned from a medium whether words, notes, colors, shading, and the like. Truman Capote observed that writing has lines of perspective, of light and shade, just as do painting and music. Nearly all of these art forms are based on some concept of organization, some discernible pattern, some relationship of parts to whole, perhaps a beginning and an end; and I believe too that the doer in each of these areas truly believes that someone who reads, hears, or sees the creation will bring additional meaning to it.

I believe then that definite parallels can be drawn between Language Arts and the other arts, and just as these are considered creative, so too is Language Arts. I further believe that the skills we look for and try to develop in the painter, the composer, the sculptress, are the same skills we should strive to develop in the English/Language Arts classroom.

We as teachers must guarantee that students are comfortable with the medium of expression in English—their language—just as the artist must feel comfortable and knowledgeable about colors, perspective, and the like. Students must be surrounded by language—not just receivers but users as well. Quiet classrooms except for teacher talk do not necessarily develop creative approaches to language or experiences in it.

Experiences need to be expanded. Mencken said that nothing can come out of the artist that is not in the man (or woman). Our students will not bring a creative response to their reading if they have not had a wide and full background of literature, which must begin at least as early as their schooling begins.

As with the recognized artist, much time must be given over to practice—the prima ballerina, the concert pianist, and the recognized author reach that point through practice—so too the student in the classroom. The language user does not develop merely by filling in blanks on worksheets; the accomplished speaker does not reach that point without opportunities to speak; so too the writer and listener. But I do not mean to suggest just practice without purpose. Direct and planned instruction must accompany this practice.

The classroom that develops the creative language arts student is one rich in language, rich in experience, and rich in adults as models. We cannot expect our students to be enthusiastic readers, writers, or speakers if they do not have role models which set examples of the joy of the use of language, the excitement of the written pages, and the richness of the writing experience.

The integrating of the language arts has not in reality moved any of the areas—listening, speaking, reading, or writing—center stage to the exclusion of all others. In fact, just the opposite has happened. We find a resurgent focus on literature, and an intensified interest in listening and speaking.

Recent discussion in the professional literature indicates that reading is an active, comprehension-centered process, and that literature provides a vital content for the process-oriented classroom. The ability to read and comprehend enables students to become engaged with literature, which, in turn, nurtures the imagination, provides vicarious experience, promotes insight into human behavior, and makes readers aware of the universal nature of human experience. Readers can learn to appreciate their own heritage and respect the heritage of others.

Connections with books must begin early—one would hope in the home—but if not, surely then in school. Children need to be read to, immersed in literature and the joy it brings. You will discover a number of interesting characteristics of books available for young children, and you can begin to appreciate the importance these characteristics have for developing readers.

SIMILARITIES OF STORY PATTERNS

We know that many of our stories begin with that famous opening, "Once upon a time." Children begin to recognize that structure of story. They understand that the story begins and moves to another point. In *The Gingerbread Man* as the storyline develops, part of the story is repeated. The gingerbread man meets a character, voices his line—"Run, run as fast as you can. You can't catch me, I'm the gingerbread man." That line is repeated as is the list of people chasing him, adding a new character as the story moves along. *Henny Penny* uses a similar pattern as well.

Our students meet this same concept in literature that they read through the grades—required and recreational. Plots are similar in development and stories fall into a recognizable pattern to their conclusion.

REPETITION

In all books appropriate for young children, you will find repetition—repetition of words, sentences, parts of the story, and repetition of ideas. Stories, songs, and poems use this device. "I Know an Old Lady" and "I

Was Walking Down the Road" are appreciated by young readers. Lest we believe that such a literary device is only found in literature for young children, we need to look again at the words of Poe, Shakespeare, Longfellow, and Frost—to name just a few—to see the importance of this literary device in works students will read in their school careers and in their life.

PLAYFULNESS OF LANGUAGE

Literature capitalizes on opportunities to play with language, to experiment with it, and to highlight the rhyme and melody of it. Dr. Seuss immediately comes to mind as an example of this type of literature. Examples of pieces of literature that celebrate the playfulness of languages, however, do not stop with children's poems and stories. We find melody, rhyme, and experimentation throughout our experiences with reading. Few children emerge from school without an encounter with Lewis Carroll's *Jabberwocky*. We all have delighted in Ogden Nash's use of language and the sound of his words.

Stories do other things for readers as well. They put them in touch with their own reality as made clear in *Living Between the Lines*. Stories expand the knowledge base, and we see this confirmed in classes where students are seeking answers to questions that have been raised in their peer conferences or class activities connected to reading and projects. Stories connect people—the young with the old, one culture with another, and individuals to ideas, challenges, problems, and solutions.

PERSPECTIVES FOR LITERACY

A definite course of action in the English/Language Arts class has to place literature as an equal component in the program. No longer can we teach reading without books. Reading is not taught through drill and practice worksheets, activity cards, or cloze passages, but primarily through books.

We have to reaffirm that students will be the main focus of education. As I sit at numerous meetings in the course of my job responsibilities, I sometimes wonder, "Where are the students in all of this deliberation?" We seem to forget that schools exist for children—not the teachers, not the administrators, certainly not for the State Education Department.

A particularly important question that each of us must ask is, "Who is it we serve?" for indeed, we are a service rendering profession. We serve the children in our classrooms. As IBM, General Motors, Proctor & Gamble, and Toyota know, in order to stay in business, they must know their consumer. We are no different. In order to teach, we must know the students we are teaching.

This socioeconomic research of the day tells us that the school population has changed.

Do you know the child who has been kept awake all night because his alcoholic parents are beating on each other; do you know the child whose mother is a drug user and seller; do you know the boy or girl who works 35–55 hours a week to bring money into the house to feed younger brothers and sisters; do you know the girl who is pregnant but does not know what choices she has; do you know the thousands of kids who come to school with empty stomachs and empty lives, those who hear nothing but the din of verbal abuse and are subjected to another 6 hours in school? Do you know these children? No, they are not only in the South Bronx or in the streets of Chicago. These children inhabit every community. So school cannot continue as usual!

Our alternative is to reorder our priorities and our children need to be at the top of our list. If we were to ask most of our citizens, "Do you think children are important?" we would be greeted by a response that would suggest we are teetering on the brink of insanity. But our record as a nation suggests that we do not value children. Poverty of children has become a national disgrace. The lack of basic health care, housing, and safety for large numbers of children condemns us as a nation. The infant mortality rate, particularly of our minority children, indicates we have not kept pace even with many of the smaller nations of the world.

Our children are our salvation as well as the world's.

We may have to reorient our classroom and our teaching, because I have yet to enter a process classroom where children were intimidated by an adult. Therefore, we will be forced to conclude that we no longer are the only dispensers of knowledge—rather we too are learners; we learn from children and each other.

We do not know all the answers, but we can facilitate learning. We create an environment where good things happen, kids are excited, and we whet children's appetites to know. We make children secure and safe, so that our literate environment can penetrate their lives.

Our children's enthusiasm is our best PR. We know good things are taking place, and we get our colleagues and ourselves to brag about those things.

Doesn't it strike you as odd that, while 50 governors assembled in Virginia several years ago to discuss what was wrong with education, just across the river 2,000 school people gathered to accept commendations for their schools of excellence? Why didn't one of our high-level planners have enough sense to bring these two groups together? Has a clear message been given that, to better our schools, we must turn to those outside of education?

Therefore, we must be scholars. We must know the underlying theory and research that support our instructional practices. One would not think of entering chemotherapy without knowing the underlying premise that supports this radical treatment. Are lives of children so less important that we willingly accept programs and materials that we do not understand and do not believe in—continue instructional practice that has not one iota of support in theory or research? Do we really believe that we can attend a 2-day whole language conference and immediately become well versed and ready to practice, and that change can be accomplished in a 9-month school year?

We may have to change some of that classroom practice. We need to realize that we are no longer the guardians of meaning—the keeper of the text. Oh yes, we have our master's degrees—our 30 credits beyond—our courses on Shakespeare, Chaucer, the Lake Poets, and the transcendentalists, but we do not possess the only reading of text. Too often as English teachers we have—because of our professionalism, because of our knowledge, because of our sheer generosity and out of the goodness of our heart—told our students what the text meant—we now know because of our probing in reading response theory that this approach does not prove us to be scholars. Scholarship mediates against what I term the DRP approach to instruction—the fill in the blank syndrome. Have you ever witnessed it? None of you, of course, are practitioners. I ask a question: The main character in "The Most Dangerous Game" is _____? What type of conflict is central to the plot in *The Great Gatsby*? The Raven symbolizes _____ in Poe's poem. I know the answer because I am the teacher. As student, you need to guess what I want in the blank. If you know, fine; and if you don't, I'll tell you anyway.

We know this approach is wrong; therefore, we must enter into an engagement with learning. We must be readers—no writer interviewed ever claims to be a nonreader. Children must see us read and interact with a book—engrossed in text. We must model what we profess to believe—we value life-long reading.

We must model how reading is handled in our classroom. Who wants to read if it means constant assessment? When you finish Danielle Steele or Stephen King, do you expect a 10-question worksheet? When you close your book at home, do you expect your significant other to murmur, "Please have a book report—both sides of a composition paper, in to me by the end of the weekend"? Do you expect your literary choices to be made by someone else without ever exerting freedom of choice yourself?

We must be writers—ready to show that we can struggle with the printed page along with the best of them. We must attempt a poem, struggle with a short story or personal narrative. As professionals we should be ashamed to admit that we cannot do or are not willing to do what kindergarten children and first graders are doing across our state and nation.

We must be proficient language users ourselves, knowing that correct usage, the turn of a phrase, the sensitivity to word choice, does in fact establish a model. I would not expect that we would always go around saying, "It was I," but I do expect that we know that is correct, and why.

We have to realize that our actions speak louder than words. So we enter the classroom with book in hand. We toss our written piece in with those of our students, and we set the tone and decorum in our speech and manners.

We are a committed group of people and we need each other's support. We can make a difference if we are ready and willing to take a different course, choose an alternative action. We can forge a different policy for literacy.

REFERENCES

Calkins, L., & Harwayne, S. (1990). *Living between the lines*. Portsmouth, NH: Heinemann.

Elbow, P. (1981). *Writing with power*. New York: Oxford University Press.

Graves, D. (1983). *Writing: Teachers and Children at Work*. Portsmouth, NH: Heinemann.

Chapter 2

Learning Considered: A Model For Literacy Learning*

Rita S. Brause

Educators at all levels are concerned with students' learning, realized, in part by our focus on language proficiencies. One indication of our concern is the extensive amount of testing we do of reading and writing. (Some would claim we "overassess" these activities, to the exclusion of promoting their development.) Implicitly we must believe that reading and writing are instrumental in learning—but precisely how they are related is obscure in most contexts. For example, many current assessments evaluate reading and writing in isolation from any specific content. Such practices neglect to recognize that outside school—in real life, when we really learn and live— reading and writing are activities in which we engage as we learn about a specific phenomenon. These literacy activities accompany our personal quest for increasing understanding.

As learning specialists located in educational institutions (schools), we are responsible for promoting learning. Reading and writing are two activities which promote learning. Literacy is one *way* of learning—there are many other ways. (See, for example, Gardner's, 1988, views on multiple intelligences.) To consider how reading and writing promote learning, we must clarify what we mean by the term *learning*. Related issues follow, namely: characteristics of effective settings for learning, characteristics of learners, evidence to document learning, and integrating literacy activities within the larger concern of learning. Each of these issues will be addressed, drawing from the theoretical work of Bruner (1989), Mayher (1990), Smith (1990), and my own empirical studies (Brause, 1992).

---

* A more expanded presentation of these concerns is provided in *Enduring Schools*, by R.S. Brause, 1992, Lewes, UK: Falmer Press.

LEARNING DEFINED

Learning has multiple meanings. Specifically, it refers to a process we engage in (Learning-1), and an outcome of that process (Learning-2).

Learning-1 is a lifelong process of making sense of situations and activities. Learning is a mental process, which we may be unable to see or recall, but we note its occurrence retrospectively as we reflect on actions and insights. Learning involves connecting personal experiences and insights to new issues and contexts. We may visualize, read, write, experiment, pantomime, participate, or engage in an infinite variety of activities as we go about learning. As we mature, we take on more complex learning tasks, seeking constantly to enhance our understanding of ourselves, our world, and the ways we may contribute to our world's changing and improvement. Learning is a complex process which learning theorists are working at describing and explaining. While many of its mysteries are unclear to date, there is sufficient knowledge about language learning to guide us in understanding the general nature of learning and the conditions which encourage learning.

Learning-2 is evidenced by new insights and understandings, outcomes of Learning-1. A synonym for Learning-2 may be *knowledge*. Learning reflects our revised understandings from our personal experiences. As evidence of learning, learners produce and understand actions, beliefs, and projects incorporating more abstract, holistic, and interdisciplinary perspectives than at previous times. These understandings are useful in broader, more generalizable contexts and incorporate multiple, possibly contradictory perspectives. What is (truly) learned is not forgotten because (true) learning connects with previous understandings, and therefore is not isolated in our minds. This (true) learning contrasts with (pseudo) learning when we memorize isolated facts for tests which we forget as we finish the test.

Every human being learns. Learning is integral to our innate biological endowment. From birth, our minds are figuring out what is happening— learning about the environment in which we find ourselves, and our role(s) in that setting.

CHARACTERISTICS OF EFFECTIVE SETTINGS FOR LEARNING-1

There are seven crucial elements in settings where individuals learn.

Settings are predictable. Settings in which learners are able to predict actions provide the learner with a sense of security. When learners successfully predict what will happen or how their actions will be responded to, they gain *confidence* in their ability to make inferences about rules, and to understand what is happening. They also gain confidence in their ability to learn. Predictable settings result from the adoption of one consistent philosophy about learners and learning. This consistency leads to predictability and confidence in learners. Confident learners willingly try new tasks and take on new challenges, essential activities in the process of learning.

Learners engage in a variety of activities which promote learning. Learners seek to discover the rules or patterns and strategies for accomplishing specific activities by speculating, experimenting, reflecting, confirming, and revising their understandings of their personal experiences. All of these activities assist in learning the unstated expectations and processes integral to the project's accomplishment.

Learning occurs spontaneously and predictably, but is not programmable. Teaching *does not* insure learning. In fact, there is no necessary connection between what is taught and what each individual learns. Although many people establish time schedules for learning, there is no evidence to support the success of that programming. Each individual, in collaboration with a guide/supporter/nurturer controls the rate at which learning occurs. Those learners who access an abundance of quality resources/guides/supporters/nurturers progress at more rapid paces than those with fewer such resources.

Learning occurs when learners are expected to learn. Guides *expect* the learner to succeed and convey this confidence subtly to the learner. And the learner *expects* to learn, investing the activity with intensive energy.

Learning happens as learners make important decisions controlling their activities. Learning happens in the process of accomplishing personally meaningful tasks for which the learner has clear responsibility and ownership.

Learners are constantly challenged to consider increasingly more sophisticated issues. Contexts which support inquiry and exploration encourage learners to adopt alternative perspectives on problems and issues. Our minds seek challenge and stimulation from new ideas and new perspectives.

More experienced learners share their expertise with the novices in the group. Learners *trust* others to help them to learn by sharing their knowledge and experiences. All group members *respect* each individual learner's experiences and motivations.

CHARACTERISTICS OF LEARNERS

Some learning results from a learner's conscious decision. Other learning occurs incidentally as an individual engages in a variety of activities. There are six crucial factors in a learner's belief system that are essential ingredients for learning to occur.

1. Learners are personally motived. Learners unconsciously or consciously decide to belong to a particular "club" (of readers, writers, singers, gymnasts, athletes, artists, a family, a gang, a class, a neighborhood, a religious group, etc.). This decision is influenced by the implicit invitations the individuals are sent in the process of engaging in these activities. People included in the club (of readers, for example) are personally and intensely motivated to do what the others in the group are doing. As learners engage in personally motivated activities for an extended time period, they become increasingly proficient at accomplishing these tasks.

2. Learning is an active process. Learning results from active engagement in projects. The projects may be serious or they may be humorous. The projects may be individual ones, collaborative ones, or a combination of the two. All contexts are potential settings for learning.

3. Learners have self-confidence that they can and do learn. Building on their successes, learners tackle new challenges. They draw on their strategies in previous endeavors and their store of personal background experiences.

4. Learners accept a long-term commitment to learning. Recognizing the complex and lengthy process of learning, learners discipline themselves to defer immediate gratification with the expectation of personal fulfillment and accomplishment in the future.

5. Learners trust their guides. Learners rely on their guides to share their personal knowledge and their personal support to enable the learner to eventually be independent of the guide.

6. Learners reflect on and celebrate their own learning. Learners realize retrospectively that they have learned and willingly share their new knowledge and strategies for accomplishing this learning with others.

EVIDENCE OF LEARNING-2:
HOW DO WE KNOW LEARNING HAS OCCURRED?

Learning is apparent in the activities and attitudes of learners. At birth we breathe and suck. From experiences starting at that point, learners make conjectures about the world, and the people in our world. With time, learners establish a rich repertoire of strategies for obtaining, evaluating, and comparing information. Learners read, write, discuss, interview, investigate, dramatize, speculate, imagine, argue, draw, paint, dance, enact, etc., to obtain this information. Each individual has a rich repertoire of experience that comprises his or her personal knowledge. Each individual uses different strategies for learning and draws on different experiences. Common to us all, however, is the evolving sense of self, of the world around us, and our roles in it. This evolving sense is stored as mental constructs or mental models which are constantly subject to revision as we add to or reinterpret our experiences. These models are in our minds, and therefore only accessible for others from observing our performances. A clear marker of this phenomenon is a learner's remark, "I didn't realize how strongly I felt about that subject until I started to talk or write about it." Educators seek to bring knowledge to a level of consciousness for the learner, so that the learner can use this personal knowledge as a basis for continued learning and exploration.

Sophisticated learners have highly elaborated and integrated mental constructs of the world. Less experienced learners have many isolated constructs which are in the main quite skeletal. The goal of integrating all this knowledge into a more simplified, cohesive model drives many of us to connect events in our society and across history, seeking to determine commonalities, universal patterns, and themes.

Early concepts focus on isolated elements of society, such as who Daddy is—using superficial criteria (see Figure 2.1). With time these early concepts become more precise and more elaborated. They incorporate superficial as well as more comprehensive elements, as, for example, distinguishing between youth and adult (as an Intermediate Stage in Figure 2.1). As this individual continues to experience life, his or her knowledge about Daddy and Adults in general is incorporated into an understanding of how these individuals contribute to the composition of a Family. With additional time, thoughtful experiences, and new insights, new concepts emerge, including how families fit into a society. Each concept is richer than the earlier ones, incorporating the concepts from the previous ones, and expanding the purview to larger segments of the world in which we live. See Figure 2.2 for a graphic presentation of this evolution.

Learning-2 represents an individual's current knowledge of disparate elements of society, for example and how these are interdependent. A less sophisticated learner will have multiple constructs—one for Daddy, one for Mommy, and one for relatives/friends. With time and insight, those constructs will overlap, and the similarities will be used to establish more holistic understandings of how people contribute to society while recognizing each individual's unique contribution. With more time we would hope the individual would consider a broad spectrum of concepts labeled "family" representing different cultural patterns. These growing concepts

Figure 1.   Sample Constructs on a Continuum: Evolution of Concept from Daddy to Society

Concept	Daddy	Adults	Family	Society	Concept

Description					Description

Daddy
+ eyes
+ arms
+ legs
+ smiles
+ speaks
+ adult
− woman

Adults
+ Mommy
+ Daddy
+ gender
+ independence
+ values
+ attitudes
− motorized
− child

Family
+ Mommy
+ Daddy
+ adult(s)
+ children
+ relatives
+ traditions
− monetary system

Society
+ Mommy
+ Daddy
+ families
+ core values
+ monetary system
+ penal system
+ traditions
+ politicians
+ intellectuals
+ corruption

+ = concept includes this descriptor
− = concept excludes this descriptor

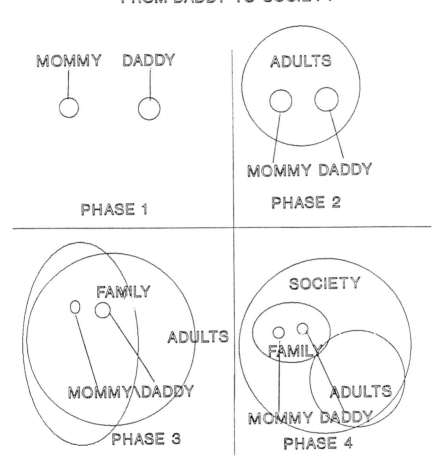

SAMPLE OF CONCEPT EVOLUTION

FROM DADDY TO SOCIETY

or constructs are evidence of learning. What we should be seeking from schooling is increased conceptual development, such as sketched in this progression.

To determine an individual's learning (Learning-2) requires studying settings where the individual displays his or her current understanding in the process of accomplishing meaningful activities. By comparing specific characteristics of these displays over an extended time period, we note that new knowledge has been acquired, when there are gaps, and where integration of previously isolated knowledge has occurred. For each individual learner at any given time we would expect to see a unique set of concepts and strategies, which represent an explanation of the world. We would note commonalities in learning strategies and for accessing an increasingly wider array of disciplines and resources to enhance society.

EDUCATORS' RESPONSIBILITIES FOR LEARNING

Educators' primary responsibility is to promote each student's learning. We are responsible for providing stimulating and challenging settings for learning to occur for our students, and for documenting what learning has occurred. We want our students to learn concepts, as well as learn-how-to-learn. Concurrently, we are charged with increasing our personal understandings about the learning process (Learning-1), and identifying increasingly more effective ways to document student learning (Learning-2). Professional educators are charged with establishing true learning communities in which all interactants learn. Recognizing that students have lives outside school that have dramatic impact on their life in school, educators need to collaborate with other caregivers in promoting the learnings of each student.

As literate individuals, seeking to share our understanding of the world, we use literacy activities to enhance opportunities for learning. We read and write as we increase our understandings. In addition, we read to and *with* our students, providing models for how more proficient individuals utilize these resources for learning specific information in a specific discipline. We model our own reading—and we model our valuing of reading and writing as activities which enhance our own learning and understanding. We also share our constant desire to learn. In essence we must be the quintessential learners we characterized earlier. By modeling for our students how we learn, by establishing numerous settings where students can actively participate, and by nurturing their learning, we will demonstrate our responsibility in enhancing our students' learning, particularly through literacy activities.

REFERENCES

Brause, R.S. (1992). *Enduring schools*. Lewes, UK: Falmer Press.

Bruner, J.S. (1990). *Acts of meaning*. Cambridge, MA: Harvard University Press.

Gardner, H.S. (1988). *Frames of mind*. New York: Basic Books.

Mayher, J.S. (1990). *Uncommon sense: Theoretical practice in language education*. Portsmouth, NH: Boynton/Cook.

Smith, F. (1990). *To think*. New York: Teachers College Press.

Chapter 3

The Reflective Teacher

Carolyn N. Hedley
Elizabeth LeBlanc

Teachers require a fresh focus for reflection about their professionalism: the knowledge that teacher development is an evolutionary process involving introspection and thoughtful analysis; a realization that success is relative, and that the gratification for progress is not immediate. A new vocabulary may be necessary to accommodate the concept of the teacher as reflective decision maker, new words that encourage a vision of teaching that has assumed reflection as one of its dimensions. Yet thoughtful deliberation about teaching by teachers has not been developed rhetorically, conceptually, or practically. Our educational preparation programs have overburdened themselves with the technicalities of teaching to the exclusion of contemplation of the strategies that foster the art of teaching. Teacher preparation programs, and teachers themselves, have paid little attention to the internal journey that teachers must take in order to be lifelong students of teaching. The internal dimension of personal reflection and professional redefinition requires long experience, insightful decision making, and societal accommodation for both teachers and students The nature of the processes, the strategic behaviors, the techniques, and the vocabulary to accommodate the dimension of thoughtful, revisionary, and constructive teaching practice is the focus of this chapter.

Through the years there has been a covert debate on the subject of the vocation of teaching versus the profession of teaching. If we consider the question closely, we will find that it is both. Teaching provides a service base for the intellectual ability and effort essential to presentation of the subject matter disciplines: Thus teaching is a profession. However, the object of teaching is learning, just as surely as the object of medicine is healing; we, as teachers, provide a service, a practical, vocational outcome for knowledge acquisition. However, teaching draws upon skills that require a relationship between knowledge and thought combined with feeling and imagination. Thus teaching has been described as an art; we discover that, when we combine the elements that give teaching the dimension of a profession with those that give it the dimension of a vocation, we produce the art of teaching.

Educators involved in the art of teaching must be reflective. They must learn to think deeply about what they are doing in classrooms, and about the children whom they teach. Teacher education programs combine both the professional and vocational dimensions of teaching, just as we combine theory and practice. This concept is at the core of the training of the teacher who is a generalist, often with a broad liberal arts background. Generalists know how to teach because they have learned how to learn. Their identity derives from their belief in the process of ongoing learning, and their reflective nature constantly demands improvement as they pass knowledge to others. An example of such a person is the teacher who remarked, "Ten years after one graduates from college, nearly all that we learned there has become obsolete, but at least we learned how to study, which is what makes life interesting."

Many people educated to be teachers do not find satisfaction in their professional role because they do not see teaching as part of their identity; it is in the formation of identity that student professionals are most weak. By such formation we mean the internal emotional journey needed to produce the identity of a person who is a reflective educator, not just a professional who is doing "things" with youngsters. We are also talking about abstractions that have emotional content and identifying symbols. This internal search for identity aids in the development of awareness of teaching as part of a personal distinction and definition. Teaching is a service that involves the development of other human beings. As such, teaching demands and transcends narrow narcissistic goals. Teaching contains the element of being for others. Teachers must see themselves as essential to the learning process, not so much dispensers of fact, but practitioners in the art of learning. The reflective educator comes across as a learned person, not as a classroom technician.

A DEFINITION OF REFLECTIVE

When describing reflective educators, the meaning of the word *reflective* becomes relevant. *The Random House Dictionary* tells us that the verb *reflect* can be used in 12 different ways; thus, the root word assumes importance. Returning to root words helps us break the crust of history and usage that gathers around every overused word. As so many words in English do, the verb *reflect* comes from the Latin. *Reflect* means "bending something back." Thus reflective educators distinguish themselves by working with culturally derived information or facts, by looking back at experience, by examining behaviors, and putting knowledge into forms that create understanding. Educators reflect on "truth" to discover its limits; reflective educators do not deal exclusively with facts or information, but emphasize processes for gaining insight and knowledge. Reflective teachers do not teach answers and reactions to questions as a way of knowing; rather they deal with concepts and ideas, the recognition of patterns and similarities, containing inclusions and exclusions, causes and effects. They look for the ways in which the current, collected knowledge of the culture expresses itself, in terms of the principles and suppositions in art and science, couched in historical perspectives and contemporary relevance.

The difficulty of measurement of what reflective educators impart is manifest. Their concerns embody values and morals, as Goodlad (1990) wrote in a recent article:

> Postulate 6. The responsible group of academic and clinical faculty members must seek out and select for a predetermined number of student places in the program those candidates who reveal an initial commitment to the moral, ethical, and enculturating responsibilities to be assured. (p. 191)

Abstract, intellectual realities, such as the smooth functioning of society, human aspirations, and human rights are the concerns of the educator-teacher. Such altruisms often defy definition. As educators pursue such generalizations as humanizing classrooms, with respect for individual intellect and the psyche that supports it, the flight of imagination, and the resulting creative behaviors, we recognize that we are vulnerable. Vulnerable, because what we aspire to do is not only intangible, unmeasurable, and, at times, difficult to define and difficult to make operational, but because we understand that we cannot let go of these ideals without losing our own value to students and to the profession. To quote Dewey (1933, p. 17), "(Reflection) enables us to know what we are about when we act."

By now it should be clear that, as reflective educators, we are not concerned with intelligence, ability, or achievement as measured by tests alone. Rather, we emphasize the processes of intelligence that look toward the generation, development, and interaction of thought, imagination, and sensitivity toward the solution of lifelike problems regarding self and others in complex contexts. Educational problems are often general rather than specialized and discrete; methods for solution are interdisciplinary and reside as much in complex processes as in facts. Reflective educators are practitioners of the art of learning; intelligence stamps their behaviors. Most university professors have been successful in creating this image, even to the point of being stereotyped. Genuine reflection needs to be developed by the whole spectrum of educators. Dewey (1904) focused on this idea at the turn of the century when he envisioned a program of teacher education that was "calculated to develop a thoughtful and intelligent teacher" (p. 27).

John Goodlad's (1990) five-year study of the education of educators is a demonstration of Dewey's concern in our time. His postulates for education are an outline of just what it will take to provide teachers who earn the respect of those in the profession and of the clients of schools: students, parents, administrators, communities and states, and the school boards and legislators that represent them. He writes:

> We regarded them as essential presuppositions—as postulates—to guide our journey through the teacher education landscape and ultimately, to shape our evaluation of it...
>
> *Postulate 7*: Programs for the education of educators, whether elementary or secondary, must carry the responsibility to ensure that all candidates progressing through them possess or acquire the literacy and critical thinking abilities associated with an educated person.
>
> *Postulate 8.* Programs for the education of educators must provide extensive opportunities for future teachers to move beyond being students of organized knowledge to become teachers who inquire into both knowledge and its teaching.
>
> *Postulate 9*: Programs for the education of educators must be characterized by a socialization process through which candidates transcend their self-oriented student preoccupations to become more other-oriented in identifying with a culture of teaching.
>
> *Postulate 10.* Programs for the education of educators must be characterized in all respects by the conditions for learning that future teachers are to establish in their own schools and classrooms.
>
> *Postulate 11*: Programs for the education of educators must be conducted in such a way that future teachers inquire into the nature of teaching and schooling and assume they will do so as a natural aspect of teaching. (pp. 191–193)

Clearly, Goodlad is calling for educational programs for educators that create the conditions and extoll the dynamics for becoming reflective, vital teachers who are able to adapt to community and who are committed to education for all of our children. The need for reform is documented in this report, which is geared to the discontent of the educational establishment. We never seem to be doing enough for our teachers and they, in turn, are blamed for lack of student learning. Where does it end? Or better yet, where does it begin? Rosovsky's (1978) description of the educated man characterizes him as spending time in meditation, evaluation, and reflection. The process takes time and most overambitious programs of teacher education do not allow for such thoughtful activity. Yet teacher training programs are part of the general educational structure, and their structures are one way that general educational values are expressed.

PROCESSES OF REFLECTION

Processes for reflective teaching are embodied in Cambourne's (1988) *Model of the Conditions for Learning*. These processes, described and developed in the following paragraphs, are: Immersion, Engagement, Demonstration, Expectation, Responsibility, Use, Approximation, and Response. The conditions closely follow the principles for teaching and learning in natural language situations. How do these qualities manifest themselves?

Immersion

Cambourne's first condition for learning, for learning change, or for being reflective, is that of *Immersion*. Teachers best become engaged in creating classroom environments and processes when they are convinced that they are potential learners about the development and improvement of curriculum content and classroom dynamics. They feel they can succeed in activities that will further their professional and life goals. Teachers appreciate that what they do has a second life or is continued in the culture and society in which they live. Thus, what teachers teach must be relevant and important, reflecting the reality of day-to-day living. Their activity integrates rationalization and abstraction processes to form concepts and principles derived from daily, sometimes vicarious, experience. In other words, not only are teachers absorbed with the practicalities of living, they are involved in the science of developing those experiences and observations to solve problems of living in rational ways. That is what is meant when we say that teachers do not deal exclusively with facts or information, but rather with processes for gaining insight and knowledge.

Thus, the reflective teacher/educator must be immersed in knowledge about teaching and learning, about content, and about materials and means. At the same time, the teacher is sensitive and knowledgeable about children, classroom dynamics, and classroom management. Teachers need to feel that they are making a deeply cultural contribution in a society that appreciates their work. During this enterprise of becoming reflective, teachers need to know that they will not be penalized for making intelligent errors, as they are learning and changing; thus they may take risks or hazard a best guess while considering educational realities. The condition of *immersion* implies the second concept in Cambourne's *Model for the Conditions of Learning*, that is, *engagement* in the art of teaching.

Engagement

Engagement suggests that the educator views himself or herself as a person who can perform, who is competent, who cares, and who can make a difference. Engagement implies empowerment of educators to enter into reflective decision making, problem solving, and creative behaviors in classrooms. To paraphrase Cambourne: Engagement occurs when the teacher/learner is convinced that:

> I am a potential doer, or performer of these demonstrations that I am observing. Engaging in this reflective planning will further my professional goals. I can engage or try to emulate without fear of abuse or psychological hurt, if my attempt is not fully correct.

Teachers should be advised to teach integratively in culturally relevant ways. Engagement suggests that teachers will be heard and respected. But such respect can only be earned when teachers are immersed in the knowledge of their profession and have demonstrated that they are fully engaged in their professionalism. Thus, teachers should not be dominated completely by state guides and state and/or college testing as the measure of their teaching and their worth. These tests should be restructured to ascertain more of what children actually know in congruence with new ways that recent and relevant information is presented. While checks of how much teachers and students are effectively integrating information must be done, the teacher must have far more latitude in measuring his or her own effectiveness and the student's competence in general learning and performance. Informal assessment is not invalid simply because it is not always numerical.

Demonstrations

The third condition for learning, not necessarily in the order presented, is that of *Demonstration*. Teachers learn from observing knowledgeable peers and other effective educators. *Demonstration* is defined as a display of how something is done; teachers need behavioral, affective, contextualized learning and teaching demonstrations that are coordinated and consistent. They need to see how good teaching is done and how such experiences become integrated into a system of curriculum experience; they need to know what is wanted and expected to gain a sense of direction about what they are doing. Demonstration is elicited in the context of the other qualities for learning change. We cannot *tell* either children or adults what to do and expect it to happen. In other words, a stand–up lecture as a constant in the classroom is not the best condition for creative learning and not the best demonstration of process learning. One creates the conditions for learning and imparts knowledge by demonstrating, by modelling, and by doing whatever it is that one expects from students. Thus the reflective teacher should become more the reader, the writer, the researcher, the manager, the cooperative listener, and the transaction expert who provides a model for students to follow. Thankfully, teachers are learning to present materials and ask students to work them up cooperatively while providing managerial direction of peer tutoring so that children may succeed in an interactive mode. But until we become more skilled in some of the methods of indirect teaching, while maintaining the art of the direct presentation, we should seek to find and to provide the means and models for acceptable scholarly behavior.

Expectation

Expectation is a fourth condition embraced in Cambourne's *Model for the Conditions for Learning*. Expectation of the success and change fostered by reflective teaching is touched upon in our discussion of *Engagement*. The teacher expects that learning will occur, that change will be manifest as he or she reflects about what is working in the classroom. Though there will be setbacks about what works for students, about what content should be presented, about the dynamics of the classroom, and about the collaborations with other professionals and students, the overall understanding of process and performance in the classroom will alter and improve. It is expected that any process that involves thinking and rethinking behavior will have pitfalls, and that these can best be overcome by joining other forwardlooking, collaborative teachers who see the classroom as a society in which human relations, general knowledge, and the maturational development of the participants is valued. Moreover, the teacher needs to feel that, when the classroom becomes more interactive, more integrative, and more relevant, he or she will not be depreciated because change is occurring. In fact, the expectation should be that others will respect his or her work.

The thoughtful teacher does not stand out in obnoxious ways, particularly if the goal is to become a model for others. The reflective role model, based on the conditions suggested here, should be unassuming and collaborative, that is, participatory without creating anxiety in others. The teacher may expect occasional adverse remarks, possibly from colleagues, parents, or an unsympathetic administrator; nevertheless, expectations for general learning and better dynamics should remain realistic and high.

Responsibility

Closely connected to the condition of positive expectation is the assumption of *Responsibility*. Gradually and easily, as he or she is trusted in the school setting, the teacher takes more and more responsibility for the well-being of his or her students, for curriculum modification, and for behavioral change. In fact, most teachers assume responsibility for their own classes; administrators, parents, and students become anxious when teachers are not in good control in their classes. But what we are speaking of here is not the disciplined class, but the class in which the teacher takes charge of ameliorated progress and thoughtfully planned lessons. As we stated in the opening paragraphs, the teacher as mechanic in control of books and students is not the objective of reflective thinking and teaching. Rather, the responsive teacher who manages learning and change based on informal and ongoing assessment is the kind of educator responsibility to which we refer. Such teachers embrace the moral and professional values of the enlightened educator. Guilt and doubt about responsible performance are not part of this professional's psychology. The teacher must be sure of his or her professionalism, grounded in knowledge and thoughtfully planned, integrative classroom action.

Jones, Tinzmann, and Pierce (1992) suggest that the educator of the future will be a high-level thinker who can contemplate and manage such areas as (a) problem-situated learning, (b) cooperative and collaborative learning, (c) considerate text and text structures, (d) graphic organizers (of which they provide many), (e) thinking skills, (f) misconceptions, (g) authentic assessment, and (h) strategic thinking. These notions will be developed in a later part of the chapter, "Strategies for Developing Reflective Behavior."

Parenthetically, if a teacher is working in a school with a traditional model of learning or is new to the school, time must elapse before this teacher can introduce other than a traditional curriculum. Other teachers, the principal, the parents, and the students probably need to understand that the educator can teach in a "front and center" mode; gradually as the classroom changes its focus, the teacher and students become responsible for learning in a more socialized and interactive mode. As the teacher becomes responsible and empowered in the contemplated class manager mode, so, too, the students must learn to take charge of their own learning.

Use

Reflective teaching requires time. The teacher tries new techniques, uses new methods, tries out dynamics, and insists on performance and products over time. Using what you have thought about, and giving it time to work, is what we mean by *Use*. Change does not occur quickly. Students must learn new modes for interaction, must become responsible themselves, must learn cooperative, goal-oriented work and study habits, and must learn to complete tasks that produce outcomes. These processes are not immediately instilled or valued. Teachers who have moved to, say, a literature-based program or theme units, state that it takes at least 2 months to get routines, work habits, and group dynamics worked out effectively. If the teacher moves too quickly either to new forms or back to old ones, students will pick up a lack of clarity and purpose; the processes of change presented here will be negated by a lack of insight and direction on the part of students and others. Therefore, *use* implies that good things take time, that the teacher does not move hastily or jump into more than he or she can artfully control. Students must practice learning processes and small-group dynamics over and over; they must understand the outlined activity, plan activities for outcomes, learn to work with their peers, and be able to assess their own learning to evaluate whether or not they are succeeding in school.

Use means that teachers and students will be able to practice and control authentic activities: to reflect in action, to orchestrate planned lessons and activities, to modify planned events, to engage in the quick integration of information, and to eliminate activities that are not contributing to achievement of a defined goal. Such demands promote personalized learning and evaluation of their own behaviors. In short, teachers should reflect on ways to help empower children as well as themselves in authentic activities. The presentation and assessment of those learning activities may take forms that are recorded by means other than scores on standardized tests. *Use* may be considered the protracted practice of "learning by doing."

Approximations

Teaching is dilemma ridden. Should we emphasize procedural knowledge (means and strategies for learning) or declarative knowledge (the factual content of the disciplines)? Should we teach theories or how to maneuver situated behaviors? How do we react to the realities of the classroom that are less than ideal? Can we engage in collaborative teaching with all students? Teachers who are reflective decision makers and problem solvers may find that their solutions don't work. They may find that they have moved too quickly with an overabundance of information and techniques to routines that children cannot yet utilize or by which they cannot truly learn. The information in content and the dynamics of classroom may be too complex for some students. We make a judgment that is approximate, but needs refining. Sometimes these judgments are less than felicitous. We are entitled to intelligent error as basic to the change process. We have to be able to talk about change and refinement in a nondefensive mode. It's part of the repertoire of reflective teaching.

We learn by our mistakes. We may experience failures in the process of becoming more independent and responsible, more idealistic, and more involved. Children, too, may fumble in the process of learning; occasionally there may be poor grades or reduced performance. This kind of faltering is part of the learning process; in the past, we, as educators, have had little tolerance for mistakes, probably because we don't see errors of judgment or lack of insight as part of the learning process. We must allow children to make mistakes and to profit from a wrong notion or a lack of perspective. We must allow ourselves the same latitude: Approximations, a close best judgment that doesn't work out, is necessary to learning. We simply use this information to revise and redo. It's an expected spin-off of change and one of the few ways that provide us information for growth.

Response

Finally, we deal with *response*, which again may be an ally of *approximation*. To learn, we need feedback from the students and from knowledgeable others. According to Cambourne (1988, p. 1), "response must be relevant, appropriate, timely, readily available, and non-threatening, with no strings attached." That is, the teacher must make reflective decisions; he or she needs feedback from his or her own reflection and assessment, from student work, from collaborators, from staff, from students and other consumers of education. The educator cannot change without good supportive information. By the same token, the teacher needs space in order to work out a plan. We have said that reflection takes time. Response implies that the educator and his or her fellow participants will have the time and the interest to continue to build the educational enterprise in the classroom.

Summary

These conditions for learning may occur simultaneously; certainly it would be a mistake to assume any order or priority with regard to these conditions. They are simply the phenomena that allow for reflection. Using these principles, the reflective educator would:

- Develop content-rich and content-deep learning environments, through demonstrations with content knowledge for children to experience and emulate.
- Develop the notion of situated, phased, and patterned learning, providing models of learning and problem solving for children to follow. Role playing and demonstrations by the teacher and other advanced adults would provide models for scholarship, reading, and writing for student and teacher alike.
- Provide for dialogue and interaction.
- Become mediators of learning, avoiding a complete return to the stand-up lecture mode as a usual method of presenting information. A period of adjustment for teachers and learners alike should be allowed for this departure.
- Insist that the teacher become engaged as a learner, and that one is responsible for one's professionalism.

- Help students to independence of learning by modelling the profession-alism that is expected of the learner.
- Realize at personal levels that learning and problem solving are, at root, social and relevant; realize that an understanding of language, the dialogue, and social interaction are a means of developing mind in society.
- Maintain positive expectations for himself or herself in terms of the practice of the profession and by the same token, maintain high expectancy for students.
- Understand that social dialogue of any kind involves approximations and risk taking, that one may not always evolve the most felicitous solution, but that attempting a resolution to a problem is more important (and more socially valuable) than being a passive dispenser of information.
- Come to terms with the notion that dialogue in the classroom must have constraints for learning to occur. Students must remain task oriented and learn to participate effectively during group work.
- Provide learners with feedback to improve their performance. Corrections are made as a means for improving personal performance and group outcomes.
- Realize the importance of formal education and the school for developing the scientific support of experience, and the rationalization of activity and phenomena. The school is an important means for developing higher level thought and the written form of language.
- Use formal testing and measures of intelligence, ability, and achievement as a point of departure for instruction. Educators should not endorse evaluation that describes fixed qualities to categorize learners. Scores exist to be modified by instruction. (Hedley, 1991, pp. 16–18).

STRATEGIES FOR DEVELOPING REFLECTIVE BEHAVIOR

Techniques for Strategic Thinking

The reflective educator is going to look for methods and techniques for succeeding in his or her progress in the process of reflection. How does one assure that reflection, or thoughtful analysis about Cambourne's conditions of learning, occurs in the minds of students and teachers? How can the teacher devise techniques to become more reflective? Our list of techniques to encourage thinking about thinking would include such items as logs, portfolios, student work samples, observation strategies, demonstrations, think-alouds, graphic organizers, freewrites, and retellings, cannot compete with Terry Salinger's very complete discussion of how to gather and validate learning in dynamic classrooms. The authors refer the reader to Chapter 9, "Classroom-Based and Portfolio Assessment for the Elementary Grades," by Salinger, who gives a thorough workup on the techniques for informal assessment, reflection, and reaction to learning tasks in the transactional classroom. To reiterate them here, in a discussion of what should be a critical point of our discussion, would be a redundancy which serves no one; suffice it to say that her discussion is as pointed and complete as any ever read by these authors.

Reflective teaching will not occur unless the teacher builds in techniques, strategies, and processes that force one to be reflective. Additionally, one needs a point of view around which to build reflection. We have described the conditions for our own thoughtful learning as professionals. What we have not developed is a projection for programmatic change. In other words, what are the components of educational practice that we want to develop? What are the functions in which we want to immerse and engage ourselves in our time? The foci that Jones et al. (1992) stress in their work, basic to the educator's reflective and strategic thinking, are: (a) problem-situated learning, (b) phased learning, (c) recursivity, (d) graphic organizers, (e) metacognition, and (f) collaborative learning.

Problem-Situated Learning. What does one need to do to engage in *problem-situated learning*? Authentic content for thinking comes from the real world. "Real world problems, for example, may not have good solutions or they may lend themselves to more than one solution; thus, they are worth thinking about" (Jones et al., 1992, p. 15).

The world is full of real problems and real examples, some of which may be vicarious (television, narration, or films, as examples). Students begin to see that what they are doing in school applies to everyday situations, a practice described as situated learning. The practice of researching and problem solving current, perplexing experiences causes students and teachers to draw upon information in many forms and from many disciplines. The introduction of the theme unit becomes a technique for just such problem solution. For example, students may discuss the systems approaches used by the military in fighting the Iraq war; they will have to utilize knowledge from science, from language, from sociology, from history, and from mathematics. They will eventually present their findings in written forms. It is not difficult to see how high-level thinking, how creative solutions, occur.

As a start, teachers may begin to use examples from everyday life and experience to salt their explanations. A rule of thumb may be that teachers in discussion with students give only examples and experiences of the last month to demonstrate meaning, or to develop analogical thought; the practice keeps one current and fresh by avoiding the tired story; moreover, the technique forces one to think anew the topic that is being developed. In a later phase, such topics as garbage disposal, cleaning up the waterfront, designing and landscaping the play area, or relating to parents should produce introductory student excursions into architecture, psychology, chemical processes, human relations, and other subjects. Information from sources such as journals, magazines, books, interviews, histories, anecdotes, television, videocassettes, and audiotapes, among others, would be utilized during the phases of learning: before learning, during learning, and after learning.

Phased Learning. A second strategy discussed by Jones et al. is to structure learning, or what the authors describe as *Phases of Learning*, supporting the notion of structuring knowledge into learning units. The first level of learning, called the *before learning phase*, requires focusing or defining the topic and the dimensions of the task with the students. Deciding what we are talking about, probing background knowledge, making connections between prior knowledge and new content, setting goals, and determining the criteria for learning, predicting, and previewing are components of the focusing stage, or the *before learning phase*.

The *during learning phase*, called *finding out*, follows this researching activity can be as simple as looking through a picture book or preparing a plan for the subsequent development of a new invention. Students are instructed to read, discuss, and "engage in activities which help them organize and think about the information they read and information from their own prior knowledge" (Jones et al., 1992, p. 17). Each lesson builds on the former lesson in a systematic way until culmination and closure of the learning unit. Each project takes on its own logic and the rationale is different depending upon the problem and the people who are researching it.

The *after learning phase* occurs when learners "summarize, review, and reflect on what they have learned." They ask new questions and apply what they have learned to new situations. As in the *before learning phase*, we often spend too little time with this kind of follow up. In the programs developed by Jones et al. (1992). the *after learning phase* is recursive and includes:

> focusing, information gathering, remembering, organizing (comparing, classifying, etc.), analyzing (identifying relationships and patterns, etc.), generating (inferring, predicting, etc.), integrating (summarizing as an example), and evaluating (verifying). Thinking is not a hierarchy of skills; rather skills are conceptualized as a pool or repertoire...students draw upon particular skills and strategies as they engage in specific cognitive processes...Furthermore, content and one's purposes or goals determine which skills and processes are appropriate to use in a particular learning task. (Jones et al., 1992, pp. 13, 18).

Recursivity. *Recursivity* implies that students will reflect in a start-stop manner during authentic thinking and learning. The learner is planning, looking ahead, reflecting, revising, and continually going back over his or her work. The teacher must build in strategies that allow and encourage this type of thinking. The demonstration of such activity by knowing, practicing, experienced peers and adults serves to model these processes. The quality of recursiveness is hard to observe and measure. Is the student daydreaming or using a pause to draw his or her thoughts together? How can you know? Should you try to find out, since both activities may have a positive function? Ultimately a product, verbal or graphic, demonstrated or written, must issue; by this product and the explanation that accompanies its development will you know if reflection is occurring.

Graphic Organizers. As the literature regarding imagery and the graphic presentation of knowledge (diagrams, forms, cutaways, semantic maps, pictures, charts, and graphs, as examples) accumulates, the technique of using graphic organizers to reflect the multiple, nonhierrarchical, complex processes of cognitive reflection becomes a way of visually portraying such complexity. The written word and the use of the computer have caused us to presume that the mind works in linear ways. Such linear projections of mental life demonstrate but one relationship to the many processes of thinking, according to Vygotsky (Rieber & Carton, 1987). Jones et al., (1992) have produced a large number of graphic presentations to help the teacher visually look at information in other than linear ways. Students and teachers may use imagery organizers (matrically, cyclically, or temporally) to graph out ideas. Graphic organizers help make connections and produce information integration and allow for metaphorical explanations and examples. There is nothing sacred about created formats; the student and/or teacher may start "drawing" solutions to problems and creating unique connections using self-constructed raw charts, produced as ideas hit. These are the self-styled graphics which are often more meaningful than those that are provided by others.

Metacognition. Thinking about thinking is requisite for strategic behavior to occur. Not only is cognitive awareness essential to teacher reflection and strategic behaviors, knowing how one knows and learns is critical to the student's acquisition of knowledge. "How did you know?" "How did you figure that out?" "Can you analyze what you did?" "Try thinking out loud as you do that information search—now, how are you going to proceed?" "How did you feel about the way you worked during this project?" Having students explain their study behaviors is as important as what they produce. Such explanation can be stifled by asking for a lengthy and self-conscious explanation or by requesting students to write down their thoughts and feelings after a task. However, strategic behaviors for learning outcomes should be developed, probably through observation, through the techniques suggested above, and most especially by modelling. The student and teacher must strive for efficiency in studying and thinking. Reflection about how one comes to process information and develop schema or knowledge frameworks effectively is critical to becoming effective as learner and teacher.

Collaborative Learning. Small-group work and classroom interaction aids student learning and motivation. Students cannot simply be put in groups and expected to learn. The teacher, as a beginning strategy, should try to have small-group sessions at least once a day. Ultimately, as a normative way of functioning in the classroom, group work may be used as the mode of learning most of the time. To work well, the group must have defined goals for learning and specific ground rules for functioning. The authors state that groups should be heterogeneous in terms of ability, that group dynamics must be attended to and worked through, that roles in groups must be defined, and that group output and productivity must be assessed, whether on an individual basis or as a collaborative process in which the same grade is given for all the participants in the group.

CONCLUSION

Becoming a reflective teacher is an evolutionary experience requiring information integration, thoughtful analysis, and creative problem-solving ability into the professional life of the teacher. This chapter has explored the dimensions of the informed and reflective teacher. The teacher the authors envision utilizes experience in teaching, an ability to observe and assess behaviors, and the facility to respond to the needs of students. We must attract people to the teaching profession who have a strong generalist background and who are committed to personal and professional growth. It is imperative not only that we create programs of teacher education that help develop teachers who are reflective, but that we encourage school administrators to nurture and sustain them in this pursuit.

REFERENCES

Cambourne, B. (1988, March). *Model of the Conditions for Learning*. Paper distributed at a workshop, Syracuse, NY.

Dewey, J. (1904). The relation of theory to practice in education. In *The relation of theory to practice in the education of teachers* (Third Yearbook of the National Society for the Scientific Study of education, Chapter 1). Bloomington, IL: Public School Publishing Company.

Dewey, J. (1933). *How we think.* Chicago: Henry Regnery.

Goodlad, J. (1990). Better teachers for our nation's schools. *Phi Delta Kappan, 72,* 184-194.

Hedley, C.N. (1992). Theories of natural language. In P. Antonacci & C. N. Hedley, *Natural approaches to reading and writing.* Norwood, NJ: Ablex Publishing Corp.

Jones, B.F, Tinzmann, M.B., & Pierce, J. (1992). How thoughts are made. In C. Collins & J. Mangieri (Eds.), *Building the quality of thinking in and out of school in the twenty-first century.* Hillsdale, NJ: Erlbaum.

Rieber, R.W., & Carton, A.S. (1987). *The collected works of L.S. Vygotsky.* New York: Plenum Press.

Rosovsky, H. (1978, March 6). Faculty of Arts and Sciences. *Chronicle of Higher Education,* p. 15.

Chapter 4
The Virtues of Digression

Thomas Newkirk

Every six months I go dutifully to see my dental hygienist. I do not look forward to these visits. I cringe at the medieval instruments she uses to chip away at my teeth; I hate the scraping sound and the continual prod to "open a little wider" and to "turn this way, please." To take my mind off my teeth and gums, I try to look at the pictures on the wall across from me. But with my head locked into place by the headrest, I can really only look at the poster of progressive periodontal disease. On the left side of the chart the gums are a healthy pink, but they redden and recede from the teeth, and I realize where the expression "long in the tooth" comes from. After the chipping and scraping, the hygienist asks, "Do you floss?" (She can see I don't), and I reply evasively, "Not as much as I should." (I usually concentrate on the 2 weeks before the visit.) I make a resolution to change my ways, and on my way home stop at the drugstore, where I may buy about a quarter mile of floss. But I have never developed the habit of flossing.

I begin with this story because it illustrates the difference between habits and ideas. I am fully convinced—at an intellectual level—that flossing is a good idea. I don't want my gums to look like those on the right side of the poster. But at a behavioral level, I have not been able to change. As we look at the way we talk to students, I think the same distinction is important. It is relatively easy to accept the concept of "whole language"; it is much harder to look at, let alone change, our habits of talking with (or at) children.

The most habitual pattern of instructional talk is illustrated well in a story from Harste, Woodward, and Burke's (1984) *Language Stories and Lessons*. In the story a theology student visits a church where the pastor is conducting a "children's sermon." Once the children were seated in the first couple of pews, he begins:

> "Children I am thinking of something that is about five or six inches high; that scampers across the ground; that can climb trees; that lives in either a nest in the tree or makes its home in a hollowed-out portion of a tree's trunk. The thing I'm thinking about gathers nuts and stores them in the winter; it is sometimes brown and sometimes gray; it has a big bushy tail. Who can tell me what I'm thinking of?
>
> Knowing proper church behavior, the children remained quiet and reserved. No one ventured an answer.
>
> Finally, Robert, age 6, slowly and ever so tentatively raised his hand.
>
> The pastor, desperate for a response so he could go on with the sermon, said with some relief, "Yes Robert, what do you think it was?"
>
> "Well," came the response, "ordinarily I'd think it was a squirrel, but I suppose you want me to say it was Jesus." (p. xv)

The literacy lesson that Harste et al. take from this story is the sensitivity of children like Robert to context, to the strangeness of an animal story in this setting. But there is a negative lesson as well.

"Who can tell me what I'm thinking of?" How often do we put students in the position of guessing an answer that is in our mind? How many of our questions are really questions, ones which we don't know the answer to? How often is the expected answer a single word? How often are children allowed to ask questions in school?

The research on these questions is, to put it mildly, depressing. We can begin with Goodlad's (1984) study of U.S. schools, reported in *A Place Called School*. Here are some of his findings:

- Seventy percent of class time was spent on "instructional talk," and nearly 75% of this talk was teacher to students. Teachers outtalked the entire class by a ratio of three to one. This is almost exactly the proportion found by Wells (1986, p.86).
- Barely 5% of instructional time was designed to elicit student response (Goodlad, 1984, p. 229).
- Not even 1% required some kind of open response involving reasoning or perhaps an opinion from a student (Goodlad, 1984, p. 229).
  Other researchers have shown that a very small portion of the children's 25% of class talk involves asking questions:
- Teachers ask four times as many questions as students (Bourke, 1986).
- Even when teachers are asking four times as many questions as students, they perceive the ratio to be 1–1 (Susskind, 1979).
- Teachers ask questions at a rate of 80/hour (Dillon, 1988).
- Almost all of the questions students ask are procedural, usually clarifying directions (Dillon, 1988).

- The percentage of student questions is three times greater in the home than in school (Wells, 1986, p. 86).

Goodlad concludes that, "If teachers in the talking mode and students in the listening mode is what we want, rest assured that we have it" (p. 229).

When I read research like this, I naturally think that it doesn't apply to me. I would never be so dominating or insensitive. But a recent experience convinced me otherwise. Last year at Ohio State I led a "discussion" of faculty and graduate students after a talk I gave there. The discussion was tape recorded and transcribed, then edited for distribution. During the latter part of the discussion it seemed to me that a graduate student dominated the talk, taking long turns, shifting the discussion to her research interests (and away from mine). It seemed to me that we got off track. A couple of months later I received the transcript. During that part of the discussion when I thought the graduate student was dominating, I was doing most of the talking—by a margin of three or four to one. My turns were far longer than hers.

I clearly had not been able to monitor my dominance of this "discussion." More uncomfortably, as I read the transcript, I began to wonder if gender played a role. If the graduate student had been male, would it have appeared so intrusive to me? Was there some bias that caused me to view her assertiveness as inappropriate? I am uncomfortable even raising this possibility, but it brings me to a point I want to make. The tendency to overtalk is probably more ingrained than we would like to believe, and that the true revolution—call it "whole language," or "reading and writing process"—requires us to look at our ways of talking with students. It requires a kind of self-knowledge and, as James Moffett has said, "self-knowledge is often bad news."

It is, after all, possible to do all the "right things"—use big books, have a literature-based curriculum, organize response journals, publish children's writing—and not transform our ways of talking with students. We can dominate discussion of trade books, just as we have traditionally dominated discussions of basal readers. I'm uneasy when I see the lavish book displays at Whole Language Conferences, because it is so much easier to focus on products, on materials we can bring into the classroom, than on the more subtle and demanding task of creating what Greene (1988) calls "public spaces" in the classroom, openings where students can talk.

READING GROUPS

Reading groups should be one of these public spaces. But for decades the potential of reading groups has been limited by unquestioned assumptions about how readers develop and learn—assumptions drawn from basal reading programs. I want to be clear—my argument is not with basal readers versus trade books. I don't want to argue one *product* against another. What I want to criticize is the impoverished language environment in many reading programs and, in general, the insensitivity of reading educators to the exploratory potential of talk. One can, for example, read a decade's worth of *Reading Teacher* without coming on one interesting, spontaneous excerpt of student talk.

I want to look briefly at three bedrock assumptions in traditional basal programs that profoundly limit the potential of reading groups to be public spaces.

The first is the *assumption of segregation by ability* for the purpose of providing appropriate instruction. Oakes (1985) notes that the concept of "equity" shifted in the 1920s and 1930s from providing the same opportunities to all students to providing "equally appropriate" opportunities to all students. The standard technique for accomplishing this differentiation has been "ability-level" grouping. But as Rist (1973) has shown, grouping is often based on the behavioral traits (forms of politeness, dress, and language) that put minorities and lower socioeconomic groups at a serious disadvantage. The groupings are remarkably stable despite the claims that changes can be made when assignments are inappropriate (for a vivid illustration of what happens when a mistaken assignment occurs, see Rose, 1989). Within the lower reading groups students often get less instructional time, and they are corrected more frequently by the teacher, even if an error makes semantic sense (Allington, 1980). In effect, grouping accentuates— rather than mitigates—racial and economic divisions in our society.

The necessity for grouping in traditional reading programs is related to another assumption, one upon which the basal reading industry rests—and I will call it the *calibration assumption*. Briefly stated, children must progress along a carefully calibrated continuum of difficulty, and determining the appropriate reading selection for the child is too complex a matter for either the child or the teacher to make. Textbook companies and their consultants are the ones to make these decisions (Shannon, 1989). By moving along the prescribed path, the child will be appropriately challenged at every point.

But are children so poor at calibrating their abilities? I think not. Watch them on the playground. Are they puzzled about the difficulty of the monkey bars? Do they wait for guidance from the recess monitor? Moreover, they experience difficulty in different ways—there is no scientifically verified threshold of difficulty for each student. Part of what we mean by *learning style* is the style of dealing with difficulty; some children are cautious, taking small incremental steps. Others plunge into tasks we would never dream of asking them to do.

A third assumption I will call the *question assumption*—children learn by answering questions posed by those in authority. "Can anybody tell me what I am thinking?" Public schools are monuments to our belief in children answering questions. In theory the questions move from recall to "higher level" inferencing, evaluative, and application questions. In practice, most questions call for an informational answer from the student (Goodlad, 1984, p. 229).

But the issue is not simply one of replacing poor questions with better ones, of asking higher level questions instead of lower level ones. Rather it is looking at questioning as a cultural practice. As Heath (1983) has shown, questioning is a common practice in mainstream homes—often beginning with display questions: "What is this?" "Doggee." "Oh, a doggee. How does a doggee sound?" By contrast, the black families in her study explicitly rejected questioning as a way of bringing up children. Stories of Hawaiian children (Au, 1980) and Native American children also show that traditional school questioning routines may run violate norms of conversing. Philips (1972) has observed that Sioux and Cherokee children did not feel comfortable in a system where they "learn by making public mistakes" (p. 381).

Even if we look at "mainstream" conversations, I believe we will find that, when they are working, when they flow, when we seem to effortlessly find our way into the stream of talk—we are not constantly asking or answering questions. Or think of conversations that were mostly questions, when you were continually being asked questions. I think to the times when I was picking up a date, and had to talk for 5 or 10 excruciatingly long minutes with "the girl's father." (Now as I enact the role of father, I realize the discomfort was on both sides.) "I hear that you're on the swimming team?" "Yep." "How's the team been doing?" "Well, we've won a couple this year." And on, and on. Always the unstated question, "What are your plans for my daughter?" (If he only knew how appallingly safe she was with me.) The persistence of questions is the sign of a failed conversation and of one in which participants are not on equal footing. Conversations work when one turn builds off another, and when we cannot fully predict the order of turns. They work when there is a sense of openness and narrative possibility.

Taken together, these three assumptions undermine the potential for talk in the reading classroom. Grouping limits the possibility for interaction among diverse students, the need of certified calibration of reading difficulty limits the possibility for student choice of books, and the assumption about questioning forces student talk into a scripted set of answers to questions that are really not questions: "Can anybody tell me what I am thinking?"

AN ALTERNATIVE

In the rest of this chapter I will present an alternative way in which reading groups can be conducted—a way (and clearly not the only way) of making them into public spaces. Because I want to focus on the talk in discussion groups, I will only briefly describe the classroom itself and the procedures used to organize the groups.

- The classroom is a first–second combination in an elementary school in Lee, New Hampshire. The school, while the site of Donald Graves and Jane Hansen's Reading/Writing project (Hansen, 1987; Hansen & Graves, 1986), has begun to shift back to a basal program. Pat McLure's classroom is a tolerated exception to this trend.
- The classroom contains a sizable library (probably 600 books) organized alphabetically in bins.
- For their reading "work" (as opposed to the reading they might do for sustained silent reading) students are expected to read a book on their own, read it to a partner, and draw a picture from the book and write a comment—either a summary or evaluation of the book. Each step is noted on a form the student keeps in a reading folder. Once these steps are finished, the student is "ready" to share in a reading group.
- For 30 to 40 minutes each day Pat meets with a group of four students to discuss the reading they have done. These groups are picked by a student. To be chosen, a student must be "ready" and not have been in the share group recently (a clipboard is maintained to indicate when students participate). Typically, groups include both first and second graders, and a range of books, from predictable books for beginning readers to Roald Dahl and Patricia Reilly Giff.
- The person who chooses the group assigns the order of presentation, usually putting himself or herself last. The presenter begins by naming the book and author (Pat records it) and by giving a brief summary of the book. The student then reads a section of the books (or, in the case of shorter picture books, the whole thing) and then asks for questions or comments. During the discussion the students calls on others in the group, including the teacher.
- In addition to participating in the group, Pat keeps a record of what children said. She also serves as timekeeper to see that turns do not go on too long.
- The pattern of sharing parallels exactly other sharing events in the day, the two times when classroom share either reading or writing to the entire class, at the beginning of the afternoon when Pat shares a trade book with the class. This sharing format is usually called "the author's chair" (Hansen & Graves, 1983).
- During the sharing group time, other children are at some point in the cycle of reading, sharing their reading, or doing their sentence paper.

EXPECTING THE UNEXPECTED

What follows is a transcript from an actual discussion group led by Cindi, a first grader and beginning reader. In the group with her is a very proficient first-grade reader, a second grader who has been coded learning disabled, and another second grader who, if placed according to reading scores, would be in the middle. It is a group, in other words, that would never assemble in a calibrated reading program. The book shared is *Stop* (Cowley, 1981), a predictable book in which a runaway milk truck goes down a hill as people exhort it to stop. The text is a repetition of the line. "'Stop,' said the _____ but the truck wouldn't stop." The discussion occurs early in the year, September 21, and some of the children are not yet familiar with the format. The transcript starts after Cindi has finished reading the book to the group:

Cindi: Any questions or comments? Richard.
Richard: What's your favorite page?

(*This becomes a standard question during the year, asked in almost every sharing group.*)

Cindi (shows crash): I like this one myself.
PM: Why do you like that one?

(*Later on in the year students will ask this question. One of the unwritten rules is that you give reasons for preferences. Cindi is not yet familiar with this question and at a loss how to answer it.*)

Cindi: I don't know I just like it.
Caren: Why did you choose the book—because it was funny or something?

(*This is another question that becomes a standard in sharing groups. And again, Cindi is not familiar with it.*)

Cindi: I just wanted to choose these because—I don't know but—I don't know really what it is but I like to read these books and stuff. Stacey.
Susan: Why wouldn't the truck stop?

(*Here Susan asks the central comprehension question.*)

Cindi: I don't know? I guess there's no driver.
Richard: He didn't put the brakes on.
Cindi: I guess there isn't any driver. (Points to the page.) See there's no driver.

(*Susan's question has forced Cindi to go back to the book and look for evidence for her answer.*)

Richard: Ahhh. I guess he didn't put on the brakes or his brakes doesn't work.

(*Richard has a different answer to Susan's question. He knows that just getting out of the truck is not enough of a reason for the truck to slide downhill.*)

PM: Do you know what a milkman does?

(*Pat gambles with a shift in topics. She feels that children in the group are unfamiliar with the idea of milkmen. In a traditional reading group this background knowledge would come first: Pat prefers to monitor the discussion before coming in. This shift initiates a string of milkman stories.*)

Cindi: Well, I guess he drives around and delivers milk to people.
PM: Does anyone here have a milkman?
Caren: I, I, I used to have a milkman when I was about three. Actually when I was

a baby. I used to sit on the steps and wait for the milkman to come and then my mom and dad were always inside and then when he came and delivered the milk he always gave me a little bottle.

PM: I didn't know we have milkman around here now. I didn't know there was anybody you could call.

Caren: I saw a milk truck a couple of weeks ago.

PM: Did you? Are there milk trucks around here that deliver milk to houses? I didn't think so.

Susan: (unclear about her cousin): . . . that a milk can comes to their house. But he just quit his job because—I don't know why—but he just quit it and it's called king of the mountain.

PM: Is that close by here?

Susan: Well, yeah. It's where I used to have an old baby sitter when we weren't in school.

Caren: We're going to soon have a milkman around our house soon because Chris Winslow, the one in my room in kindergarten, his mom is having a baby October 20.

Richard: I have lots of babies in my neighborhood. But I don't never see the/

PM: The babies?

Richard: The milkman go by.

(*Richard is skeptical that all babies get milk the way Caren has described.*)

PM: You haven't seen the milkman go by?

Susan: I have.

Caren: I have.

PM: When the milkman brings the new milk to the house, in the story it shows that he is picking up the empty bottles? Why do you suppose he is doing that?

Cindi: I don't know.

Richard: Maybe the cat drank it.

PM: That's what people used to do when they had a milkman. They put out the empty bottles and then they take them back and wash them out and fill them up with new milk.

Richard: Is it like a glass bottle or plastic?

PM: It was a glass bottle. (Cindi: See I just noticed.) That's different from what we have now.

Cindi   (excited): These are new milks. These are new milks. These are new milks, and he's delivering those but he forgot to stop the truck so it's going on the road.

(*Cindi hasn't forgotten Susan's question. This talk about what milkmen do has helped her to answer it better. She now understands why the driver was out of the truck.*)

PM: That's right, it took off without the driver.

Cindi: Yeah.

Richard: It took off because he didn't have his brakes on.

PM: I bet he didn't put the emergency brake on.

Susan: Trucks can do that, for true?

(*Susan is trying to determine how realistic this fiction is—a major interest at this age.*)

PM:	What, for true, trucks can start rolling without a driver?
Susan:	Yeah.
Richard:	That happened to my car.
PM:	That's why drivers have to be very careful.
Caren:	Hey Richard, how'd that happen in your car? (Overlapping talk here. Richard tells how his mother's car started going backward. Pat explains to Susan where the emergency brake is located.)
Richard:	My mother forgot to put on the brake and the car started going. But my mother put on the emergency. (To Pat) Did it roll backwards?
Pat:	No I think it ran down the hill. It took off going down the hill because on every page they've got the uphill line.
Richard:	It's a good book.
Pat:	I guess we're all finished.

In some ways Pat assumes a traditional role in this group, particularly when she asks about what milkmen do. But one feature of this discussion that is not characteristic of conventional reading groups is the "right" of the student to bring in associated topics, ones that Pat does not plan and indeed could not anticipate. She could not have guessed that *Stop* would turn into a discussion of emergency brakes. In many cases students exercise this right to shift the topic of conversation from the story world to their own experienced world, and in some cases the most interesting talk occurs, not about the text, but about a child's story *suggested* by the text.

In the next excerpt the discussion takes a similar unexpected turn. A student has shared *Arthur's Tooth* by Marc Brown (1985). In the book Arthur is self-conscious about not having lost a tooth and for that reason being called a "baby." A dentist convinces him that in time his teeth will come out, and sure enough, Francine, his usual tormentor, accidentally knocks one out at recess. Unlike *Stop* a number of discussion points come to mind—teasing, feelings of being a baby, of being different. The children in Pat's share group focused on none of these—they focused on blood. Arthur's tooth would have bled—a topic that inevitably led to stories of lost teeth, blood, and the Tooth Fairy. Pat, rather than redirecting the talk back to the book, helps elicit these stories.

Megan:	I've lost eight.
Pat:	Did they bleed quite a bit?
Megan:	Well, the first two did but the others didn't.
Pat:	I don't think they always bleed a lot.
Martin:	When my tooth fell out I didn't even know it and I couldn't even find it so I had to write a note to the Tooth Fairy and I put it under my pillow and I still got a half dollar for it.
Pat:	Even though you didn't have the tooth there.
Martin:	Yeah.
Megan:	I lost a tooth once and I really lost it and I wrote a note to the Tooth Fairy and the next morning I did find a dollar under my pillow but I also found the tooth under my pillow.

Pat: Ohhhhh. Did the Fairy explain how the tooth turned up under the pillow? (Megan indicates "no.") Brian, how did you get your tooth back?

Brian: Well, I know because the Tooth Fairy doesn't know. I know it was my mom because the Tooth Fairy doesn't know I practice the violin.

Pat (laughing): So how is that connected?

Jimmy: The Tooth Fairy might.

Pat: Why? Did she leave a note for you?

Brian: Yeah. It was my mom. She wrote it. The Tooth Fairy I don't think writes in cursive.

Jimmy: You never know.

And then Jimmy tells his story. It is at points like these that the discussions become the most lively, when stories topple over stories, when students tell their versions of the story that has been shared. Typically talk of this sort is considered "off task" if it strays from the text; the book, the published story, is the only one that matters. But the conversational conventions of this classroom allow for a meeting of story tellers. Marc Brown is given a turn with his Arthur story, but others in the group can take their story-telling turn as well. This talk is "off task" only if we ignore the ways we all gossip and share stories outside school settings.

In the next excerpt the students have taken over the discussion. (Pat's only comment in this string is "yeah.") The book is *Arthur's Nose* (Brown, 1976) in which Arthur deals with another of his insecurities, his concern about his large and running nose. Much of the discussion focuses on the pictures in the book, particularly one that shows Arthur at the "rhinologist's" office, where he is given a choice of animal noses that might replace his own. Jed begins with a summary:

Jed: The name of this book is *Arthur's Nose* by Marc Brown. And he's worried about his nose and he wants to change his nose because he's worried about it and he goes to this place but he doesn't change his nose. He keeps the same nose and Francine says, "I still want to change my seat at school." Because his nose is always dripping and it's bothering her. This is Arthur's house. (Reads.)

Becky: Wow, that was probably the first book. (Jeffrey: I know.) It tells all about their family.

Jed (Reads. Stops at picture of Arthur's running nose): I don't think his nose looks funny because my nose sometimes looks like that. (Reads.)

Richard: Achooo.

Jed: It doesn't say "achoo." (Reads.)

Susan: Picture, picture!

Jed: I think Francine is making a little model of his nose.

PM: Yeah.

Becky: And with purple clay. I thought he had a brown nose.

Jed (Reads): Look at his sharp fingernails.

Becky: Wow!

Adam: Oh, my God!
Susan: It looks like pencil sharpeners sharpened them.
Jed   (Reads).
Becky: Can I see the noses?
Adam: Picture. Picture.
Becky: I've got to see these noses. Elephant.
Richard: Fish.
Adam: Where's the emu?
Becky: Where's the fish? Where's the fish?
Richard: Emu, right here.
Susan: A fish.
Becky: Where's the fish, Jed?
Jed: The fish is right there.
Becky: No way. I think the mouth is a little too big.
Jed   (Reads).
Susan: The mouse.
Jed: I like the mouse.
Richard: The mouse is pretty good.
Jed: Yeah, but look at his nose. Look how big his nose is compared to his mouth.
Susan: It'd be better if he gets whiskers.

So for 3 or 4 minutes they crowd around *Arthur's Nose* and imagine which nose they would pick. This episode illustrates a practice, common when a popular picture book is shared, of carefully attending to pictures to see all that can be seen—"milking the picture." Another variant is trying to find something hidden in a picture (e.g., Marc Brown put his children's names somewhere in the pictures in his books). The phenomenal success of the *Where's Waldo* (Hanford, 1987) books is explained by children's delight in attending to pictures. This episode also illustrates a method of response that appeared in mid-year, particularly when the books shared were popular picture books—the "running commentary." Students interject comments after each page, evaluating, kibbitzing as the book is read. It seemed that this form of response allowed them to react spontaneously, as it was read, like the "amens" and "preach it brothers" that punctuate the African-American sermon. Response should accompany reading, not follow it.

These three excerpts suggest the evolution of shared groups during the year that I recorded. As students became familiar with the rituals and kinds of questions that are asked, increasingly they took over the groups. They talked more, and Pat talked less. These transcripts also suggest that the sharing is most animated when it leaves the interrogative mode. Even when children are asking questions, there was often something ritualistic about the way they did it. And to say that they were ritualistic does not mean they were not in some way meaningful—why else did many of the ritualistic questions persist? It often seemed that these ritualistic questions allowed anyone to participate without the necessity of "invention"—just as anyone can talk to anyone about the weather. It's a risk-free (and thought-free) opening.

But once the door is open, if the sharing session was to work, a breakdown in question–answer decorum had to occur, and there needed to be a shift to some other mode of sharing—story telling, making comparisons between the story world and the world they know, kibbitzing, poring over pictures for details, wordplay. Many of these activities which engaged them seem to go off the point, off the text. How, for example, are we to respond to the following exchanges? It occurs around *Thomas the Rabbit*, by David Lloyd (1984), when students discussed a segment in which Thomas is caught but then escapes. Adam says it is too bad that Thomas got away and Sharon, the book's presenter, comes back, "Want them to cook him in a stew?"—a comment which led to a discussion of exotic and semigross foods:

Martin: Have you ever had rabbit stew?
Sharon: Unuh. My mother has had pickled rabbit.
Adam: Is it good?
Sharon: I never had it before. I don't even want to eat it.
Jed: My mom likes froglegs.
Adam: My mother loves them. And she loves snails.
Sharon: Has she been to Canada yet?
Adam: Yes.
Sharon: No wonder. Jed.
Jed: Well, Thomas is sort of like Dumbo but he's a rabbit.
Sharon: And he can't fly. He can sort of fly he can go so fast.
Jed: Yeah. Ooup (sound effect indicating speed). And then you couldn't say he has froglegs.
Phillip: It kind of grosses me out. If I hear it more than five times in one day I get sick.
Martin: Froglegs, froglegs, froglegs, froglegs, froglegs.
Phillip: No that's not what I'm talking about. The other way will do it.
Jed: I eat froglegs. I eat froglegs. I eat froglegs.
Adam: You eat froglegs. You eat froglegs. You eat froglegs. You eat froglegs. You eat froglegs.
Phillip: I eat froglegs (pretends to be sick).

We can make a case that serious booktalk is going on in this excerpt—evaluating the consequences of Thomas's possible capture, Jeffrey's comparison of Thomas to Dumbo, and even the enumeration of adult delicacies that children find gross. But what of the last ritual, the way Jed and Adam play off Richard's claim to be sick if he hears *froglegs* five times? How does that fit in? Or is this "off topic"?

To understand these groups, we must see them as open spaces where there is a meeting of formalized, adult question–answer patterns and the oral traditions of 6- and 7-year-olds. Some of the patterns are modelled by the teacher and taken over by the student, for example, asking questions of the reader. But other patterns—for example, the "milk the picture" pattern, the running commentary pattern, kinds of wordplay—are part of the children's culture. By making a place for both, I believe that Pat taps the conviviality and humor of her students. They socialize the act of reading and sharing reading. By contrast, the traditional reading group, with its rigid focus on decoding and comprehending the text, drives this child culture into the hallways and playgrounds.

The children in these groups were decidedly middle class, and it is only fair to ask if the openness I am advocating is appropriate for nonmainstream students. It seems to me it might be even more crucial to minority students who, as research has shown, are often unfamiliar with question–answer formats where every answer is evaluated by the teacher. We need to ask what alternatives to question–answer formats would be more congenial to these groups. Based on my own work in inner-city schools, where I began my teaching, I would predict that story telling and running commentaries would be far more "natural" than answering questions the teacher knows.

By viewing the reading groups as a mingling of cultures, we can abandon the binary mentality that separates student activity neatly into "on task" and "off task" behavior. We can ask whose definition of *on task* should count. We can begin to uncover (and respect) the conversational rules and routines that children bring to these groups. Much of the supposed "off task" or "off topic" talk is central to the effectiveness of these discussion groups. Dyson (1987) has written:

> Talk about academic tasks is often contrasted with social talk: individuals achieve because the time is spent "on task." My observations suggest that the "academic" and the "social" are not so simply—or profitably—separated. The social laughing, teasing, correcting, and chatting that accompany children's academic work are byproducts of the need to link with others and be recognized by them. But they can also be catalysts for intellectual growth. (p. 417)

It is the same for all of us. Think of those people we know who are always "on task," who seem to resent small talk as time wasting, who always act as if they are double parked. In the long run, it is hard to work efficiently with these people because we cannot share the stories, digressions, jokes, and family pictures that will make for intimacy and caring. Without that sense of mutual enjoyment that comes with these digressions, we never quite feel comfortable. We always feel rushed. There is no bank of good-will to draw on in critical times.

Maybe Holden Caulfield said it best in *Catcher in the Rye*. At one point in the book he recalls a teacher he had, Mr. Vinson, who taught "Oral

Expression." Students in the class were trained to yell "digression" whenever any speaker went off the subject:

> There was this one boy Richard Kinsella. He didn't stick to the point too much, and they were always yelling "Digression!" at him. He got a D plus because they kept yelling "Digression" at him all the time. For instance, he made this speech about the farm his father bought in Vermont. They kept yelling digression at him the whole time he was making it and this teacher, Mr. Vinson, gave him an F on it because he hadn't told what kind of animals and vegetables and stuff grew on the farm and all. What he did was, Richard Kinsella, he'd *start* telling you all that stuff—then all of a sudden he'd start telling you about his uncle, and how the uncle got polio and all when he was forty-two years old, and how he wouldn't let anybody come to see him at the hospital because he didn't want anybody to see him with a brace on. It didn't have much to do with the farm—I admit it—but it was nice....I mean it's dirty to keep yelling "Digression" at him when he's all nice and excited. (Salinger, 1951, p. 185).

Holden is asking that we redefine what we mean by being on-topic. He is reminding us that, without a sense of openness, of story-making possibilities, we can only recite the names of animals and plants. We never get to the good stuff.

REFERENCES

Allington, R. (1980). Teacher interruption behaviors during primary-grade oral reading. *Journal of Educational Psychology, 72*, 371-377.

Au, K. (1980). Participant structures in a reading lesson with Hawaiian children. *Anthropology and Education Quarterly, 11*, 91-115.

Bourke, S. (1986). Class of questions: Questions of classes. *SET Research Information for Teachers* (Australia), No. 1.

Brown, M. (1976). *Arthur's nose.* Boston: Little Brown.

Brown, M. (1985). *Arthur's tooth.* Boston: Little Brown.

Cowley, J. (1981). *Stop.* Auckland, NZ: Shorthand.

Dillon, J.T. (1988). *Questioning and teaching: A manual for practice.* London: Croom Helm.

Dyson, A. (1987). The value of "time off task": Young children's spontaneous talk and deliberative text. *Harvard Educational Review, 57*, 396-420.

Goodlad, J. (1984). *A place called school.* New York: McGraw-Hill.

Greene, M. (1988). *The dialectic of freedom.* New York: Teachers College Press.

Hanford, M. (1987). *Where's Waldo.* Boston: Little Brown.

Hansen, J. (1987). *When writers read.* Portsmouth, NH: Heinemann.

Hansen, J., & Graves, D. (1983). The author's chair. *Language Arts, 60*, 176-183.

Hansen, J., & Graves, D. (1986). Do you know what backstrung means? *Reading Teacher, 39*, 807-812.

Harste, J., Woodward, V., & Burke, C. (1984). *Language stories and literacy lessons.* Portsmouth, NH: Heinemann.

Heath, S. (1983). *Ways with words: Language, life, and work in communities and classrooms.* Cambridge, UK: Cambridge University Press.

Lloyd, D. (1984). *Thomas the rabbit.* New York: Scholastic.

Oakes, J. (1985). *Keeping track: How schools structure inequality.* New Haven, CT: Yale University Press.

Philips, S. (1972). Participant structures and communicative competence. In C. Cazden, V. John, & D. Hymes (Eds.), *Functions of language in the classroom.* New York: Teachers College Press.

Rist, R. (1973). *The urban school: A factory for failure.* Cambridge, MA: MIT Press.

Rose, M. (1989). *Lives on the boundary.* New York: Penguin.

Salinger, J. (1951). *Catcher in the rye.* Boston: Little Brown.

Shannon, P. (1989). *Broken promises: Reading instruction in twentieth century America.* Granby, MA: Bergin & Garvey.

Susskind, E. (1979). Encouraging teachers to encourage children's curiosity: A pivotal competence. *Journal of Clinical Child Psychology, 8,* 101-106.

Wells, G. (1986). *The meaning makers: Children learning language and using it to learn.* Portsmouth, NH: Heinemann.

PART II

STRATEGIES FOR READING AND WRITING ACROSS THE CURRICULUM

Chapter 5

From Workbook to Workshop: Increasing Children's Involvement in the Reading Process*

Cora Lee Five

The most dramatic change I have made as a teacher occurred in the last 6 years, in the area of reading.

In the past, my emphasis in reading was on reading skills. My fifth graders were divided into three groups based on a timed reading test I gave at the beginning of the year. I relied on workbooks that included endless pages on finding the main idea, selecting supporting details, determining the correct meaning of vocabulary words printed in bold-faced type, choosing an appropriate title from a list of four, and numbering sentences in the order in which they occurred in a given paragraph. My fifth graders filled in the blanks, guessed at multiple choice answers, and tried to make sense out of the sequencing exercises. I felt secure that at least I was teaching reading skills, the same skills that would show up on the reading achievement test at the end of the year.

But were these children learning to read? Where they even learning isolated skills? I didn't know. What I did know for sure was that they hated reading workbooks, and I hated correcting them.

*An earlier version of this chapter appeared in *Harvard Educational Review*. (Five, C.L., "Fifth Graders Respond to a Changed Reading Program," *Harvard Educational Review*, 1986, *56*, 394–405. Copyright© 1986 by the President and Fellows of Harvard College. All rights reserved.)

In those days I also gave my class a reading period for 20 to 30 minutes a day. Students had to have a book to read for the reading period. I often suggested or assigned books that I thought would be appropriate for their reading level—not their interest—their reading level, based on the test at the beginning of the year. During the reading period I would see five or six students a day. They would come to my desk individually, and I would hear them read their books aloud, checking to make sure they could pronounce every word and teaching them to sound them out if they couldn't. If they didn't know the meaning of isolated words or couldn't pronounce some of the words, I suggested they return the book and get an easier one.

That was my reading program, and I worked hard at it. I wanted my students to become good readers, which meant to me, at that time, that I wanted them to have high scores on the end-of-the-year reading test. Yet, despite my hard work, I heard from their parents, "Michael doesn't like to read," or "She doesn't read at all at home." And I observed my students during the reading period as I corrected their workbooks. They turned the pages of their books, but they looked out the window, sighed, whispered to each other, passed notes, and watched the clock. They did not like reading. In fact, the reading period was a chore for them.

Today my reading program is dramatically different, and so are the results. Today my students read between 25 and 160 books a year. Children listen to each other and seek recommendations for their next book selections. They wonder about authors and look for feelings, for believable characters, for interesting words, and they are delighted with effective dialogue. And my students and I always talk books before school, during school, at lunch, and after school, something we never did in my "workbook" days.

Test scores are gratifying, too. With this program that departs from the teaching of isolated skills, test results remained constant or showed gains of from 2 to 6 years in reading comprehension.

What caused the changed in my reading program? What caused my growth as a teacher of reading? When I reflect on myself as a teacher, I see myself as a learner. And my learning started with the process approach to writing. I did not know how to teach writing 10 years ago. Again, I relied on language arts textbooks and workbooks and the assigned topics they offered. My students did not like to write, and, once again, I did not like to correct.

Then I learned about the writing process and my professional life changed. My students and I became involved with each other. We talked, and we listened. We became a community of writers. I saw how they responded when they could select their own topics. I saw how they loved to write when they had time to write and revise. I saw their enthusiasm when they conferred with one another, offered suggestions, explained their feelings, made revisions—in effect, took control of their writing and improved it. And I saw their pleasure in sharing their own work, writing that was meaningful to them. The daily conferences turned me into a listener. Their pieces provided me with insight into the mind and heart of the 10-year-old. Their needs and interests became the basis of my teaching. When there was a need to know how to use quotation marks, they wanted to learn. When there was a desire to experiment with suspense, humor, similies, or new vocabulary, they needed the freedom and support to take risks. They loved writing. It became their favorite subject, and it became my favorite subject to teach.

Could reading be a favorite, too? I wondered about the connection between writing and reading. Could the same elements found in the writing program, time, ownership, and response, be applied to reading?

And so I began to study the connection between reading and writing. Inspired by the insights of three people, Nancie Atwell, (1985), Mary Ellen Giacobbe (1985), and Jerry Harste (1985), I embarked on a new venture 6 years ago—the creation of a reading program that would give children time to read and time to make meaning through writing and talking about books. I hoped my students would turn into readers who loved reading, just as they had turned into writers who loved writing.

The first thing I did was the most difficult. With much trepidation, I gave up those reading workbooks—and set up a reading program that has the crucial elements of my writing program—*time, ownership,* and *response.*

It was essential to establish a reading period or workshop. I increased the amount of school time children had for reading to 45 minutes every day. I begin each reading period with a minilesson on an element of fiction—character development, setting, titles, flashbacks, and other techniques writers and readers need to know. Often I use the books that I read aloud to them each day as the basis for my minilessons, allowing time for discussions, for making predictions and interpretations, and for discovering characteristics of a particular author's style that students may wish to apply to their own writing. Different genres are also introduced during these lessons.

Early minilessons focus on how to select a book. We share our methods of book selection and learn that many students rely on recommendations from friends. Others use the cover, title, or information about the book that is included on the inside flap or back cover. These discussions have proven to be especially helpful for those students who could not "find a good book."

In another minilesson we talk about abandoning books, how students decide to change one book for another, how long they try a book before they give it up. At first, their comments center on "when it gets boring," which we soon realize means different things to different readers. Some students notice books could be "boring" if they are too difficult. They also begin to realize the importance of a good lead, one that grabs the reader's attention right away (this ties in very well with a minilesson on leads during my writing workshop!). Immediate action seems important to my fifth-grade readers at the beginning of the year. They reject books with long sections of description, although toward the end of the year description was more interesting to them as writers and did not present problems in their enjoyment of reading.

Many minilessons are of a sharing/ discussion nature. Others, however, involve more directed teaching on my part. I teach the class about the meaning and importance of copyright. Students then look for the copyright date in their own reading books and share this information with the group. We also look at names of publishers, places of publication, and where and why this information is noted in a book.

In other minilessons, specific activities are done together. In one minilesson, we made a time line of the life of one of the characters from a book I was reading aloud. We starred those events that seemed to have a significant effect on the character. Later, students made time lines for characters from their own reading. In another minilesson we graphed the plot of *Little Red Riding Hood*, using a continuum of smiling to sad faces. This activity was based on a lesson called "The Fortunes of the Protagonist" in *Literacy Through Literature* (Johnson & Louis, 1985). Not only did students learn the word *protagonist*, they began to notice an interesting, involving plot was not a straight line of happy events but was, instead, one with peaks or climaxes. The children then graphed the plots, "the fortunes of the protagonist," from other books I had read aloud. They shared their individual graphs with each other and were often surprised at the many possible interpretations of the same book.

After the minilessons students read books of their own choosing. They maintain ownership because *they* decide what to read. Books come from home, the school library, and from the extensive classroom library I have been developing over the past few years. Children read the books they select, not those assigned by me.

During the reading period I confer briefly with each child about his or her book. As with the writing, I become a listener who asks questions that truly interest me. This daily contact with each child involves me with my students and their reading—just as I am involved with them and their writing. Once I confer with each student, I spend the remainder of the reading period reading a book of my own choice. No more correcting papers during reading period! Now I have the pleasure of reading, too. We end the period with either a group sharing-time, often related to the minilessons, or discussions among two or three students, who talk about some aspect of their books.

The third element, response, is the most interesting part of this new approach to reading. Discussions during the reading period are not the only way the students communicate about what they read. They also respond to their reading in a variety of ways in their literature journals. The primary response is based on Atwell's (1984, 1985) model. They write letters to me each week, and I write letters back to them. (Spelling errors are not considered and not corrected. I look for their ability to make meaning and personal connections to their reading.) What a joy to read and respond to these letters and to observe their development as readers!

At first, journal responses were similar to the book reports students had written in previous years. They summarized plots and recommended books. Gradually the topics presented in minilessons and in our discussions of the books I read aloud began to appear in the children's letters.

After 2 months of school, Danny, who did not like reading at the beginning of the year, was making personal connections with the characters.

Dear Miss Five,

This letter is about *Norman Schurnam—"Average Person"*. The things I liked best about the book were, feeling and comedy. Especially feeling. Because when I read the part about when he told his Dad he didn't want to play football. I think he deserved "Ten Medals"! Because if I had a Dad like that I would have probably played the whole season even if I was that bad and got hurt alot. Because I wouldn't have the heart to watch him put his head down in disappointment. And if he did put his head down, I would have felt so guilty I would have come back ten minutes later and said Dad I'll play. No matter how bad it felt. But I guess me and Norman are different people. And I thought the author had a good ending because it made you in a way forget about the incident with his Dad.

Truly yours,
Danny

By March, Danny loved to read and write and had developed an interest in the authors of the books he was reading. He discovered Betsy Byars (1979) through *Good-bye, Chicken Little*.

I thought this book was so true and this may have happened to a kid. I think I might send a letter to Betsy Byars to see if this book was based on experience. I thought his biggest mistake was fighting with Conrad. this book was so good I wish I could read it forever.

Danny wrote to Byars and treasured the letter he received from her, stapling it into his literature journal. He read all the rest of her books, and he decided to write in his journal every night, because "In case I really do become an author, I want to remember all my experiences so I can put them in books for kids my age."

As the year progresses, many students begin to experiment and struggle with interpreting the ideas in the books they read. Josh described Jess, a character in Paterson's (1977) *Bridge to Terabithia.*

Dear Miss Five,

Jess has so many feelings its hard to describe him. Let's say he had three stages. First, a normal, hardworking stage at the beginning, and feelings, if he had any, would never be shared with anyone else. The second stage, when Leslie came into his life, turned into kind of a magical stage in a way for him. The third stage, when Leslie died, he began to relate to adults. These three stages make him real.

> Sincerely,
> Josh

Etay began to interpret and extend his ideas in the fall. His response to *After the Goat Man* by Byars (1974) and his other letters show his developing ability to look beyond the story line.

Dear Miss Five,

On Thursday I finished *After the Goat Man.* I thought it was better than all the other books I read by Betsy Byars. I think she got the idea of the goat from as goats are supposed to be stubborn and the character is stubborn. I think thats her symbol for the character. I also like the way she puts Harold as a kid still in his fantasys and still dreaming about himself. I like the way she puts her characters. There is also something that I liked about an anology about life. Figgy puts life as a spider-web and everybody's all tied up except for him, and he's only tied up by one string which is his grandfather (the Goat Man.)

> Etay

He found a connection between Byars's 1980 *The Night Swimmers* and Paterson's (1977) *Bridge to Terabithia:*

In the end of the book Roy asked his oldest sister "is the Bowlwater plant really a big gigantic plant with bedspreads for flowers" and he went on explaining his fantasy. His oldest sister answered "no." At that moment I thought about the book. I thought maybe that was Roys' bridge (like Bridge to Terabithia) from his fantasy world to reality world.

> Etay

It appears that students attempt to search for greater depth in their books if their responses are accepted and not treated as comprehension problems. Just as they experiment and take risks in their writing, they do the same thing with their reading.

Three or four times a month each child writes a letter to another child in the class about his or her book. These letters are often of a different nature than the ones they write to me. David and Etay began to write to each other at the beginning of the year.

Dear Etay,

I just finished *A Wrinkle in Time*. It is a great book. I think you should read it again. Some parts of the book are pretty confusing though.

> From,
> David

Dear David

I hate science fiction!!!

> Etay

A few months later there was more of an exchange of ideas between the two boys.

Dear Etay,

I am reading a book called *Alice's Adventures in Wonderland*. I don't like it very much. I think it is too boring! It seems that it takes forever. I have always liked Alice in Wonderland, but I don't like this one. Even though it is by the original author, Lewis Carrol. I am up to The Mock turtle's story. My favorite parts so far is when she was playing croquet and when she kept growing and shrinking when she ate the mushroom, even though these parts are not so good. I am not going to read, Through the Looking Glass.

> David

Dear David,

I can see that you didn't like this book. I didn't like it either. I thought it was just an adventure after an adventure and then all it lead to was a dream. It was written the best way it could but I don't think it was made for our age. I think it was made for smaller kids (who see it as a cute little fantasy) or for grownups (who see it with some meaning). We're in the middle because we're too big to see it as a cute fantasy and we're too small to see it with some meaning.

> Etay

It was through these letters to partners and their journal responses to me that I became convinced that children need to have control over their book choices rather then receiving specific reading assignments from me.

In addition to letters about books, I provide other opportunities for students to respond to their reading. They can express their interpretations through art, drama, and "mapping" (Krim, 1985, 1986). Mapping proved to be especially interesting due to the variety of responses. Two examples of mapping Paterson's (1977) *Bridge to Terabithia* demonstrate the range of strategies used for interpreting the book.

Bridge to Terabithia is a story about a fifth-grade boy, Jess, who has difficulty relating to other people. He befriends Leslie who moves in near his home. Together they create a special kingdom called Terebithia. Jess loses his friend when Leslie has a fatal accident in Terebitia. As he tries to adjust to her death, Jess grows and begins to build a closer relationship with his father and others.

Josh used lines and numbers to connect his drawings of important events. He made large drawings of the two events he felt were most significant. In picture 7 he made a bridge between Jess and his father and in picture 9 he showed Jess rebuilding Terrabithia for his sister Maybelle (see Figure 5.1).

Amy mapped the story through a chart of the character's feelings (see Figure 5.2). She placed Jess and Leslie at the top and described their meeting at school where Jess is "anxious" and Leslie feels "different and out of place." She continued her chart expressing the events in the book through the characters' feelings until Leslie's death. Then she included all the emotions Jess experienced as he tried to deal with his best friend's death.

Student responses to me and to each other made me think about he classroom context needed to support their reading. I realized that they read with greater depth when they selected their own books, ones that appealed to them rather than those I thought they "should" read. Because they had

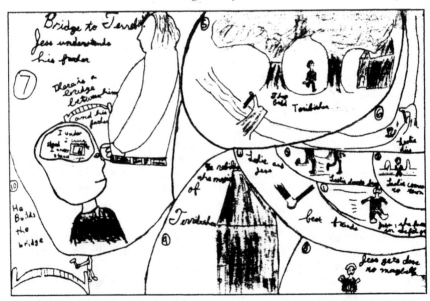

Figure 5.1.   Illustration by Josh

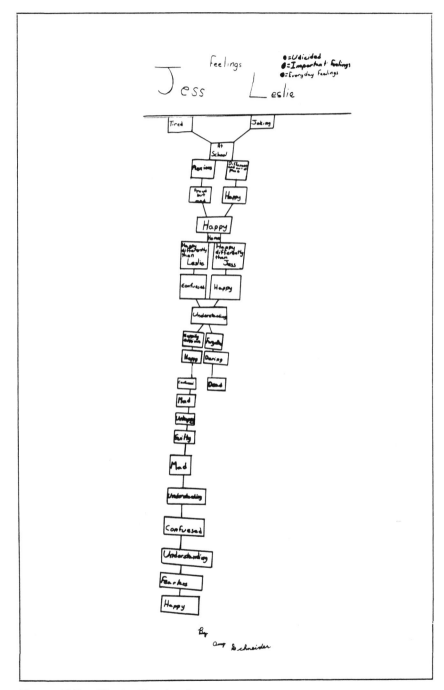

Figure 5.2.   Illustration by Amy

the freedom to choose their books, I think they felt the freedom to experiment with their own ideas. I also realized that they probably took risks to find ways to express themselves, because I did not label their comments as "correct" or "incorrect." I learned that children have different ways of making meaning and that they benefited from exposure to different strategies. And as in their writing, they expressed what was meaningful to them. There wasn't one right answer or interpretation as in the teacher's guide for the reading workbook. A classroom environment that accepted and respected what children said about books was necessary for my students' responses and their increased interest in reading.

This new approach to reading had an important effect on me. My students and I began "talk books." Their enthusiasm was infectious. I was constantly drawn into their discussions and especially their thinking, as I became more and more involved in their reading and their responses. This approach helped me to continue to learn more about my students, their reading processes, and their attitudes. As I grew and moved from reading workbooks to reading workshops, I learned the importance of giving students freedom to read and opportunities to explore and experiment with their own ideas. As a result my students turned into readers who loved books.

REFERENCES

Atwell, N. (1984). Writing and reading literature from the inside out. *Language Arts, 61,* 240–252.

Atwell, N. (1985, July). *Reading, writing, thinking, learning* [course]. Institute on Writing, sponsored by Northeastern University, Martha's Vineyard, MA.

Byars, B. (1974). *After the goatman.* New York: Viking.

Byars, B. (1979). *Good-bye, Chicken Little.* New York: Harper & Row.

Byars, B. (1980). *The night swimmers.* New York: Delacorte.

Giacobbe, M.E. (1985), July). *Reading, writing, thinking, learning* [course]. Institute on Writing, sponsored by Northeastern University, Martha's Vineyard, MA.

Harste, J. C. (1985), July). *Creativity and intentionality* [course]. Institute on Writing, sponsored by Northeastern University, Martha's Vineyard, MA

Harste, J.C., Woodward, V.A., & Burke, C.L. (1984). *Language stories and literacy lessons.* Portsmouth, NH: Heinemann Educational Books.

Johnston, T.D., & Louis, D.R. (1985). *Literacy through literature.* Melbourne: Methuen Australia Pty Ltd.

Krim, N. (1985, March). *Integrating reading, writing, and critical thinking skills in the teaching of literature: Focus, mapping, and sequencing strategies.* Presentation at the annual spring conference of the National Council of Teachers of English.

Krim, N. (1986). *Where do we go from here? Try mapping.* Unpublished manuscript.

Okimoto, J.D. (1982). *Norman Schurman, average person.* New York: Putnam.

Paterson, K. (1977). *Bridge to Terabithia.* New York: Crowell.

Chapter 6

Classroom Environments for Reading and Writing Together*

Ruth Nathan
Charles Temple

THE TEACHER GOES FIRST: ESTABLISHING A TRUSTING ENVIRONMENT

Teachers often tell me their children don't want to share their writing, especially when they're approaching the upper elementary and junior high years. I don't need research to tell me why. And they often say, even if their children do share, that share time is nebulous: not much gets done. Often these same teachers follow their statements about timidity and lack of peer-conference content with the question, "What can we do about it?" When my workshops bend in this direction, I usually look to the teachers I'm working with for answers. Generally I find the collective group knows exactly what to do.

The Teacher as Writer

I ask, "How many of you write and share your writing with your children?" A few teachers nod, and so we ask them to tell us why. The answers are often long and passionate. Teachers who write tell us things we know are true because we're writers ourselves (Nathan, 1988). Usually they begin with the effect their authorship has on how they talk to their students and thus how their students begin talking and sharing with one another.

---

*This chapter is reproduced from T. Shanahan (Ed.), *Reading and writing together: New perspectives for the classroom.* Norwood, MA: Christopher-Gordon. Reprinted by permission.

If you are a teacher, they say, holding a conference with a young writer is not easy. The problem is twofold. Authors break easily, and teachers tend to criticize. Authors, especially authors who happen to be children, do not want advice right away. Teachers who write know this. Authors want readers to tell them they've done a good job. A fourth grader recently put it simply: "I want people to say that's 'EXCELLENT!'"

Teacher writers also understand that advice, while necessary, must be given at the right time and by a trusted individual. The know how a writer feels when a piece is shared—the chemical twang, the wildly beating heart, the mental involvement, the "I'm out there and feeling vulnerable" sensations. We find it doesn't really matter if teachers write well: that's almost (but not totally) irrelevant. What does matter is that teachers attempt to write something well and that they share their drafts as they ask their students to do.

Another reason teachers tell us they write in order to encourage quality sharing is that only after they have seriously attempted to get an idea across on paper does the difficulty inherent in the writing process become obvious. We agree; ideas, far too many of them, enter our minds all at once, and writers (unlike the computer on our desks) must eke them out one at a time—slowly. Furthermore, we don't have gestures to help us get our points across, as we do when we're talking. Gestures, and other cues like intonation, help our audience understand us. When we write, all we have is a blank sheet of paper and our ability to handle the English language. Most know this is natural. The difficulty in matching what's in one's head with what's on the page is difficult to explain to anyone who hasn't grappled with the problem, really caring to get the ideas right.

Teachers who write are the best conference partners in the world, because they respect their children's efforts. It's that simple. When it seems as though a piece is breaking down, a teacher who writes is more apt to ask himself or herself, "What's this writer doing that's new?" instead of thinking, This piece is impossible.

All of this—knowing that modeling is important, feeling vulnerable, and understanding the difficulty inherent in getting your paper to say what you mean—adds up to an honest workshop environment where writing takes the shape of the craft it is meant to be.

The Teacher as Reader

Establishing a trusting reading environment is to risk monster behavior: Children who chomp at the bit to read; tell their peers *what* to read, emphatically; roar for new titles; make connections between books; and demand time *in class* to talk books, write books, and *read*. Teachers who do not routinely find the time to read for pleasure or information themselves may not understand what all this means or how to bring it about. For those who do, it comes naturally.

Fearing that many teachers don't carve out niches of reading time for themselves often enough, I routinely give an assignment to my summer graduate students at Oakland University, where I teach a master's course, "Literature/Writing Connections." The assignment reads:

> Choose a book you'd like to read but have put aside due to lack of time. Bring it to class. It will be one of your three textbooks.

My graduates are both amazed and thrilled. A typical response to the syllabus is, "I haven't touched my professional literature in months, let alone Le Carre!"

I tell them, "Take your guilt and throw it out with the trash!" The notion that one shouldn't or *that one need not* be a reader to teach reading, or writing for that matter, needs shedding. "Say goodbye to that 'I've not time' skin, and look in the mirror," I say. "First remember yourself as a child, perhaps when you read *The Hardy Boys, The Bobbsey Twins, Mr. Opper's Penguins, The Secret Garden, The Thirteen Clocks.* Do you remember reading," I ask, "under the covers with a flashlight in hand?"

"Now, bring up an image of listening to your fifth-grade teacher reading to you. Do you see yourself and your class in that mirror? Recall how you felt hearing Wilbur in *Charlotte's Web* would be spared, how you roared over Toad's escapades in *The Wind in the Willows*, how you gasped when you realized Johnny Tremain was in love. Do you remember hearing the incredible story of Galileo or Leonardo da Vinci? did your class ever get a class-size subscription to the local newspaper? Did you read about Martin Luther King in one of those issues? Or Sputnik?

"Teachers who gave you all those opportunities to read were readers themselves, just as surely as I'm standing here," I assure them. So, in that university class each summer, I give my students time to read something they choose for themselves. I also give them time to write about their books in dialogue journals (Atwell, 1987; Five, 1988). These logs, as they're often called, are places where readers write reactions, suspicions, questions, and predictions; where they digress, just as often, about the books they're reading to a trusted other-often another student but sometimes the teacher.

Here are two sample entries running between one of my students and me (Nathan, Temple, Juntunen, & Temple, 1989) last summer. Linda and I were reading *Collaborators* by Janet Kauffman.

Dear Ruth,

> ...I especially like Chapter Two, which took place at Rehobeth Beach. It reminded me of the time I was living near Washington D.C. and working at

the National Institute of Health. On weekends, I'd take my daughter, then about two, to Rehobeth Beach for the day. We liked it best in the spring or the fall when it wasn't full of tourists. What fond memories...

Back to the book...

I thought it was interesting how Kauffman used the tobacco farm surrounding the prison as her main setting. I know if I were reading this in Professor Fitzsimmon's class, he'd find all kinds of symbolism in that and know exactly what it meant, but I haven't figured it out yet. I'm just enjoying Kauffman's colorful use of language.

I haven't yet decided why she titled her book *Collaborators*. I'll have to look for more clues as I continue to read. What do you think? I'm also curious about who you think Andrea Doria's mother is referring to when she refers to her three lovers—grandfather, father, and son.

Dear Linda,

Reading the first few chapters, then your letter—what fun! I've never done this before.

...Yes, you talk of language. Kauffman is an acrobat. "Every singsong she treats as a crowd of words, and she is vigilant, gulping, ready for trouble," tells us so much about this lady, this mother. And, "if all my loved ones were drowning, she says to me—to me that is no one—and I had the strength to save one, I'd save Ruth." Kauffman hasn't used more than one adjective in those two quotes, yet we know so much about this woman. Think of that—

...I also loved Chapter Two, the beach chapter you mention. You know, that chapter is a short story in her collection, *Places in the World a Woman Could Walk*...On page seven, "I calculate how to touch a collapsing wall...," she's talking about waves—what an apt metaphor. And she uses "tag" rather than "touch"— how to tag it, and how to rush off within my own splashes...I wish I wrote like that! So fresh.

Regarding lovers, I'm not sure. I'll have to read on and let you know next letter swap. Ditto regarding the tobacco farm.

Getting serious about books with your students collapses the wall between you, as surely as Kauffman's waves collapse upon her shore. Linda could have as easily been a fourth grader as my student; I could have been her fourth-grade peer as easily as her teacher. Teacher as reader, reader as teacher, young and old, it doesn't matter. As with needing to write in order to create a healthy writing environment, being a reader is *the issue* when it comes to creating a trusting reading environment. Your students need you to read books you choose, and for *you* to become famous, perhaps infamous, for talking "books" in the teacher's lounge, at your dining room table, at the parties you go to. Shed your "I've no time" skin—if you're someone who needs to—and take time, make time, to read.

Children and Teachers Sharing Writing Strategies

We begin this section with a story. One of us (RN) walked into a fourth-grade class the other day with a draft in hand called "The Last Windy Night." "Kids, come over here," I said. "I have to show you something." The children gathered around. "I went up to Torch Lake this weekend, alone. I stayed at a friend's cottage. At dusk, I walked out the back door and headed toward the pier to watch the sun set. As I left, the door squeaked in a funny way, sort of like, "Eee...eee...eeek...hmm...m.' I went back inside to try it again. Same sound. I tried it again, and again. Same thing. I sat down on the back porch steps thinking about how I might use it in a story. It was such a sound! Forgetting the sunset, I ran inside and started to write; I had no idea what I was going to say.

"I plopped down on the floor with a paper and pencil and scratched out a beginning. Before I knew it, I had an idea. The sound would be a trapped ghost trying to tell me it wanted out! Once I tripped upon my idea, the rest was easy."

The children were astounded by my telling them I had no idea what I was going to say before I began my story. They were used to planning their stories on work sheets before they wrote. "Next time you get a feeling you have a story," I said, "you might forget your plan sheet and just start to write. While you may need it later, occasionally those things get in the way. Sometimes I just need to write lots of words before a good idea comes into my head."

The spontaneity of my sharing was catching. Soon the other children in the class began to share things that happen to them as they write before they write. One youngster said she needs to take a shower! ("I think so well then!" she said.) These sharings become natural minilessons before a writing workshop. A child would tell me something, and I would say, "Would you begin our writing workshop with that story tomorrow?" The children know I'm dead serious over wanting to learn all I can about their writing strategies, and they know, absolutely, that I think we all will learn from those stories. That's because we're all readers and writers; it's the bottom line.

Another telling story. I received Wallace Stegner's (1987) novel *Crossing to Safety* one afternoon last month. It is a beautiful, poignant novel from a Pulitzer Priz-winning author about friendship. Do you remember what Holden Caulfield said in *The Catcher in the Rye* about a good book (Salinger, 1951)? "What really knocks me out is a book that, when you're all done reading it you wish the author that wrote it was a terrific friend of yours and you could call him up on the phone whenever you felt like it."

Oh, how I wanted to call Stegner *A thousand* times as I read *Crossing to*

Safety. I found myself spellbound as Aunt Emily read *Hiawatha* to the children, frightened as the novel's foursome almost perished on Lake Mendota, astonished over the author's "snake in the grass" and dazzled by Stegner's continual reference to literature across cultures through the centuries. I went to class the next day (this time my students were in middle school) and started "reading time" by sharing Salinger's line. Then I read from Stegner's novel in hopes that my students would understand my Caulfieldian response:

> We have been tacking back and forth, ducking under the swinging boom. Sid is very busy, for the boat handles badly and the wind seems to come from every direction. The sun has gone under, too, and the warmth has left the afternoon. The sky to the left is full of bruise-colored clouds, and the hospital towers on the north shore are lost in gray shrags of rain. In the hostile airs we come almost to a standstill. The canvas flaps. Sid grates out, "Oh God, don't *luff!*" The boom comes over, we veer sluggishly onto another tack. (p. 116)

In no time we were all talking at once, my students calling out names of authors they wish they could met—Pearl Buck, Jane Yolen, Lloyd Alexander, Roald Dahl, Katherine Paterson, Laurence Yap—me telling them others I'd like to know, and not letting on, just yet, about Buck. (I've written authors after they died, by accident, and am none the worse for it.) All this started a lively discussion about writing authors and, more important, about perusing the newspaper for writers giving readings at our local universities, colleges, and community centers. I said that, while I might write Segner some day, I didn't know, because I'd not yet finished the book, but that I had written Fielding Dawson (1984) a few years ago after reading *Tiger Lillies: An American Childhood*, my all-time favorite collection of childhood remembrances. "Bring the letter in!" they yelled. I did, hoping Fielding Dawson wouldn't mind (he has since given me permission to quote it here). Here is a short excerpt from his note:

> In the fall of 1984 I was invited to a college in upstate New York to give a talk to a class, and a reading to the students. There was a good turnout for both, and the kids were eager. I read from *Tiger Lilies*. Their teacher, who invited me, asked me to read the section about Popeye, in grade school, so I did, and became so moved I wept. I couldn't read. I stood up there, not knowing what to do, wiping my eyes, clearing my throat, the guy who invited me in tears, the whole room, a lecture room, upset, confused, embarrassed, some of the girls crying. I at last got hold, and went on, etc. and they sent me a copy of the school paper with a picture of me, and an article, no mention of you know what except a line that I have an emotional involvement with my work.

"An emotional involvement with my work." The children were genuinely touched by that line. Me, too. Surely, it says what being a teacher should be all about. Just as we walk into writing classes as writers and share our enthusiasms, strategies, and frustrations, we walk into reading classrooms as readers with our questions, excitements, and desires—desires to know authors we admire, how others feel about a book, how a book might affect the way we live our very lives. The day I received Dawson's letter I wept, too, from sheer relief that another human being would open his heart to me, a stranger; and, too, that I apparently hadn't made a fool of myself in sending him those few carefully chosen words. This behavior, because it's honest and natural, sets the stage for all that's to happen, or not happen, in our language arts classrooms.

"Guilty?" Because we take time to read Stegner, Dawson, Kauffman, Le Carre? The notion needs challenging. Guilty? Because we treat ourselves to a public reading once in a while instead of correcting papers? Guilty? Because we write an unrequired letter? I say, let happen what happened in Sendak's *Where the Wild Things Are*—let the monsters roar their terrible roars.

Teacher and Children as Readers and Writers

Karen has just finished a piece about her dog. Most of it is what you might expect from a fourth grader. But out of the ordinary comes this line:

"My dog looks like a ghost with curls."

Karen's teacher turns to her and asks how she thought of that description. "He's white and curly," came Karen's reply.

The children press, "But the ghost part."

Karen smiles and whispers to her teacher, "He's light as a feather, too," and laughs.

"What did you say?" the children shout. And Karen tells them, in this authentic place, because she knows they want to know. Like her they are writers who published at their work, and Karen knows they want their work to be read and loved, too. Class opinion has it that Karen has done something extraordinary, and they'd like to write something extraordinary as well.

Karen's exchange with her classmates and her teacher took place in a matter of a minute or two, but the authors of this chapter are of the decided opinion that small incidents like this are what teach in a reading-writing classroom. Teaching effective word choice, like most other reading-writing lessons, happens throughout the course of the day as opportunities arise. The hard part for teachers who don't write or read very much is to know what to notice and, therefore, what to teach. This is why workbooks are still so inviting to so many.

Another room, another day, by the same idea: effective word choice. The teacher is reading a passage from a book that's hooked her, *Reading the River* by John Hildebrand (1988). It's about a man who decides to canoe the length of the Yukon in order to know the people he had not become. The teacher had typed a paragraph from it the night before and later made copies for the class:

> Gathering in the brackish water of the Yukon Delta, the salmon undergo a transformation. Their coloring changes from bright silver to muddy red: their stomachs shrink as they cease feeding. Already they've begun to die from the tail up. (p. 79)

She reads the excerpt aloud, after telling the children a little about the book's themes. Then she asks them to do something. "Read this passage again slowly to yourself; then underline your favorite line or passage. Plan on telling us why you chose it." The children read and mark their pages. Several have chosen the same line, others the same phrase. The children like "Already, they've begun to die from the tail up" because "That's a new way of saying dying," or "It's like 'bottom up,' but different." The children recognize fresh language. Several mention the phrase "stomachs shrinking"; they've not thought of that before: "stomachs shrinking." Like the teacher who recognized "ghost with curls," this educator knows, because she is writing herself, that children are able to detect words that "mean more." Word choice is part of what makes writing worth reading.

The kids catch on. "Can we do that with one of our paragraphs?" one youngster asks. They can and do. The students take a ditto master from the ditto box and proceed to copy their favorite paragraphs from their own handwritten books. When one finishes, he passes it on to the next youngster, who adds her paragraph, and so on. The teacher runs it off after school, and the next day, writing workshop starts with this:

> The next day we went to Walt Disney world. We went on a lot of rides. One of them was haunted mansion. fack ghosts that were white and we saw spider webs that were torn up. There were loud noises that sounded spooky and like the wind. by Aaron Fry 3rd grade.

> I jerked it up I took a step and I thought there were some more boards there but there weren't I'll tell you what was there. Yucky. smelly. dirty water. And when I took that step—Cusplash! by Dale King, 4th grade

The children underlined their favorite parts, talked about "Spooky and like the wind," and Dale's smelly, dirty water. They talked about Aaron and Dale's work just as they talked about Hildebrand's.

Modeling Writing Dialogue

Recently one of us read Paul Darcy Boles's (1984) book *Storycrafting* and got an enriched awareness of what makes dialogue work. While there are many answers to why talk flows in one story and not in another, Boles taught this author that *surrounding description* and *explanatory action* help bring an exchange to life. Consider this excerpt from *Twenty and Ten* by Claire Bishop (1952, p. 25), the story of 20 Christian children who help conceal 10 Jewish children during World War II:

> We sat down in silence. We did not feel like talking. Soon we could tell by the very sound of the spoons that everybody was getting to the bottom of each bowl pretty quickly—too quickly.
>
> Henry sat across the table from me. He was counting the spoonfuls and swallowing very slowly to make it last: nine, ten...He sighed, and I heard him mutter to himself. "Perhaps three more." He threw a glance at his new neighbor, who had already cleaned his bowl. He was a small blond boy, doubled up on his chair, and he had large dark circles under his eyes.
>
> "What's your name?" asked Henry in a low voice.
>
> "A-A-Arthur," said the boy.
>
> "I'm Henry. Look Arthur. Do me a favor. Eat the rest of my soup." Arthur shook his head vehemently.
>
> Henry compressed his lips and said, "Please. To tell you the truth, I hate the stuff."

Take a look at the action and the description surrounding Arthur and Henry's short exchange. (Sometimes we ask the children to underline description and action in different colors.) We have seen Henry counting out each precious spoonful of soup. We have heard him sigh and mutter for the sake of his own painfully hungry belly. At the same time, we have caught his furtive glance toward the small boy who's doubled up and laden with black circles. Against this background, the beautiful gesture offered through the words, "To tell you the truth, I hate the stuff," takes on the profound meaning it's supposed to. Children everywhere understand the importance of that line. Boles, in *Storycrafting*, helps us understand how it's done: how dialogue rings true depends on how it's dressed.

One of the authors (RN) took Boles's lesson to the children's teacher, this time with my own rough draft in hand. I purposefully left my dialogue as it was and worked in front of them by adding surrounding description and explanatory action to make it better. The children reminded me that characters' thoughts also surround talk, so I considered that, too. Here's my piece before I worked with it, followed by my revision based on Boles's suggestions, as well as the children's. The story is the same one we mentioned earlier, "The Last Windy Night," a ghostly tale for second, third, and fourth graders. Suzanna, the main character, has just run from her bedroom after hearing a scary noise coming off the lake and through her window.

First Draft

Suzanna was not to get far, however, for just beyond the bedroom entryway stood a real, live ghost blocking her way. "Ahhhhh! Ahhhhhh" and

"Ahhhhh!" again Suzanna cried. "What do you want?" she said, as she tried to make her way out of the door. "Eeeeeee, irrrrrrk, irr, ir, ki, ki, ir, eeeeeeeee." What did you say,—you thing, you!"

The children said, "Let's see the ghost! Your'e telling, not showing." (Out of the mouths of babes, I thought.)

Second Draft

Suzanna was not to get far, however, for just beyond the bedroom entryway stood a real, live ghost, blocking her way. The white mist of the thing towered over her, its arms moving slowly in strange circular strokes, its legs doing a moonish walk. "Ahhhhhhhhhhhhhhhhh!" Suzanna screamed. "What do you want?" she bellowed as she tried to make her way past it.

Suzanna was not to go far, however, for the ghost blocked her way. At first it tried to speak, but nothing came out. Its two lips moved in its face, disconnected somehow. But slowly its cheeks began to fill; its lips tightened; bigger and bigger they grew until Suzanna heard something coming from between them in a raspy, whispery voice, "Eeeeeeeee, irrrrrk, irr, ir, ki, ki, ir, eeeeeee."

"What did you say, you thing?" she snapped.

My doing this spurred some action in the classroom, enough to have warranted my doing it. Children began to look for dialogue in famous authors' books and to point out Boles's lesson. Chris Van Allsburg's (1985) *The Polar Press* was seized upon early, especially the part where the boy first sees the train outside his window:

I looked through my window and saw a train standing perfectly still in front of my house. It was wrapped in an apron of steam. Snowflakes fell lightly around it. A conductor stood at the open door of one of the cars. He took a large pocket-watch from his vest, then looked up at my window. I put on my slippers and robe. I tiptoed down the stairs and out the door.

"All aboard," the conductor cried out. I ran up to him.

"Well," he said, "are you coming?"

"Where?" I asked.

"Why to the North Pole, of course," was his answer. "This is the polar express." I took his outstretched hand and he pulled me abroad.

After noticing the well-written dialogue, the children became more critical of their own. The children most affected in this class were those whose stories were all dialogue or those whose stories had none. Everyone, however, was eager to play with whatever he or she had done. In our view, that's the spirit we want to cultivate.

Publishing Children's Work

Nothing has changed us more as writers (other than computers) than seeing our work published. Teachers who write tell us it is the same for them. Recently a writing consultant friend of ours, Kathy Juntunen, (1989) had a small vignette (a few paragraphs) published in *The Reading Teacher*. While Kathy has written a book on writing, this first "juried" piece making it into print was a boon. She was extraordinarily overjoyed and called to tell us about it—she even turned our search for it into a riddle!

Children bubble over being published, too, but even more over being read. A second grader stopped one of us in the hall a few weeks ago, grabbed an arm, and pulled to get our matching ear close to her lips. "You'll never guess what I just saw," she said.

"What?"

"Somebody reading *my* book." Karen had passed by the library, where her class' books were on display, on her way in from recess. "It was a *sixth grader*," she added. We understood just how Karen felt, primarily because we're writers. But her teacher understood, too, because she recently published *her* first book, which is right in the library along with her children's, on display.

There are many publishing alternatives that can be found in several books already in print (e.g., Nathan et al., 1989; Routman, 1988; Turbill, 1988), but there are a few principles that need sharing:

1. Teachers need not be involved with publishing final products beyond second grade. Too many simple publishing alternatives exist that children can use by themselves or with the help of a friend or a parent.

2. Publishing does not always have to occur in book form. Getting the word out can take many forms: all-school loudspeaker radio shows once a week (Friday afternoon for 5 minutes), school newspaper entries, classroom thologies (literary as well as content-oriented work), news flashes that go home, all-class sharing, bulletin board displays, school hall displays, stories turned into play form and acted out, letters to editors, and letters to published authors (famous, but don't forget local authors). Of course there are more.

3. Published work often contains errors and teachers need to accept this fact. Try as we might, things slip our attention.. When parents detect an error, and they will, this is what we say: "it is a statistical impossibility that you will see fewer errors in my children's work than in the work of children who do not publish on a regular basis. In my room *millions* of words get into print. In rooms where only a *few thousand* words are published, you are bound to find fewer errors. Which is often for their teacher's eyes only, or a room where writing is prolific, authentic, and read by tens of eyes, not just two?" This quotation has never let us down!

Modeling How to Ask Questions and Collect Information from an Expository Place

Mrs. Raymond's class was about to begin a class book about the Civil War, a subject they were studying in social studies. Each person in the class chose a topic that interested him or her, and when Mrs. Raymond gave the word, they were to begin collecting data. Before they began, however, Mrs. Raymond went to the overhead projector and modeled asking some questions that she hoped would drive her report on the Underground Railroad. She pulled a chair next to the overhead and slowly began to talk out loud about what she wanted to ask, and why. She said she'd often wondered just where the railroad was—were there several paths to the North, or just a few? She wondered about the people who helped the slaves gain passage. Who were they? And what dangers did they face? She'd heard about certain heroic characters but knew very little about the specifics of their heroic deeds. Mrs. Raymond went on. When she was done, she asked the children to do the same. She said that, unless they were answering questions that truly interested them, they wouldn't be likely to do a good job. They wouldn't be able to see it through. The children sat fascinated, not only by Mrs. Raymond's honesty about her own questions but also by knowing she was writing a report right along with them.

After a few days, when all the children had narrowed their questions down to four or five, Mrs. Raymond modeled again. But this time, she thought out loud (at the overhead) about where she'd be most likely to find the answers to her questions. She did something else, too. She invited the school librarian in to watch along with the children. Mrs. Raymond played the innocent in need of help. The children said the encyclopedia would give her information about some of the heroes she wanted to know about, and library books would, too. One child suggested *Who's Who*. The librarian suggested *The National Geographic* for a map of the Underground Railroad—she had seen an article about it there recently. The children, Mrs. Raymond, and the librarian took the whole social studies period to brainstorm possibilities and help Mrs. Raymond find some books. The next day the children worked in small groups reading questions aloud and gathering information from the library for each other. The scene was remarkable!

Modeling Proofreading Techniques

Chidlren in reading-writing classrooms are encouraged to write freely all the time, relegating proofreading to its proper place in the writing cycle.

Many texts aren't proofread at all, such as the content area journals or log entries; prewriting cluster sheets, free writes, or lists; literature dialogue journals, and the like. But when a piece needs proofreading—it's going to be published in book form, on the bulletin board, in a home new flash, or in the school paper—it helps to know what to do. Modeling this procedure for children fosters a spirited attitude. Children learn to do one thing at a time and a few other tricks of the trade, as well as make the important discovery that a piece can be punctuated several different ways. Figure 6.1 is a page from one third grader's draft that this author (RN) uses frequently in class demonstrations.

I began by listing what the children think they can do themselves. Most third and fourth graders tell me they think they can look for misspelled words, capitals, and periods. Some say they can tell run-on. I give all the

Figure 6.1.

children a copy of the draft and make one transparency of it. I ask them to underline word spellings they were unsure of and invite them to work in pairs if they'd like. Then someone comes to the overhead and underlines the words that he or she thinks need to be looked up. Sometimes a child underlines a word that's actually spelled correctly, but that doesn't matter—the point is to make the children feel comfortable taking risks. Then I ask the children to try what I do, read the draft backwards by sentences and listen for complete thoughts. It's amazing how much going backwards helps. (Having them circle the periods first makes this a little easier.) The children soon discover the run-on, "Then my cousin was babbling about a ride it was called the tilt 'a' wirl." When they do, I ask them to fix it. They come up with several options:

1.   Then my cousin was babbling about a ride called the tilt "a" wirl. (I might comment, "You've done what some writers call sentence combining.")
2.   Then my cousin was babbling about a ride. it was called the tilt "a" wirl. ("You found the problem.")
3.   Then my cousin was babbling about a ride—the tilt "a" wirl. ("Have any of you used a dash before? Let's look it up in the *Write Source*." (Sebranek, Kemper, & Meyer, 1987, pp. 172–174)

While we could go on and share other writing techniques, we hope our discussion had led you to conclude that language arts teachers who read and write lend a credibility to their work that invites mutual respect and nurtures children's growth as writers and readers . Reading and writing classrooms are not places of anarchy; they're highly structured environments framed by teachers and constantly modified to meet students' needs and developmental levels. They are benevolent places, and they are remarkably effective places for children to learn.

Making Connections Across the Curriculum: The Real Use of Reading and Writing

In *Writing to Learn*, William Zinsser (1988, p. 11) writes, "Over the years I've written or edited hundreds of articles on subjects I had never previously thought about." Think about that. How is it possible that a man of Zinsser's stature could do such a thing? How irresponsible. But Zinsser knows what all writers know, that writing leads to clearer and deeper thinking. In this confession, Zinsser is not alone. Carl Sagan (1977) expresses the same eagerness to use inquiry in his book, *The Dragons of Eden*. In the introduction, Sagan tells his readers that the book gave him the opportunity to revise and expand his earlier thinking about the origins of intelligence. He says:

> The subject is a difficult one... I proffer the following ideas with a substantial degree of trepidation... At the very least, this inquiry has provided me with an opportunity to look into an entrancing subject. (p. 5)

In this country, no one has expressed this concept more succinctly than Toby Fulwiler (1987), editor of *The Journal Book*. In his introductory remarks to that text, Fulwiler lists several cognitive activities people engage in when they take the time to write freely with the intent to learn. While there is no suggestion the list is complete, he shares these activities: observing, questioning, speculating, becoming aware of oneself, digressing, synthesizing, revising, and informing. Consider this entry by a fifth-grade child, Courtney Baker, who was asked to write about how she felt dissecting a pig's lungs in class that day. Her journal entry reads:

> When I came to school today I was so excited because today my class was going to dissect pig lungs. I introduced my Dad and he called everyone up to the table and showed us how to dissect the pig lungs. I felt my heart pounding so hard, it almost came out of my chest. When it was my turn to cut, I took one deep breath and started cutting down one of the tubes. A bronchial tube is like a little pipe that the air goes in and out of. I kept cutting and cutting, the bronchial tubes getting smaller and smaller until finally you could barely see them. Afterwards I felt like I had saved a life for some reason, like looking for a little boy in a dark tunnel and finding him and feeling so glad you did. That's how I felt about cutting the bronchial tubes.

We gasped when we read Courtney's entry because of the digression at the end, the poetry and the human response that one could almost taste. Look at the entry yourself, and reflect on Toby Fulwiler's list. Share the entry and list with a colleague, and decide if Fulwiler might be on to something. Into how many kinds of thinking has Courtney been inviting by writing this journal entry?

CLASSROOM ROUTINES THAT ENCOURAGE READING AND WRITING

The first thing that needs to be said is that the lion's share of instructional time should be devoted to real reading and real writing. As a rule of thumb, from second grade on, three quarters of each language arts block should be thus devoted, with the remainder being set aside for focused lessons on some aspect of reading or writing.

Research is beginning to show that being a reader is the best way to learn to read. Reading instruction should focus on cultivating in students that habit of reading and giving them time to read. There should be classroom libraries with at least three to five titles per child. Teachers should get to know the books and take an opportunity to match books with children's interests. It is possible to get help building a book collection from several fine annotated book lists and from the regular book reviews in *Language Arts, The Reading Teacher,* and *The New Advocate.* But when it comes to telling children about a book in order to arouse their interest, book reviews are not a substitute for the teacher's having read hundreds of children's books and reading more all the time.

Teachers in reading-writing classrooms see to it that every child is reading a book for pleasure, and then they see to it that they have time set aside to read them. Lyman Hunt's idea of *uninterrupted sustained silent read* (USSR) is still a good one: setting aside 20 minutes or more each day in which everything else stops and everybody reads.

In order to make sure that every child does read, and also to encourage the children to think about what they read, many teachers use response journals. In these, the students make notes about what they are reading. In Midge Burns's third-grade class, these notes take the form of letters to Mrs. Burns in which the child tells her what she is reading and what she thinks about it. Mrs. Burns is careful to answer each child's letter with a letter of her own—and to do this, of course, she has to have read the same books the children have read.

Diane Barone (1990) often has students respond to a book using a *dual entry diary* (DED). In these, they draw a vertical line down the middle of a journal page. On the right-hand side of the paper, students recorded direct quotes, lists, and other pertinent information; on the left-hand side, they say what they thought about it. Dr. Barone is careful to write comments in the students' Dual Entry Diaries, too.

In a similar vein, time should be set aside daily for children to write. Lucy Calkins has argued eloquently for the need to fix this writing time regularly in the schedule. She notes that while the act of creating can require us to be flexible in our thinking, it helps if the setting of our creativity is stable and predictable. In a moment of inspiration, the sculptor shouldn't have to hunt for a chisel. Likewise, a child who feels a story coming on shouldn't have to wonder whether or not she'll get time today to write it down.

Many reading-writing classrooms, then, have a period of up to 45 minutes each day set aside for writing (see Figure 6.2). Ruth Nathan divides this period up in the following way. For the first 5 minutes, everybody writes, including the teacher. If the teacher, too, is writing, he can insist on a period of concentration at the outset, and other students are likely to need this quiet time to get started. Then for the next 10 minutes, the teacher moves around the class to encourage students who may be having trouble.

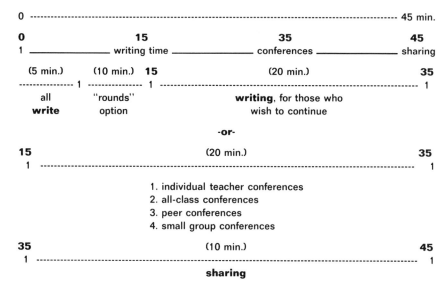

Figure 6.2. Writing Period.

Then follow 20 minutes in which the teacher has individual conferences with students to talk about their writing drafts. During the final 10 minutes, students who have works completed will share them with the class from the Author's Chair, a piece of furniture set aside to give special, somewhat ritualistic flavor to the sharing of the finished piece.

A schedule of this sort is easily adaptable for reading as well. The period can begin with uninterrupted sustained silent reading (5 minutes), in which everyone, including the teacher participates. Then the teacher can move around the room to visit individuals who are having problems or need encouragement (10 minutes). Then he or she can invite five or six students who are reading the same book to come to the circle and discuss it (20 minutes). Finally, the teacher can invite one student to come forward and share with the whole class a book he or she is reading (10 minutes). Alternatively, the teacher might use this final interval to call attention to one strong feature in an author's work that the students may wish to try in their own writing, or to teach a minilesson on reading. A further alternative would be to begin the period with a minilesson on reading (for example, noting how authors use the context to suggest the meanings of words), and end the period with a checkup to see how the students were able to employ the lesson in their reading that day.

In the writing and reading workshops we just described, the lion's share of the time is spent in real reading and real writing. While some time is set aside for direct instruction, there is a delicate relationship between this instructional time and the sustained reading and writing. During instructional time, information is shared and skills are taught. During sustained activity time, information and skills may (or may not) be put to use; and during the sharing period that often comes at the end of the sustained activity time, the use of this information and these skills are commented upon.

Let us give an example. Let us say that a teacher wishes to call the students' attention to the role of conflict in adding suspense to stories. She does this by reminding them of a story they have read; say, "Jack and the Beanstalk." Then she points out that stories often contain a character who is the hero, and that sometimes working against the hero is the enemy or the rival. She asks who is Jack's rival. The students agree it is the giant. Then she asks how the story of "Jack and the Beanstalk" would have seem if there had been no giant. "You mean if Jack just got to go up to the castle and help himself to the treasures?" someone asks. "There wouldn't have been any danger," someone says. "Pretty boring." The teacher mentions another story many students have read: *Captain Najork and the Hired Sportsmen*. The children quickly agree that Tom was the hero and that Captain Najork was the rival. After some discussion, they agree that the rivalry between the two was what made the story fun to read. "It wouldn't have been interesting if it had just been about Tom without Captain Najork," someone says. "Or about Captain Najork with Tom," another adds.

Now the teacher goes a step further. "I know that some of you are going to write stories today during writing time; some of you are starting from scratch, and some of you are working on stories you had already begun. You probably know who your story is about—that's probably your hero. If it fits, without changing your idea around too much, see if you can find a person in your story who can be the rival—who can work against your hero a little bit to make your story more interesting. As I said, writing time is your time, and I only want you to try this if it seems to suit what you're writing. Tell me if you do, though, and maybe we'll get you to share what you wrote during sharing time at the end of the period."

At the end of the writing period, the teacher asks if anyone wrote a rival into his story. Someone says he did, so the teacher invites him to share. The students remark on how the struggle between the hero and the rival affected the story. Some make suggestions for ways the conflict could have been made stronger. Some think of other ways the conflict could have been resolved.

There are several things we should point out about this example.

- The teacher has used the lesson to introduce an idea that the students may use during their sustained writing time. She believes they will benefit from having this idea now so she introduces it, rather than waiting for the idea of rivalry to develop spontaneously in their writing.

- She uses stories they know well as models of the device she wants to teach them (more about this later).
- She is very careful to leave it up to the children whether or not they wish to use this new device on that particular day. Writing time is *theirs* after all: by long-standing agreement, writing time is governed by the students' ideas and not by the teacher's assignments.
- She plans to follow up during the sharing time to discuss the uses the children made of this new idea. We should note that, now that the idea of the rival has been introduced, the teacher will point out the use of it in children's writing or reading whenever a rival appears. A purpose of these lessons is not just to teach skills but also to introduce them as each arises—often to discuss the occurrence of these same concepts in the writing and reading children are already doing.
- Though this example related most directly to writing, it might also have been used in conjunction with reading. Let's suppose the teacher were to have done this same lesson before the students' free reading time. She could have summed up the lesson by inviting them to look for rivals and heroes in the story they were reading, and she could have invited the children to talk later (or to write in their response journals) about the rivalries they found and how these rivalries affected the stories they read.

CONCLUSION

A teacher contemplating setting up a reading-writing classroom wants to know how to do it. In this chapter, we have tried to provide some guidance but have stopped well short of providing any supposed formula for success. Why? Because such formulas are almost always recipes for mediocrity. Lately we have heard more than one author of popular books for teacher publicly wishing they had never been so specific in telling others how to set up reading-writing classrooms. Too often they found that others were following their procedures with disappointing results. Almost invariably what was missing was the teacher who was reader and writer, or, as Nancie Atwell put it recently, a person to whom learners of literacy would want to apprentice themselves. Such a person could make a success of any number of approaches. Conversely, none of the approaches are likely to make for success without such a teacher.

REFERENCES

Atwell, N. (1987). *In the middle: Writing, reading and learning with adolescents.* Portsmouth, NH: Boyton Cook.

Barone, D. (1990). The written responses of young children: Beyond comprehension to story understanding. *The New Advocate*, 3(1), 49–56.

Bishop, C. (1952). *Twenty and Ten*. New York: Viking Press.

Boles, P. (1984). *Storycrafting*. Cincinnati, OH: Writer's Digest Books.

Dawson, F. (1984). *Tiger Lilies: An American childhood*. Durham, NC: Duke University Press.

Five, C. (1988). From workbook to workshop. *The New Advocate, 1*, 103–113.

Fulwiler, T. (Ed.). (1987). *The journal book*. Portsmouth, NH: Boyton/Cook.

Graves, D. (1982). *Writing: Teachers and children at work*. Portsmouth, NH: Heinemann.

Heath, S.B. (1983). *Ways with words*. New York: Cambridge University Press.

Hildebrand, J. (1988). *Reading the river: A voyage down the Yukon*. Boston: Houghton Mifflin Company.

Juntunen, K. (1989). Literacy vignette: The singing puppet. *Reading Teacher, 43*, 41.

Kraffman, J. (1986). *Collaborators: A novel*. New York: Knopf.

Nathan, R. (1988). Effective teacher-child conferences: The importance of writing yourself. In R. Hubbard, B. Mullen, & J. Whitney (Eds.), *The writing and reading process: A closer look*. Portsmouth, NH: Heinemann.

Nathan, R., Temple, F., Juntunen, K., & Temple, C. (1989). *Classroom strategies that work: An elementary teacher's guide to process writing*. Portsmouth, NH: Heinemann.

Routman, R. (1988). *Transitions: From literature to literacy*. Portsmouth, NH: Heinemann/Rigby.

Sagan, C. (1977). *The dragons of Eden*. New York: Random House, Inc.

Salinger, J.D. (1951). *The catcher in the rye*. New York: Little Brown.

Sebranek, P., Kemper, D., & Meyer, V. (1987). *The write source*. Burlington, WI: Write Source Educational Publishing House.

Stegner, W. (1987). *Crossing to safety*. Franklin Center, PA: Franklin Library.

Temple, C., Nathan, R., Burris, N., & Temple, F. (1989). *The beginnings of writing* (2nd ed.). Boston: Allyn & Bacon.

Turbill, J. (1988). *Now we want to write!* Rozelle, New South Wales: Primary English Teaching Association.

Van Allsburg, C. (1985). *The polar express*. Boston: Houghton Mifflin Company.

Zinsser, W. (1988). *Writing to learn*. New York: Harper & Row.

Chapter 7

Images: Partners with Words for Making Meaning

Ruth Hubbard

Consider this problem: to show on a two-dimensional surface the sound, movement, and action of a ball exploding into a million pieces. How do you do it? If you take out a piece of paper and experiment with showing in some way the sound, movement, and action of a ball exploding apart, you'll find that it's a complex task with endless possible representations.

Take a look at 6-year-old Robyn's solution to the problem (Figure 7.1). She shows pieces of the ball material that you could push back together to show the original ball shape, but there are lines to show that the ball is in the act of exploding and is moving outward in all directions, but still in a circular shape. Next to this exploding orb is the circled word *POP*, to represent the sound at the moment of bursting. Even the placement on the page is planned: to the right of the center, isolated from the rest of the setting and the words on the page.

Think of the problems like this that children solve every day in their effort to use that two-dimensional space to depict a three-dimensional world. Imagine yourself immersed in a world based half on reality and half on fantasy as you write. Yet your hands won't always do quite what you want them to, and you don't have years of learning the conventions that other people understand as signs; you don't have that wealth of verbs and action markers to get the excitement you feel across on the page.

In order to really understand literacy, we need to do just that—put ourselves in the children's place and invite their interpretations to see the problems that are being solved, the ingenious inventions that are created. We need to stop looking at the paper as a two-dimensional entity and see the enormous space it represents to the children. And we need to stop drawing

Figure 7.1.

such a clear line between the verbal and the visual—between words and pictures, because both play key roles in literacy, in reading as well as writing.

Lots of practitioners—adult writers—*do* stress the way words and pictures are intimately related. Think of e.e. cummings, for example, who called himself "an author of pictures, a draughtsman of words." Besides practicing the craft of writing, cummings sketched and painted daily: oil portraits of his wife and himself, watercolors of his farmhouse, line drawings of elephants, anatomical studies of animals and people. When asked by an interviewer, "Tell me, doesn't your painting interfere with your writing?" he replied, "Quite the contrary, they love each other dearly" (Hjerter, 1986, p. 109).

For the last few years, I have investigated the importance of picture as well as word symbols in literacy by spending time in elementary and middle-school classrooms. The 6-year-old children in Patricia McLure's classroom were my first guides, and they helped to show me the visual and verbal systems that children create in order to expand the page to communi-

Figure 7.2a.

cate the important realities of dimensions like time, space, movement and color.[1]

Early in the year, for example, Kelly used a combination of print and pictures to get the concept of passing time (Figure 7.2). The words in her

---

[1]For a full report of the research on which this chapter is based, see R. Hubbard (1989), *Authors of pictures, draughtsmen of words*. Portsmouth, NH: Heinemann.

The Mississip
river in p st
orom.

Figure 7.2b.

story hint at the passage of time: "The Mississippi River in a storm" (Figure 7.2) places the time as in the present, and "A Mississippi River boat docks after a storm" (Figure 7.2) uses the linguistic time marker "after." But Kelly has created a more powerful symbol to show the sequence of events through her drawing itself. She uses the black of the coming and going storm quite consciously to reinforce and extend the words she has written. And when

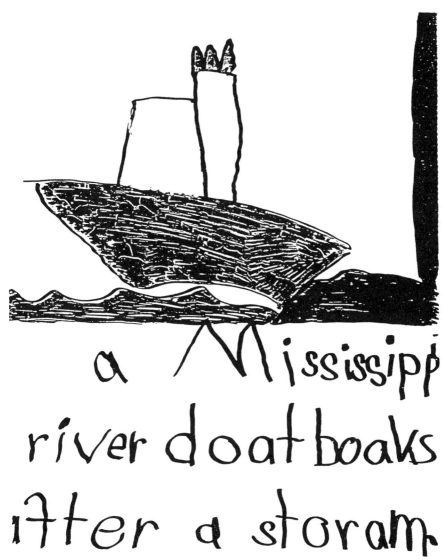

Figure 7.2c.

she explained her story to me, she began with the present, then worked backward and forward.

"You see, the steamboat here [Figure 7.2] is *in* the storm," she began. "This is the water coming down here. On the page before [Figure 7.2], you can see, the storm is just coming. I'll make the black on the other side now, going away, to show the storm is going away [Figure 7.2]."

And that use of color was extremely important to her. When I commented that she seemed to like to draw in pencil, then color it in, she replied, "Yeah, so I know how to color it, and it also helps me to remember what to write there. See, the different pages, the steamboat is always different colors. It fades into different colors by the rain." Without Kelly's explanation as she worked, I would never have known how deliberate her color changes were in this story, chosen to represent the reflection of light as it changes through a storm.

Sometimes those color meanings come from the larger culture. One example is Eugene's fascinating drawing showing the end of the day (Figure 7.3). He explained what he meant to show on this page: "See, the day is over. There's some of the light from the moon, and it comes out as this light." He pointed to the lines reflecting off the car. "A tree's in front of the moon," he went on. This is a big harvest moon—that's why it's orange, or you wouldn't know it was fall. And the moon shows that the day is over. Sometimes I watch the moon, and the falling stars with Paul—that's my Dad."

To Eugene, a big orange moon is a symbol of the autumn season. He doesn't need to say that it's fall, because he assumes that his audience shares the same cultural meaning for an orange moon.

Ming knows that her audience will associate the color blue with water, even though water is often colorless. In her flower story, she explained about her "fancy watering can." "This is the watering can," she told me. "I wanted to make it fancy. It's glass, so you can see the water inside. Blue water." She looked up at me from her coloring to explain, "You can tell there's water in it, so I made it blue."

This use of color may be a learned convention. Many of the books that surround Ming and the other children *do* use blue to represent water. Linda uses another color convention in her apple story, and again, I can only speculate that she has learned this from the books she has seen and read. As she drew and colored in her "fake apple that you can eat," she carefully made white semicircles on the side of the red apple. "These are the shines on the apple," she explained. "They almost make it look like it's smiling!"

These children are learning the uses of color in the books that are read to them and that they read themselves. In an interesting conference between Sarah and Sally early in September, I was able to observe them as they struggled, and ultimately came to terms with, the use of black line drawings with some water color tints in an illustrated "Snow White" story.

"This story is pretty much the same as mine at home, but the pictures are real different," Sarah told Sally. "Her lips—" she pointed to the cover picture of Snow White—"should be more red. See, they're pale here, not real red."

She flipped through the book, and together, Sarah and Sally scrutinized

THE DAY IS OVR

Figure 7.3.

the lips on each illustration of Snow White. "They're black here." Sarah shook her head. "And black again and again."

The illustrations on these pages were mostly outlined—Snow White's lips drawn in black but never filled in with color. Although I would not have interpreted these lips as black, clearly Sarah and Sally did.

Sally was adamant. "Her lips should be red. Red like in the movie."

But Sarah kept trying to figure out what the illustrator had in mind. "They're always black here, though." She looked closely and pondered for a minute. "They're not really black inside, they're actually white inside."

"They're just supposed to be pale, then, I guess. Like on the cover," Sally decided.

Besides color and time, the children have ingenious solutions to the problems of both representing and reading three-dimensional space. One of the ways they represent space is to create drawings that allow the viewer to see through an object to something behind or inside it. Nick shared an example one morning a few days before Christmas. He had drawn his Christmas tree with all the presents under it. Even though they were wrapped, we could easily see the inside, but his brother, Mark—in the picture—can't (Figure 7.4).

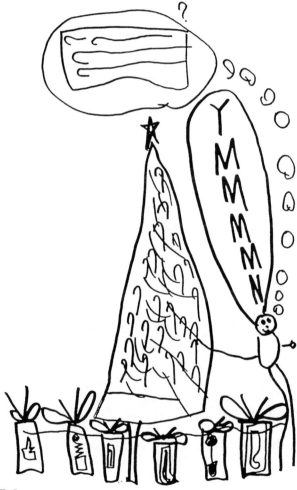

Figure 7.4.

"There's something inside all the presents, see?" Nick explained. "That's a fish, Jack-in-the-box, candy canes, new stockin', a rattle for Will. And that guy is my brother Mark. He loves candy canes.. He's thinkin' he's gonna ask Mom if he can have the biggest candy cane on the tree."

Linda used a similar "transparency" technique when she recorded in her choice book what she had worked on during free choice time in the afternoon. "Me and Ashley used the computer," she wrote (Figure 7.5). In her picture, she wanted to show what it looked like to an observer watching her and Ashley working—a view of their backs as they faced the computer screen with the Logo turtle on it. But she also wanted to show how she was creating the Logo drawing, using the keyboard their backs would have kept

Figure 7.5.

from view. She solved the problem by giving the figures that transparency, so that the observer can have a simultaneous perception of different spatial locations.

These kinds of drawings have been termed *X-ray drawings* by some researchers (Freeman, 1980; Gardner, 1980; Winner, 1982). These theorists conclude, as Winner (1982) does, that the children "are simply unable to draw in a more realistic way" (p. 158). Although Winner admits there are parallels between the child's use of space and that of some adult artists, she concludes that they have "no alternative but to make X-ray drawings. And they may not intend the strong visual effect they create" (p. 160).

I disagree with these conclusions, and the notion that these are X-ray drawings. These researchers did not talk to the children whose drawings they examined, nor did they know the children's other work. In the case of Nick and Linda, these children do have alternatives to showing space, but chose in these instances to use transparency to solve the particular visual problem at hand. In reviewing Nick's writing folder from September to January, I found this was the only time he chose to use this kind of transparency, and he used it because he specifically wanted to show that we knew what was in those presents, but that his brother didn't.

I prefer to use the term *transparency* for this solution to showing space on the page, because this is a technique artists purposefully use. Although psychologists like Winner would term the similarities to Chagall's "Pregnant Woman"—where the artist draws the baby inside the transparent uterus of its mother—only *surface*, I believe they are all consciously solving the problems of space.

Sally's theory about her trip to visit her grandparents provides more evidence. She wrote about the car they rented "since they ran out of little cars" (Figure 7.6), and she wanted her readers to know what it was like inside the car as well as outside. First she drew the car, with all its occupants in the right order, her bearded Dad in front driving, and she and her sister in the back seat looking out at the craters in the moon. But inside the car, she told me, "It was a mess! We had Pepsi on the floor, crayons, books, blocks." And in the rectangle drawn under her Mom, we can see all the items she has mentioned—we get a view of both the inside and outside. At this point, I thought she was done with this page, and I made a copy of it during recess time.

I was premature in my judgment, however, as I believe other researchers may have been in the past. The next day, when Sally returned to her writing, she had come up with a modification; she preferred to show the inside and outside of her car. She cut out and taped a door over the car's side, which opens and closes to reveal—and to hide—the mess on the floor inside (Figure 7.7).

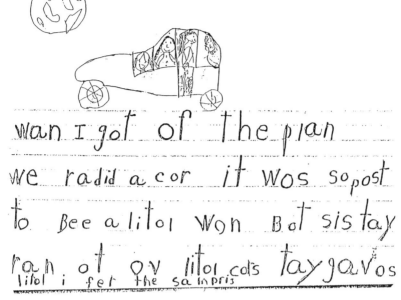

wan I got of the pian
we radid a cor it wos sopost
to Bee a litoi won Bot sistay
ran ot ov litoi cds taygavos
litol i fer the sa in pris

Figure 7.6.

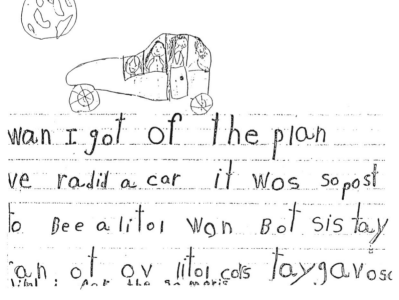

wan I got of the pian
ve radid a car it wos sopost
to Bee a litoi won Bot sistay
an ot ov litoi cds taygavosc
litol i Aor the sa moris

Figure 7.7.

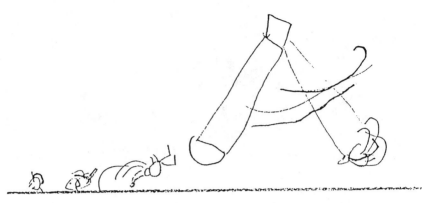

Figure 7.8.

Related to the problem of showing space and time on a flat piece of paper is the question of showing movement. As children attempt to communicate their action-filled stories, memories, and mental images onto the surface of a page, they create a wide variety of ways to show their "pieces of the action."

One morning, Graham was intent on communicating a "terrifying" experience, and he explained to me his drawing of falling off a swing (Figure 7.8). "That's the swing at different times," he told me pointing to the two swings on the page. "It was going up and it had to go down." He

Figure 7.9.

rolled his eyes and gave an exaggerated shudder. "I did a backwards somersault right off the swing! Boy, did that give me a headache! See? I'm going' back. I'm goin' up, I fall back, I roll over, and that is it."

One way to represent movement on a page is to show an object or a person in successive movements over time, as Graham did. These multiple images indicate movement that occurs in a brief amount of time. I found that the children often used this technique to show movement, especially that of the human body. Nick found it helpful in his epic circus chronicle, *I Went to the Circus* (Figure 7.9). As he explained it to the class during whole-class sharing time, "This guy was walkin' on this tightrope, walkin'.... And he's there, and he walked across, and then he fell. *Boom! Oh, no!*

For me, the most exciting way of representing movement that the children taught me is their sophisticated use of picture metaphors that they were able to create as well as interpret when they wanted to communicate motion and movement in their stories.

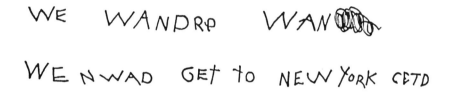

Figure 7.10.

Graham was hard at work one day writing about his trip to New York City (Figure 7.10). "We wondered when we would get to New York City," the text reads, and the picture metaphorically explains the situation.

"That's my family in our car right there." He pointed to the vehicle in the middle of the page. "See all those marks around the wheels? They're like on tanks. You know, they show the tires are, like diggin' in slow."

I must have looked confused, because he looked to Ethan for help in his explanation. "Ethan, you know those things on tanks? What are they called?"

"Oh, I know what you mean, like on tanks? Aren't they caterpillar wheels or something like that?"

"Yeah, that's what I mean. You know? Our car was goin' along real slow, like a tank would go."

"Oh, I see what you mean," I responded. "Tell me about he rest."

"Well, see, that's my dad driving. He's going 'Mmmm,' singing away, 'cause he doesn't care that we're going slow. But that car behind us—" he pointed to the car behind them, drawn with a huge angry mouth full of teeth on its hood—"that's a new York car! He's saying, 'Hey you!!! Beep!"

Graham's pictorial metaphor immediately struck home for me—a timid country driver who has experienced the Jaws-like aggression of impatient city drivers!

Figure 7.11a.

Figure 7.11b.

Kelly relies on picture metaphors to show movement and action, too. Her entire dog sled story is an example of trying to make clear the movement in her story within the limits of her medium, incorporating the elements of time and space to help her (Figure 7.11).

Her title page uses time: She draws just part of the dog to show he's

Figure 7.11c.

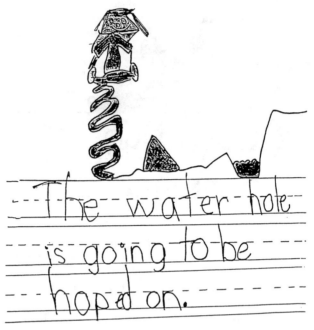

Figure 7.11d.

moving (Figure 7.11). "This picture just has part of the dog, 'cause he's gone ahead," she explained to me (Figure 7.11).

Later in the story, she also struggled with finding the right technique to represent the motion of the water in all its dimensions. "Over here's the side view of the water hole, and over here's a top view." Then she created a pop-up version of the water hole and attached it to the page with an accordion of folded paper. "I want to make it look like it will swing and make waves right off the paper" (Figure 7.11).

Kelly is in control of the conventions she chooses to use. Although she wants to continue to show that movement that's essential to her story, she decides not to continue with pop-ups. As she explained, "You're gonna see what happens to the water hole on the next page. But the rest of the book is going to be flat on the page. No more pop-ups."

But it wasn't until she shared the story with the class the next day that I saw the metaphor she chose to show "what happened to the water hole." First she read the pages I had already heard and seen, then concluded with, "The water hole is going to be hopped on" (Figure 7.11). Above the words is a picture of the sled driver, legs outstretched, atop a recently released coiled spring—a perfect metaphor to show that the water hole indeed can't escape being hopped on now!

The use of "action lines" is another convention many of the children use to show motion and movement. In a sense, this convention is used as a kind of metaphor as well. Notice, for example, the swirling, stylized lines that Paul uses to show the rolling snowballs in his work (Figure 7.12).

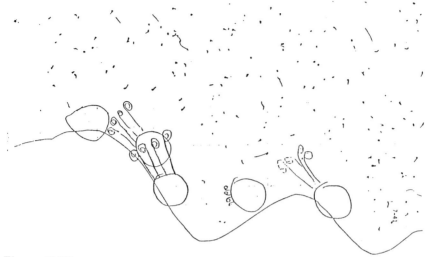

Figure 7.12.

Graham also uses lines to represent the path his sled has just taken as it flies down the hill (Figure 7.13). "I bumped into a stump," he explained. "I did not like it. See, I hit the stump and I went right up. Here's the ground level...it got so much speed!"

Then Graham explained his other use of lines in this picture. "These lines, they show you're going fast!"

But the children also found that there are things that words can do that pictures can't. Kelly relies on words—especially strong verbs—*with* her pictures. One morning she sat down to write about a bus accident that may of the children had witnessed. She began with a picture, with part of the bus shown, the tree crashed into it, and a loud exploding sound, "Bang!" (Figure 7.14). Then she wrote the words, "The bus crashing into a tree."

Figure 7.13.

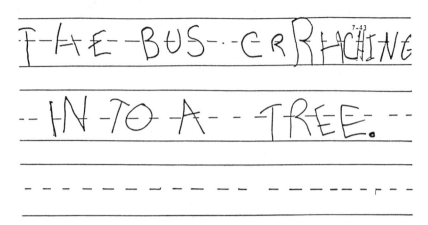

Figure 7.14.

Unlike some of the children who write first and then illustrate their words, Kelly chose to draw first to show the movement of the crash, then felt she needed a caption to further explain her picture.

Although Kelly's vocabulary is quite sophisticated, she continues to rely on pictures to complete the whole story in most of her writing. Her "adventure story" is another example (Figure 7.15). "While I was watching my sun, a volcano erupted behind me," she wrote. "Choke," sputters the volcano in her picture as the lava pours out behind Kelly.

Figure 7.15.

Kelly doesn't always draw first, then illustrate. Often she goes back and forth between the words and pictures. One day, she began by writing the words, "I am at Debbie's trailer" (Figure 7.16), then drew the picture of herself approaching Debbie's door. Dissatisfied, she added another sentence with a more precise verb to show the action she wanted to communicate: "Another way to say it is, I arrived at Debbie's trailer."

These children are creating symbols that will work to communicate motion for their particular purposes. They create metaphors like Graham's angry New York car biting at his heels, and create pop-ups to make the water seem to splash out of the pages of the book. They are using both verbal and visual languages as tools to help them sort out, understand, and cope with their environment, learning ways to translate and communicate the three-dimensional, movement-filled world to the limited dimensions of a page.

Picture-book author/illustrator Trina Schart Hyman echoes e.e. cummings' claim that his paintings and poetry love each other dearly, when she writes that her text and pictures "are absolutely married to each other" (Saul, 1988, p. 8). Pictures as well as words are important to human beings in their communication; we need to expand our narrow definition of literacy to include visual dimensions, answering the call of researchers for

Figure 7.16.

the recognition of multiliteracies and ways these literacies can work to complement each other (see Gee, 1987; Green, 1984; Heath, 1983).

Most classrooms deny to the children the very tools that adult authors find helpful in their work. Not just picture-book authors, but many writers rely on drawing to help them. The drafts and manuscripts for E.B. White's classic novel *Charlotte's Web* are full of sketches of pigs, barns, and of Charlotte herself, labeled with diagrams of the different parts of a spider, such as coxa and trochanter, which were later incorporated into the novel (Neumeyer, 1982). D.H. Lawrence found in oil painting a medium to work out visual images which were later transformed into metaphor; John Dos Passos's and William Faulkner's pencil sketches filled their notebooks; and writers as diverse as S.J. Perelman, Gabriel Garcia Marquez, and Flannery O'Connor began as cartoonists (Hjerter, 1986). In an account of his writing process, John Updike (1986) stresses how drawing and painting can be important tools for writers:

> The subtleties of form and color, the distinctions of texture, the balances of volume, the principles of perspective and composition—all these are good for a future writer to experience and will help him to visualize his scenes, even to construct his personalities, and to shape the invisible contentions and branch-ings of a plot. A novel, like a cartoon, arranges stylized versions of people within a certain space; the graphic artist learns to organize and emphasize and this knowledge serves the writer. The volumes—cloven by line and patched by color—are imitated by those dramatic spaces the inner eye creates, as theatres for thoughts and fantasies. (p. 8)

It isn't just poets and novelists who rely on combinations of words and pictures to make their messages clear. Evans-Pritchard's ethnographies are full of his sketches, "rimming like visual footnotes, the edges of the text" (Geertz, 1988, p. 67). Stephen Jay Gould (1987) claims that pictures provide a key to his understanding, and he urges readers not to consider the illustrations in his book "pretty little trifles included only for aesthetic or commercial value" (p. 18). He argues that scholars have been too slow to recognize "another dimension to their traditional focus upon words alone."

Curriculum directors will ask, if the language of literacy is expanded to include the visual dimension, how does this set of conventions and the "sequence of development" fit into the "hierarchy of skills"? Unfortunately, human development—and literacy—are messier than this. Tom Newkirk (1985) argues that there simply isn't a convenient scope and sequence into which educators can plug children; instead, we need to allow for considerable variability in the development of literacy.

Instead of looking for ways to isolate particular skills and plan mastery-learning sequences, we can turn to classroom teachers who are successfully opening these new roads to literacy for their students. Besides early elementary teachers, there are teachers at the upper elementary, middle school, and high school levels who are expanding the dimensions of literacy in their classrooms, and learning with their students.

In writing about the process of teaching, Donald Murray (1982) stresses that students must be given four freedoms: "The ability to find his own subject, to find his own evidence, to find his own audience, and to find his own form" (p. 142). Teacher-researchers like Cora Five (1986), Donna Lee (1988), Paul Nelson (1988), and Linda Rief (personal communication, March 15, 1988) have all given these four freedoms to their students, including, within the freedom of form, the ability to use visual as well as verbal solutions to their problems.

In Cora Five's (1986) fifth-grade classroom, for example, the children often write her letters in response to the books they are reading, as well as journal entries to each other. But they are also encouraged, if they prefer, to sketch important parts of the book they are reading, map out characteristics, or create flow charts. "By collecting, sorting, reading, and rereading their letters, maps, and sketches," Five writes, "I found for myself a much closer view of how children struggle and then succeed to find meaning in books. The process also kept me engaged in learning because it led me to new questions" (p. 405).

In the sixth-grade classroom they team teach, Donna Lee (1988) and Paul "Chip" Nelson also invite children to use whatever symbol system works best for them. Lee describes Andy as a "reluctant writer who had no idea that writing could turn to discovery. His belief that he had nothing to say entered into every conference and prevented him from ever writing unless forced to do so" (p. 7). Instead of focusing on the difficulties Andy had with

```
          Chapter 2 - Trout

     Trout are mainly fish that live in fresh
water.
     There are three different types of trout
that live in the Squamscott River:  the rainbow
trout, brook trout, and the brown trout.
     A rainbow trout can be identified by the
bright colors on their side.  The colors form
a rainbow.
```

Figure 7.17.

written conventions, they instead validated the sketches that filled his writing folder, encouraging him to include these drawings in order to communicate the things he did know about—particularly fish. His careful pencil drawings illustrate his nonfiction piece "Salmon and trout of the Squamscott" (Figure 7.17), and his sketches are an integral part of his plans to cross-breed fish from a local river (Figure 7.18). His sixth-grade classmates' writing folders, too, are full of maps and diagrams, like the detailed layout drawn in Jim's "The Place Intact" which accompanies his writing (Figure 7.19), or Grant's description of the way to fix a bicycle (Figure 7.20).

"With my help as a facilitator and as part of a writing community," writes Chip Nelson (1988), "the children are responsible for their own learning" (p. 8). One of the ways that Chip acts as a facilitator is by surrounding the

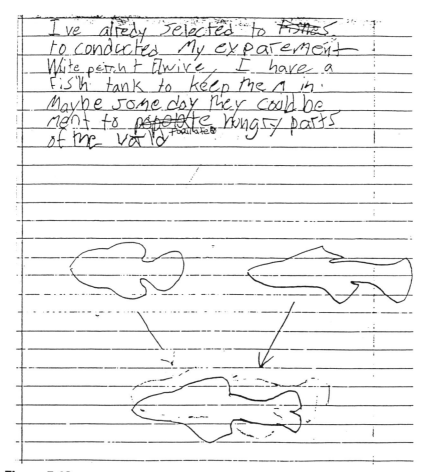

I ve alredy Selected to Fishes
to conducted My exparement
White pernt Elwive, I have a
Fish tank to keep men in.
Maybe some day they could be
ment to populate hungry parts
of the vorld

Figure 7.18.

children with pictures and print. The walls are covered with posters, charts, and graphs, and the children are immersed in the works of fine adult authors and illustrators. "Surround the children with literature," urges Donald Graves (1983), reporting the variety of connections children can make to their own work. The children in Donna and Chip's sixth-grade classroom are surrounded by the literature of master writers and illustrators, and aspects of their work turn up in the writing of the children, from Tad's Tolkein-like map of his fictitious world, to the drawings of knights and damsels in Christine's novel, dressed in intricate medieval costume reminiscent of Trina Schart Hymen's artwork.

The atmosphere in these classrooms encourages "total communication" in the students' literate behaviors. Much of the debate about children's "preferred mode of thought" has focused on diagnosing a learning style,

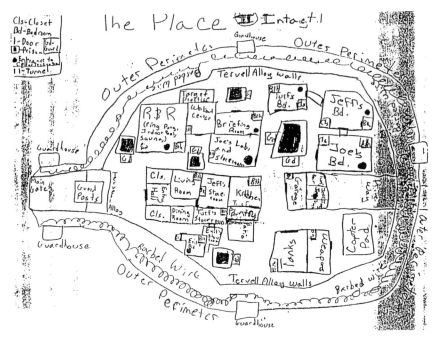

Figure 7.19.

then teaching encouraging one particular mode. In the history of deaf education, a similar polarization occurred: Some deaf educators believed solely in preparing their students for a hearing world, banning sign language, and teaching lip-reading and oral speech only; on the other end of the continuum were the educators who believed in teaching only American Sign Language. In the last decade, the school of "total communication" has gained prominence in deaf education; educators of this persuasion argue that their learning environments and teaching activities should encourage children to use whatever modes of communication will work best for them, including combinations of sign language, lip-reading, and finger spelling. The idea of "total communication" should spill over into mainstream public school classroom environments as well, allowing children to learn to communicate in a range of modes and with a combination of media that will work best for them, experimenting and altering techniques to meet the changing demands of the tasks at hand.

Teacher-researcher Linda Rief (personal communication, March 15, 1988) encourages this total communication in her middle-school classrooms, and she finds that her students often rely on visual as well as verbal solutions. She reports that some students, for example, find photographs helpful tools for describing people they have interviewed. "In their journals, some kids

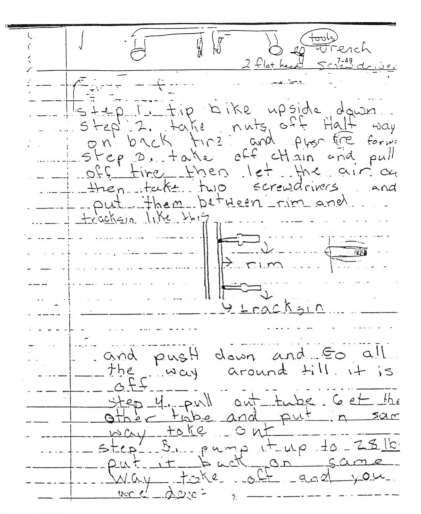

Figure 7.20.

have told me about studying photos they've taken in order to add the details that will create a vivid description on paper," Linda reports. "I've never given them directions or assignments that ask them to use pictures or drawings in the ways they have, but I've made it clear that they should use whatever works to communicate their messages, or to show me they've understood what they've read."

After reading "Romeo and Juliet," Alan's journal entry contained a "comic strip" rendition of the parts he had read (Figure 7.21). "I had fun writing/illustrating in my log," he wrote, and the pages that followed reflected both his enjoyment and his understanding of the story.

Figure 7.21.

Sandy, on the other hand, used words and pictures in quite another way: She chose to borrow the picture-book format of an old Dick and Jane reader to write about Ann Hutchingson's flight from Massachusetts for religious freedom in her book entitled "Dick and Jane Visit the Massachusetts Bay Colony." Using the stylized words and pictures of this genre, she shows her knowledge of the historical event she studied (Figure 7.22). Her readers learn about Ann Hutchinson's escape to Rhode Island as she reports Dick and Jane's time travel in the machine they built "with a spatula, macaroni, paper mache...and the red wagon" (Figure 7.22).

Other examples, like Stacy's porcupine brochure (Figure 7.23)—including "Eating Habits Poem" alongside the diagramed characteristics—or Ann-Marie's autobiographical chart (Figure 7.24), show the range of solutions and the strength of communication these teen-agers demonstrate when literacy is viewed as a process of "total communication."

These classrooms can give us the opportunity to see what is possible—for students and for teachers. Drawing is not just for children who can't yet write fluently, and creating pictures is not just part of rehearsal for "real writing." Images at any age are part of the serious business of meaning-making—partners with words for communicating our inner designs.

THE MEN WITH POWER ARE SAYING BAD WORDS TO ANNE. THE MEN WITH POWER ARE MAKING ANNE SAY BAD THINGS SHE HAS DONE. THE MEN WITH POWER SAY ANNE CANNOT LIVE WITH THEM ANYMORE. THE MEN WITH POWER SAY ANNE MUST GO.

RUN, ANNE, RUN! RUN TO RHODE ISLAND!

ANNE RUNS TO RHODE ISLAND WITH HER FRIENDS. ANNE IS SAFE

Figure 7.22a.

REFERENCES

Five, C.L. (1986). Fifth graders respond to a changed reading program. *Harvard Educational Review, 56* 395-405

Freeman, N. (1980). *Strategies of representation in young children.* London: Academic Press.

Gardner, H. (198). *Artful scribbles: The significance of children's drawings.* New York: Basic Books.

Gee, J.P. (1987), October). *What is literacy.* Paper presented at the Planning Session for the literacies Institute, Cambridge, MA.

Geertz, C. (1988). *Works and lives: The anthropologist as author.* Palo Alto, CA: Stanford University Press.

Figure 7.22b.

Gould, S.J. (1987). *Time's arrow, time's cycle.* Cambridge, MA: Harvard University Press.

Graves, D.H. (1983). *Writing: Teachers and children at work.* Portsmouth, NH: Heinemann.

Greene, M. (1984). The art of being present: Educating for aesthetic encounters. *Journal of Education, 166,* 123–135.

Heath, S.B. (1983). *Ways with words: Language, life, and work in communities and classrooms.* New York: Cambridge University Press.

Hjerter, K.G. (1986). *Doubly gifted: The author as visual artist.* New York: Harry N. Abrams.

Lee, D. (1988), March). *Emotions unleashed.* Paper presented at the annual conference of the National Council of Teachers of English, Boston.

Murray, D.M. (1982). *Learning by teaching.* Montclair, NJ; Boynton/Cook.

Nelson, P. (1988, March). *Who's in control here?* Paper presented at the annual conference for the National Council of Teachers of English, Boston.

Neumeyer, P.F. (1982). The creation of *Charlotte's Web*: From draft to book. *The Horn Book, 58,* 489–493.

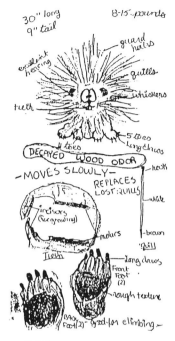

The eating habits of the porcupine,
Are really, quite honestly, truely devine.
In spring, she eat's buds, twigs and leaves
And munches on acorns from the acorn trees.
Also on the menu are wild onion, and
                                    mushroom,
And also geraniums if there is
                            enough room.
She will wade in a pond, holding tril cril
And munch on a lilly pad without a fret.
Salt is by far her most favorite treat,
And to get it she'll go through impossible
                                        feat.
How can she hold all this food? Do you
                                    ask?
Her 25 foot intestine preforms the hard
                                    task.
Her large incisors grow as she sits
                    on her haunches,
And brings her food up with her hand
                she sits quietly and munches.
Her stomach can hold one pound of food,
which her large liver stores for the winter
                                interlude.
When snow hits the ground, and grasses
                        are covered.
She climbs up a tree and sits there:
                            Hovered.
She gnaws on the bark in her thick coat
                        she grew
And stays up there for days, stuck to it
                            like glue,
Yes, this vegetarian is very unique,

Figure 7.23.

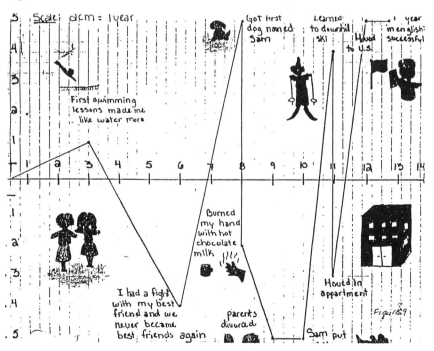

Figure 7.24.

Newkirk, T. (1985). The hedgehog or the fox. *Language Arts, 62,* 593–603.

Saul, W. (1988). Once-upon-a-time artist in the land of now: An interview with Trina Schart Hyman. *The New Advocate, 1,* 8–17.

Updike, J. (1986). Foreword. In K. Hjerter, *Doubly gifted: The author as visual artist* (pp. 7–9). New York: Henry N. Abrams.

Winner, E. (1982). *Invented worlds: The psychology of the arts.* Cambridge, MA: Harvard University Press.

Chapter 8

Strategies for Leading Readers into Text: The Prereading Phase of a Content Lesson

MaryEllen Vogt

In many intermediate, middle, and high school classrooms, students frequently complain, "But I *read* the chapter! I just can't remember what it said!" Faced with this familiar lament, teachers often resort to having class members read the content text aloud, one paragraph at a time. Yet few students master and retain material when this frequent oral reading is monotonous, boring, and unproductive.

Another common approach to the teaching of a content lesson is to post the assignment on the chalkboard, or to direct students to the selection in a textbook. Perhaps a few vocabulary words are introduced, and the teacher may ask questions that the students should think about and attempt to answer during the text reading. The students then silently read the text selection and conclude the lesson by answering questions from worksheets, study guides, or the textbook chapter. While the purpose of the teacher-generated questions appears to be on focusing the students' attention on the material to be read, often students skim to find the answers and fail to comprehend the overriding concepts discussed in the chapter (Readence, Bean, & Baldwin, 1989).

This lack of comprehension and retention of information may be attributed to poor content lesson design and ineffective utilization of instructional time. Informal observational research data collected in approximately 200 junior high and high school content area classrooms over a two-year period suggest that approximately 25% of content area instructional time is utilized with students completing workbook pages or teacher-made worksheets, while another 23% is spent on procedural activities such as taking attendance, issuing materials and instructions, and classroom management. During only 5% of the time are students writing texts longer than one to two sentences; during only 7% of the time are they reading passages longer than one to two sentences (Vogt, 1986).

These findings concur with those of Applebee (1981), who additionally found that secondary teachers generally spend less than 3 minutes preparing students for a writing assignment. It appears that the preparation of students for reading, if present at all, fares little better. The prereading instructional comments of teachers often consist of the assignment of text pages to be read and the answering of questions about the mechanics of the assignment. The students are then left on their own to comprehend and retain information from their textbooks (Vogt, 1986).

From the student's perspective, it may appear that content text assignments are to be read in order to answer either the teacher's or the text's questions. Because the assignment is *inauthentic*, in that the student's goal is simply to fill the teacher's requirements, the student never completely involves himself or herself in the reading. *Authentic* assignments, on the other hand, are "couched in the student's own terms" (Dyson, 1984, p. 619), and the goal setting for the assignment is determined by the student rather than the teacher. Assignments in which students have a sense of personal involvement are the ones that are most successful, both in terms of mastery of content and the student's sense of accomplishment.

This chapter will respond to the following questions: How can we involve students in their own learning? How can content lessons be designed so as to foster this involvement? In what ways can we insure content mastery while providing a sense of the authentic in assignments?

BACKGROUND

For over 200 years, philosophers and psychologists have discussed how teachers connect students' present understandings to new information. Kant, in 1781, suggested that "mental structures that incorporate general knowledge" assist learners in processing new information (Anderson, Spiro, & Anderson, 1978, p. 434). The philosopher Herbart, in the 19th century, believed that a teacher should not present entirely new information to students. Rather, Herbart suggested the teacher should "recapitulate beforehand what is going to be said" (Smyth, 1983, p. 9). Mulliner, in 1898, said that teachers should "give the pupil a definite tendency to arouse expectations, stimulate interest, and give intellectual activity from the beginning" (Moore, Readence, & Rickelman, 1982). Further, Morrison in 1926 and Bartlet in 1932 stated that instruction should consist of associating previously learned ideas with new ones (Smyth, 1983).

Cognitive psychologists, including Piaget and Pascual-Leone, have contended that information is processed through the instantiation of schematic slots or frames. When we learn something new, we simply "fill in" the existing slots with our new information (Ammon, 1977). The brain receives the stimuli, which it sorts out and schematically arranges in these slots prior to storing them in memory. These schemata are not isolated bits of information that we store in memory and then retrieve, but previously learned concepts, facts, and ideas that constantly interact with new information we learn.

Comprehension of text occurs when we recognize items and are able to "bind" them to appropriate slots. In order for this binding to occur, prior knowledge of the world, of the uses and functions of language, and of procedures for processing text must be activated and utilized (Ruddell & Speaker, 1985). Further once this activation takes place, ideas must be focused, maintained, and refined in order to develop an interpretation of the reading that is complete and plausible. When this occurs, the reader comprehends the text, because there is a match between the reader's world and that of the material he or she is reading (Cooper, 1986; May 1990; Tierney & Pearson, 1985).

This match can be accomplished when teachers assist students in utilizing schemata to build bridges between prior knowledge about a subject and new information which is read (Johnson, 1986). If students have poorly developed schemata, the integration of new and known information is difficult (Langer & Nicolich, 1980). Having appropriate schemata allows the reader to allocate attention, elaborate, search the memory in an orderly fashion, edit and summarize, and reconstruct inferences (Anderson, 1984).

THE PREREADING PHASE

The teacher's conscious and planned activation and utilization of students' prior knowledge during every content lesson is of critical importance. This preparation for reading is a type of "frontloading," teaching that assists students in constructing meaning from text (Vance & Buehl, 1990). With this type of instruction, the teacher no longer asks, "What does the student not know that I have to help him or her learn?" Rather, the teacher asks, "What is it that the student does know that I can use as an anchor point—a bridge—to help develop the concepts that he or she needs?" (Tierney & Pearson, 1981, p. 16). Once this anchor point is in place, nearly all students, even those who are less able readers or who are second-language learners, should be ready to read an assignment. Hopefully, internal goals and expectations, rather than external such as the teacher's, will guide a student's reading.

The teaching during this prereading phase is active, interactive, meaningful, and authentic. If possible, when strategies are selected for use during this phase, attempts should be made to integrate the language processes: reading, writing, listening, and speaking. Students should be encouraged to interact with other students and to share prior knowledge, thus assisting each other in connecting with the topic at hand.

Further, strategies for leading students into the text should enable them to predict what the reading will be about, generate questions about the topic within their minds, and assist them in reflecting about their own feelings regarding the subject. In essence, strategies selected for the prereading phase of a content lesson should provoke students to ask of themselves: What do I know about this topic? What do I think about it? What do I predict it will be about? How do I presently feel about it?

STRATEGIES FOR THE PREREADING PHASE

The following activities are especially effective in the prereading phase of a content lesson and are appropriate for use in all grade levels. Some of them may also be used effectively as postreading activities and for literature selections. Teachers may use nearly any grouping configuration with these activities: whole class, partners, small groups, or cooperative learning groups. With each the teacher serves as a guide or facilitator so that the student's eventual reading becomes self-directed rather than teacher-directed.

1. *Anticipation-Reaction Guide* (Readence et al., 1989). The purpose of the *anticipation-reaction guide*, which introduces a topic by asking the reader to reflect on thoughts and feelings about the topic prior to reading, brings misconceptions or misunderstandings to the surface, and allows the reader to take a stand on the subject.

Directions:

a.   Identify major concepts and supporting details in a text selection;
b.   Identify students' experiences and beliefs that will be challenged and/or supported by text;
c.   Create statements which require students to take a stand in regard to topic discussed (three to five statements suffice);
d.   Write statements on paper, transparency, or chalkboard;
e.   Students respond positively or negatively to each statement ("+" or "−") in the "Anticipation" column;
f.   Justifications for responses are discussed with the whole group, with small groups, or with a partner;

g. Following the reading, students record reactions in the "Reaction" column; responses are discussed.

Example: Science unit on space exploration

Anticipation   Reaction

_____   _____   The United States must continue to explore our solar system regardless of cost.

_____   _____   If citizens are asked to volunteer to live on a space station, I'll be one of the first to volunteer.

_____   _____   Space exploration should be a joint effort between all the countries of the world.

2. List-Group-Label (adapted from Readence et al., 1989). The purpose of this activity is to allow all students to contribute and classify their prior knowledge about a topic at the same time that they are listening to their peers' contributions. Additionally, they are able to add their new knowledge to the classification system they devised from their prior knowledge. Their reading becomes interactive as they attempt to link new knowledge with old.

Directions:

a. Select topic that has vocabulary which can be classified into broad categories;
b. With whole class, brainstorm list of words and/or concepts students may have culled from previous readings, discussion, and instruction;
c. Individually or in groups, students label and categorize groups of words;
d. Discuss classifications and put all subgroups on board until all unique groupings have been discovered;
e. Students write words on paper, placing in appropriate categories;
f. During reading, students mark with " + " previously brainstormed words or concepts that are mentioned in text;
g. Following reading, students add new words/concepts under categories; new categories may be added, if needed.

Example: Social science lesson on the Revolutionary War. Brainstormed words: Paul Revere, Stamp Act, Minutemen, Lexington, King George, Valley Forge, Redcoats, George Washington, Boston Tea Party, Tories, Declaration of Independence, taxation, Loyalists, muskets, bayonets, French, cannons, right to bear arms, Concord.

Categories:

People	*Places*	*Weapons*	*Issues*
P. Revere	Concord	muskets	taxation
K. George	Lexington	bayonets	right to bear arms
G. Washington	V. Forge	cannons	

Groups	*Consequences*
Minutemen	Stamp Act
Redcoats	Boston Tea Party
Tories	Declaration of Independence
French	
Loyalists	

3. Brainstorming with a Twist. This activity gives a new dimension to brainstorming by providing students an opportunity to activate their broad knowledge about a subject. The teacher assists them in specifically focusing on a limited piece of the broader topic, as defined by the text to be read. Directions:

a. With partner or whole group, students brainstorm all words/concepts they can think of related to topic covered in text;

b. Following brainstorming, teacher narrows topic according to text subtopics;

c. Together, through discussion, teacher and students eliminate words that do not fit narrowed topic; students predict which words/concepts they think will be discussed in chapter/story and mark with " + "; words are left on board during reading so students can refer to them during reading.

d. Following reading, students refer back to words to eliminate or group words which do or do not pertain to particular reading passage; new words learned from text may be added; for writing assignments, students may be required to use as many of the words/concepts on list as possible.

Example: Geography lesson on deserts
Brainstormed words: sand, dunes, scorpions, tarantulas, sunshine, hot, lizards, snakes, drought, camels, cold, mirage, rocks, sagebrush, cactus, sandstorm, sheiks, wind, oasis.
Narrowed topic: American deserts
Eliminated words might be: camels, sheiks, oasis

4. Feature Analysis (Readence et al., 1989). *Feature analysis is a versatile, fun activity that can be used at any time during a lesson, but it is an especially good motivator when used during the prereading phase. Once again, brainstorming is utilized, though the teacher can vary the strategy by presenting words and features* to the students on a grid. It is a great way to teach and reinforce vocabulary but can also be very effective as a means of assisting students in developing concepts and relationships.

Directions:

a. Select category with multiple words associated with it and which can be described with multiple features;
b. Brainstorm and select words for "Words" and "Features"; students write *words* down left side of grid and *features* across top of grid;
c. Students then match *words* with *features* and mark matches with " + "; if no match, mark with "-";
d. Class discussion follows (thumbs or pencils up/down for matches or mismatches); corrections can be made as necessary;
e. For concept development, teacher selects words to use for *words* and *features*; for example: qualities of heroes, properties of elements, freedoms guaranteed by Constitutional amendments;
f. Use as prewriting activity: Students use matched words and features as material to write about.

Example: Unit on Our City; Topic is Transportation
   Brainstormed modes of transportation: car, elephant, shuttle, motorcycle, bus, hot air balloon, dirigible, airplane, feet, rickshaw, rowboat, horse, train, cruiseship, subway, bike, rocketship, rollerskates, Concorde, tricycle, camel, skateboard.
   Brainstormed features of transportation: engine, rails, gears, tires, brakes, pedals, wheels, driver, tracks, fuel, steering wheel, wings, windows, sails, fumes, seats, keys, propellers, tickets, compass, bathrooms, shoes (see Figure 8.1).

5. Interactive Cloze. The *interactive cloze* motivates students through their interest in a topic to want to read more. It also provides for active discussion of synonyms, context clues, and grammatical structure of text. Students actually argue about words, their meanings, and their appropriateness when completing an interactive cloze. Prepare for enthusiastic students!

Directions:

a. Select paragraph from content area of story;
b. Keep first and last sentences intact;
c. Delete every "nth" word (teacher chooses which words to delete);
d. Students work in groups to determine best word for blanks; groups must arrive at consensus for word replacements;
e. Teacher reads selection with author's words in blanks;

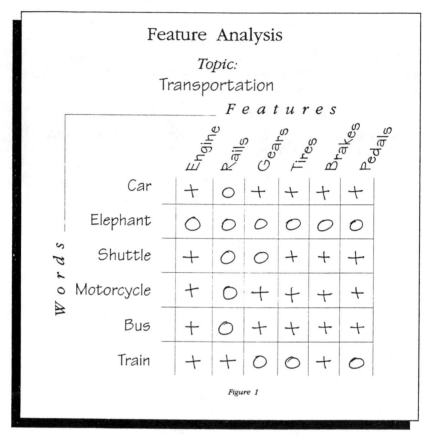

Feature Analysis

Topic:
Transportation

F e a t u r e s

Words	Engine	Rails	Gears	Tires	Brakes	Pedals
Car	+	O	+	+	+	+
Elephant	O	O	O	O	O	O
Shuttle	+	O	O	+	+	+
Motorcycle	+	O	+	+	+	+
Bus	+	O	+	+	+	+
Train	+	+	O	O	+	O

Figure 1

Figure 8.1.   Feature Analysis   Topic: Transportation

f.   Compare groups' choices with "author's choices"; discuss synonyms, use of context, etc.

g.   Alternative (Whisler & Williams, 1990): Select or write cloze sentences which include key vocabulary students will encounter in their reading; sentences should have rich context. In groups, students determine a word to fit in each blank. After vocabulary is introduced by teacher, students insert newly learned words into blanks. The context will already be familiar to them.

Example: Social Science—World War II

Battle of Britain

One thousand German airplanes droned toward England on August 13, 1940. It was "Eagle Day," the day the Germans had —1— to destroy Great Britain. The greatest air battle ever was about to begin. The German pilots —2—

nothing about England's newest weapon, however. For on the ground, alert British soldiers and air crews —3— over their top-secret instruments in darkened rooms. They were —4— at radar screens.

Soon British fighter planes took off to battle the invaders. Without error, the English —5— their pilots to the large formations of enemy airplanes. For many hours, the skies above English —6— to the sound of machine-gun fire. The surprised Nazi pilots were no match for the well-directed British.

Authors' choices: 1. Decided; 2. knew; 3. hunched; 4. staring; 5. directed; 6. echoed.

6. Yays and Boos (Mason & Au, 1990). In order to respond aesthetically to what they read, students need to care about the topic. One way to promote this aesthetic response is by introducing *yays and boos* prior to text reading. When there is disagreement about a word, notion, or concept, active discussions can result.

Directions:

a.   In a content area, determine pairs of emotionally laden words (e.g., Fascists/Democrats; virtuoso/tyrant; Abraham Lincoln/Adolph Hitler);
b.   Teacher reads pairs of words aloud; students respond orally with "Yay" or "Boo," depending upon the words' meanings and emotional quality;
c.   Discussion of responses follows.

Example: Science or Social Science Unit on Atomic Energy. Word pairs: nuclear energy/coal fuel; invention of atom/invention of atom bomb; invasion of United States/bombing of Nagasaki; meltdown/radiation.

7. Prereading Question Strips (adapted from Whisler & Williams, 1990). As previously mentioned, prereading questions tend to suppress students' overall comprehension if they are related to specific information in the text (Readence et al., 1989). Therefore, in order to activate and utilize prior knowledge, as well as improve comprehension of text while motivating students to read, the *prereading question strips* are suggested.

Directions:

a.   Prior to introducing a chapter or story, write on tagboard strips four yes or no questions that probe students' background and experiences related to the text;
b.   Hold up strips one at a time, reading questions aloud if necessary; students respond to questions with thumbs/pencils up or down to indicate a "yes" or "no" response; they then share and elaborate their responses with partner for 1-2 minutes;
c.   Students write responses to one of the questions which have been posted on wall or pocket chart;

d. Students then predict how questions will be related to topic which will be read; predictions are listed on chalkboard or overhead;

e. Following reading, students orally share responses they previously wrote; class members try to guess which question matches the response (with number of fingers held up or with number wheels); students learn to formulate responses clearly and concisely;

f. Teacher and students relate their own responses to the events discussed in the text.

Example: Social Science or Literature lesson on Abraham Lincoln

Sentence Strip questions:

1. Were you or anyone in your family named after a grandparent?
2. Can you remember the names of your earliest teachers?
3. Do you remember the most frightening time you had as a very young child?
4. When you were a young child, were you an expert at something?

During their reading, students will learn that Abraham Lincoln was named after his pioneer grandfather who was shot dead by hostile Indians in 1786. They will also learn about Lincoln's first teachers, Zachariah Riney and Caleb Hazel, and will discover that when Lincoln was a small boy, his family lived in a leanto. Every night he and his sister Sarah were frightened by the howls and screams of wolves and panthers. Last, they will read about how Lincoln became an expert at using the ax (Freedman, 1987).

8. Five-Minute Write. Of all the prereading activities described here, the *five minute write* may be the most powerful and effective. It integrates writing, activates prior knowledge, enables students to self-generate questions about the topic to be studied, and focuses the reader on specific text structure and material. Originally conceived by the Bay Area Writing Project, it has been adapted for use as a prereading activity. The *five minute write* presented below is the actual work of a 10th grader in a biology class. Directions:

a. Prior to introducing lesson, students write in paragraph form everything they know about the topic for the day;

b. After 5 minutes, the teacher says something like, "As a result of your writing, you probably thought of some questions about (topic). At this time, write down any questions that come to mind."

c. Teacher tells students chapter subtopics and asks them to mark which of their questions they think will be answered in the chapter;

d. Have them mark these questions with "1," "2," "3," etc., corresponding to the chapter subtopics previously introduced;

d. Students share their writing and questions with partners, generating more questions about the topic if they can;

e. As students read text, they answer their own questions, if possible; unanswered questions may be used for independent, partner, or group research projects.

Example: Topic for Writing: Pollution; Chapter subtopics: Solid Waste, Chemicals, Sewage.
    Pollution is what one would call dirtying the air and/or atmosphere. Pollution can be caused by such things as factories, cars, disposing of wastes improperly and many other things. America is starting to have a serious problem with this and people need to pay more attention to it. It not only looks bad on the outside, but it is also bad to humans, plants, and animals on the inside. Breathing dirty and unclean air isn't good. It can cause internal lung problems.
    Student's self-generated questions:
    1. Why don't more people try to prevent pollution?
    2. How dangerous can it be to your health?
    3. Why aren't cars made so they don't contribute to the pollution problem?
    4. Is there some kind of fuel that will help decrease the pollution put out by cars and factories?

9. Your Own Questions (adapted from Vacca & Vacca, 1989). Whereas most prereading questions are generated by the teacher or textbook authors, these are generated by the students themselves, based upon their own prior knowledge and careful examination of the text chapter. Students need to be encouraged not to peek at end-of-chapter questions during their previews! Directions:

a. Students preview title and/or listen to or read portion of text from beginning of text selections;
b. Students write or ask as many questions as they can that they think will be answered by reading the remainder of selection (question-generation is most effective when students are working with a partner or coopera- tive learning group);
c. Teacher writes questions on board and discusses them in terms of what students already know about the topic; some students may know or think they know answers to the questions; if so, they should record them on their papers;
d. Students read text to find answers; after reading, discuss which questions were answered, which were not, and why; unanswered questions may lead to independent or group research projects.

10. Knowledge Chart (adapted from Macon, Buell, & Vogt, 1990). The purpose of the *knowledge chart* is to activate prior knowledge and then to connect it to new learning. This simple chart can be reproduced on worksheets, transparencies, or even on a large sheet of butcher paper. Avoid using it as an individual worksheet. Rather, it is intended to be used with the whole class, with partners, or with cooperative learning groups. The strategy is especially effective to use with students who have some prior knowledge about a topic, but not a great deal.

Directions:

a. Students brainstorm all they know about the topic to be read and list what they know under the "What I already know" column;

b. The list can be shared with partners or with groups so that everyone has access to everyone else's prior knowledge;

c. During a 1-2 minute preview of the chapter, students can mark with a " + " any of their brainstormed words or ideas that they think will be discussed in the text;

d. Following reading, students brainstorm and record all new information they learn during the reading;

e. If erroneous information has been recorded prior to reading, it should now be corrected.

f. Each individual student records and determines how he or she can put newly learned information to use.

Example: Social Science Lesson on the Gold Rush (see Figure 8.2)

CONCLUSION

When teachers conscientiously strive to incorporate a carefully prepared, interactive strategy into the prereading phase of a content lesson, students respond with eagerness, sensitivity, and sometimes surprising amounts of prior knowledge. All learners can become engaged in the learning, not just those for whom the reading task comes easily. Students with limited prior knowledge, and those for whom English is their second language, are exposed to vocabulary, concepts, and content before they ever have to tackle the text. Additionally, for those who are less prepared readers, the opportunity to share their own prior knowledge can be stimulating and gratifying.

Hopefully, the days of a teacher announcing, "Read the chapter and answer the questions" is over. Our present understanding of Schema Theory, as well as our own first-hand experiences with students who are motivated to read about content subjects, quickly convinces us that we must, every day and in every lesson, carefully lead our students into text. This can best be accomplished by including a well-structured prereading phase in every content area lesson.

Knowledge Chart
The Gold Rush

What I already know:

Search for gold

California

Wagon trains

Greed

Panning for gold

"Way out West"

Sierras

San Francisco

Missions

What I have just learned:

Many Chinese people came

Some were rich

Some were poor

Children had to work

Life was hard

For fun, people danced

Men hunted for food and fur

How can I use what I just learned?

I learned how to pan gold in a river.

I might pan gold when we go camping.

Figure 8.2.   Knowledge Chart

REFERENCES

Ammon, P.R. (1977). Cognitive development and early childhood education: Piagetian and Neo-Piagetian theories. In H. Hom, Jr. & P. Robinson (Eds.), *Psychological processes in early education*. New York: Academic Press.

Anderson, R.C. (1984). The reader's schema in comprehension, learning and memory. In H. Singer & R. Ruddell (Eds.), *Theoretical models and processes of reading*. Newark, DE: International Reading Association.

Anderson, R.C., Spiro, R.J., & Anderson, M.C. (1978). Schemata as scaffolding for the representation in connected discourse. *American Educational Research Journal, 15*, 433–450.

Applebee, A.N. (1981). *Writing in the Secondary Schools*. Urbana, IL: The National Council for the Teaching of English.

Cooper, J.D. (1986). *Improving reading comprehension*. Boston: Houghton Mifflin Company.

Dyson, A.H. (1984). Research currents: Who controls classroom writing contexts? *Language Arts, 61*(6), 618–625.

Freedman, R. (1987). *Lincoln: A photobiography*. New York: Clarion Books, Houghton Mifflin.

Johnson, D. (November 1986). *Guidelines for vocabulary development*. Paper presented at the annual conference of the California Reading Association, Fresno, CA.

Langer, J.A., & Nicolich, M. (1980). *Facilitating text processing: The elaboration of prior knowledge* (Preliminary Draft). (ERIC Document Reproduction Service No. ED 188 171)

Macon, J., Buell, D., & Vogt, M.E., (1990). *Responses to literature: Grades K-8.* Newark, DE: International Reading Association.

Mason, J., & Au, K. (1990). *Reading instruction for today*. Glenview, IL: Scott, Foresman/Little Brown Higher Education.

May, F. (1990). *Reading as communication: An interactive approach* (3rd ed.). Columbus, OH: Merrill Publishing Company.

Moore, D.W., Readence, J.E., & Rickelman, R.J. (1982). Pre-reading activities for content area reading and learning. In *IRA Services Bulletin*. Newark, DE: International Reading Association.

Readence, J.E., Bean, R.W., & Baldwin, R.S. (1989). *Content area reading: An integrated approach*. Dubuque, IA: Kendall Hunt Publishing Company.

Ruddell, R., & Speaker, R. (1985). The interactive reading process: A model. In H. Singer & R. Ruddell (Eds.), *Theoretical models and processes of reading*. Newark, DE: International Reading Association.

Smyth, T.J. (1983). *The effects of two types of pre-reading instructional activities on the reading performance of middle school students..* Unpublished doctoral dissertation, University of South Carolina.

Tierney, R.J., & Pearson, P.D. (1985). Learning to read from text: A framework for improved classroom practice. In H. Singer & R. Ruddell (Eds.), *Theoretical models and practices of reading*. Newark, DE; International Reading Association.

Vacca, R. T., & Vacca, J. L. (1989). *Content area reading*. Glenview, IL: Scott, Foresman, & Company.

Vance, D., & Buehl, D. (1990). Active learning strategies: Developing critical and creative thinking. In N. Cecil (Ed.), *Literacy in the 90's: Readings in the language arts*. Dubuque, IA: Kendall Hunt Publishing Company.

Vogt, M.E. (1986). *Reading and writing activities in the secondary schools*. Unpublished paper presented to Dr. R.B. Ruddell, University of California, Berkeley.

Whisler, N., & Williams, N. (1990). *Literature and cooperative learning: Pathway to literacy*. Sacramento: Literature Co-Op.

PART III

LITERACY INSTRUCTION AND ASSESSMENT

Chapter 9

Classroom-Based and Portfolio Assessment for Elementary Grades

Terry Salinger

There is widespread discontent these days with standardized literacy assessments. Brenda Engle (1990) of Lesley College has summarized the situation quite eloquently: "At present traditional evaluation is holding back the practice of teaching... preventing many teachers from teaching in ways they favor or with which they feel comfortable." At the same time, there is strong interest in assessments that can be aligned with instruction, which Engle maintains will be "informative to teacher (and parents) and encouraging to children" (p. 5). This chapter discusses the current state of assessment and makes two suggestions to improve assessment: taking advantage of the assessment opportunities within classroom instructional interactions and using portfolios of students' work to assess literacy growth.

REASONS FOR CRITICISMS OF STANDARDIZED TESTS

Questions about standardized testing have emerged for several reasons. Standardized tests may not capture all that needs to be known in order to make appropriate decisions about students' placement within schools and their subsequent instruction. Additionally, standardized tests most definitely do not allow learners to demonstrate the depth and breadth of what they know. Critics also claim that these instruments fail to look at the children themselves, at how they construct meaning from the world around them and specifically from, within, and across the content areas they encounter in school. Traditional assessments, especially those that use multiple choice items, by and large, tend to ignore how children think, a factor which diminishes their usefulness for fine-tuning instruction.

Additional criticism comes from reading educators, who cite the extensive research that has validated a definition of reading as a process of interaction between readers, the texts they encounter, and the contexts in which reading occurs (see, for example, Goodman, 1990; Valencia, McGinley, & Pearson, 1990). Tests constructed from a model that views reading as the accumulation of subskills cannot reflect the extent to which school-aged readers are developing a range of strategies to use to construct meaning from text.

Further, most standardized tests seem to serve little direct purpose in terms of instruction. Teachers may receive scores too late in the school year to make use of whatever information they provide, and the data may seem irrelevant or contradictory to what teachers themselves know about students. Standardized tests, then, cannot be said to be aligned with instruction.

To understand how assessment and instruction can be aligned, that is, how assessment can actually reinforce sound teaching practices, it may be helpful to consider the difference between testing and assessment. Testing is a technique, a way of gathering data about performance on individual occasions; a test produces a single "snapshot" of performance that reflects what a student has done on a particular date. Tests give a "slice of skills" rather than a picture of students' development (Wolf, 1989, p. 36).

Assessment on the other hand, implies an ongoing process, resulting in richer, more varied, and useful information. Initially, such data may seem less clear-cut than test scores, and teachers may have to infer what data mean. Their purpose is to present a cumulative portrait of learners' strengths, weaknesses, and capabilities within which teachers can better understand how to help each student learn more efficiently and how to better meet the needs of whole groups of children.

It is also helpful to think about the audiences for whom assessment and testing data are collected. The first audience should be classroom reachers, who should be able to use the collected information to refine their instruction. Other audiences who demand hard data as checks on accountability are school- and district-level administrators, state educational officials, policy makers in general, and taxpayers. An additional audience is parents or caregivers, who need information and reassurance about their children's progress. Finally, there is a frequently forgotten audience for assessment information: Children too need data on the headway they are making and on their particular strengths, weaknesses, and individual qualities. It is an unfortunate artifact of our current approach to educational accountability that it seems necessary to give students both in-class assign-ments and also separate, externally developed tests in order to generate the raw material from which information can be extrapolated for the various interested audiences.

SEEKING ALTERNATIVES

Recognizing all this, scholars, educators, parents, and groups such as the New York Public Interest Research Group (NYPIRG) and the Committee for Appropriate Literacy Evaluation, an outgrowth of the American Read-ing Council in New York, have called for either a ban on traditional means of testing in early grades or at least a supplemental reliance on other assessment measures. Less public in their consternation with traditional testing but perhaps even more effective in lobbying for change have been those involved in daily interactions with students. Increasingly, teachers or administrators—or, ideally, the two in collaboration—have been examining the assessment and testing requirements of individual schools or districts; and they are often arriving at decisions to seek alternatives to existing mechanisms.

Any successful assessment procedure—but especially one that is lodged primarily with teachers and students—must meet certain criteria con-cerning its purposes, the context in which it will take place, the evidence that it will generate, and the reporting mechanism that will best serve its stated purposes. For it to be effective, criteria concerning logistics and practicality will also have to be met. To meet theses criteria, teachers and administrators planning to initiate change will do well to ask themselves— and to collaborate on the answers to—the questions presented in Table 9.1. Underlying the 14 points is one basic question that teachers need to consider: What is the *smallest, most conservative* amount of information that teachers can keep on each child and still have useful data? Usefulness should be a guiding principle in shaping any assessment program that seeks to move beyond dependence primarily on externally imposed standardized tests.

Whatever the impetus for changes in assessment/testing methodology, suggested alternative measure can usually be divided into two categories: (a) assessments that spring from the instructional fabric of the classroom, and (b) evaluations that are performed on instructional artifacts or work samples after students and teachers have assembled longitudinal collections of students' work. These collections, often kept as "portfolios," may contain diverse kinds of evidence of what students have been doing and thinking and often also include the results of teachers' observations of students in the various classroom contexts discussed below and even standardized test scores.

Table 9.1. Questions to Ask Before Beginning an Alternative Assessment Program

Teachers and administrators should ask and thoughtfully consider these questions before developing an alternative assessment program.

Purpose of the Assessment
1. What specifically do you want to find out, both in terms of *hard data* such as "grade levels" and *soft data* such as attitudes about literacy?
2. Why are you going to assess children's literacy? Why do you need this information? What will you do with it?
3. What balance will there be between data needed for external reporting (accountability purposes) and classroom use (fine-tuning instruction)?

Context(s) of the Assessment
4. Where will you best be able to gather information?
5. How many cities and/or situations are there in the classroom that will allow you to gather information about children's *authentic* interaction with literacy?
6. What kinds of standardized situations might you have to devise to gather information about the children

Evidence to Be Gathered
7. What will best show you what you need/want to know? What kind(s) of instrument(s) do you need?

Reporting the Data That Are Gathered
8. To whom will you report the information you gather? There may be multiple audiences.
9. In what form(s) will the information be most useful?

Logistics and Practicality
10. How are you going to keep track of all you find out? Where will you physically store all the information?
11. What current assessment strategies will continue to be useful or can be modified to become more useful?
12. In what ways can the children themselves be involved in the assessment procedures?
13. What short-term sue will this information have?
14. What long-term use will this information have to have?

ASSESSMENT OPPORTUNITIES WITHIN INSTRUCTIONAL CONTEXTS

For assessment opportunities embedded within the instructional fabric, teachers are advised to look to what Chittenden (1990) has called the "database for literacy assessment." He suggests

> that as teachers incorporate greater variety of activities and materials into their reading program, the base can become that much more solid. It is true, sometimes, that teachers worry that they won't know "where the children are" when they shift from a single-dimension basal program to a more variegated literature–based approach. But these same teachers... are now in a

position to know much more about the child as a reader—interest, choices, strategies, skills—because the opportunities for assessment have multiplied. (p. 6)

The opportunities for this kind of assessment within a literate classroom environment are many. These contexts include:

1. Story time
2 Children's independent reading or writing work
3. Individual reading or writing conferences
4. Group dictation, reading, or discussion sessions
5. Literacy-related activities and tasks such as research projects and use of classroom books and print as resources or integral parts of literacy work or play
6. Informal setting such as self-initiated reading or writing, language play, and so forth
7. Class overview or "status of the class" reports (Atwell, 1987) that check up on each student's activities and perceptions of accomplishments.

Using diverse literacy contexts for assessment requires teachers to step back from their participatory role just enough to observe students and make appropriate notes on their behaviors, attitudes, and accomplishments. Sample record keeping/observation forms are presented in Figure 9.1. Their intent is purely illustrative; teachers should always try to tailor their forms to the kinds of observations they make and the records they need to keep. Because teachers know the students and know what they bring to their work and what they are trying to accomplish, teacher observations can indeed be rich ones. Teachers' role is to integrate information about the students themselves, the curriculum presented, the activities students engage in, and the overall context of learning in as objective as possible a way to arrive at specific decisions about individuals, groups, and classes as a whole. Teachers must be prepared to bring their best guesses, intuition, knowledge of children, and inference skills to making sense of what they observe.

Recognizing the significance of observations made within these many contexts expands teachers' range of options for assessment. Such assessments should serve the primary purpose of helping teachers offer the best possible instruction and the best possible learning environment; teachers often modify or personalize instruction to better meet students' needs. This is the essence of "kidwatching" behaviors, and the skills which a perceptive kidwatching teacher uses in observing and interacting with students are in many ways foundational to the skills needed to evaluate the contents of students' portfolios.

What is clear from this discussion of the many classroom contexts in which assessment can occur is the role teachers can and should play in

Figure 9.1.   Sample Checklist*

Sample 1: Checklist for Individual Student

Name _____

Focus of Checklist _____

Dates

Selects appropriate topics:
      When given choice
      When general topic is selected								

Demonstrates strategies for planning (e.g., brainstorming, etc.)								
Demonstrates understanding of drafting process								

Revises work:
      Adds/deletes information
      Reorganizes
      Considers vocabulary/word choice
      Considers grammar								

(ETC.......)

assessing their students' progress. Teachers who have realized that they have been preempted from this important function have recently attempted to regain some of their authority as assessment agents, to find assessment methodologies which they can control, strategies which will affirm the effectiveness of their observations.

PORTFOLIO APPROACHES TO ASSESSMENT

Helping students assemble portfolios of work samples which will be systematically evaluated is one way in which teachers have attempted to gain control of assessment. It is important to note that, as teachers have initiated portfolios to regain control of assessment, they have invited their students into the process. As will be discussed, students must participate fully in the portfolio process. A positive consequence of the approach, then, is that two of the audiences for assessment/testing data—two of the major stakeholders of the process—become the chief architects of the assessment strategies.

---

*In order to take advantage of the many opportunities for assessment within the fabric of the classroom, teachers need to decide what they *want* to observe and then to develop means to record their observations. These checklists are *only* samples.

Sample 2: Checklist for Group of Students

Name of Checklist: _____

Date Compiled: _____

Fill in students' name

Reads familiar material fluently						
Reads with appropriate intonation						
Reads with appropriate expression						
Self-corrects						
Uses punctuation to guide reading						
Takes risks in pronouncing unfamiliar words						
Demonstrates strategies for decoding unfamiliar words:						
Skips word and continues to read						
Rereads entire sentence						
Uses picture clues						
Uses context clues						
Sounds word out						
Asks for help						
Other strategies evident						

(ETC.......)

Portflios are increasingly being used as an alternative to or augmentation of traditional evaluation procedures. Compilations of students' work samples and thoughts about their work collected over a year's time, portfolios profile what and how students have learned. Denny Wolf (1989) has written, "Thinkers and inventors often keep longitudinal collections of their ideas, drafts, and questions. They use these as a kind of storehouse of possibilities for later work, valuing them as a record of what they have been and reading them for a sharp sense of their own signatures and uncertainties" (p. 37). Different from a work folder in which students keep drafts and records of reading and writing information to use while working, this "storehouse" of best works can also be the means of assessing student growth when teachers and students analyze and reflect on what is included in each portfolio and what the contents mean. Wolf continues "Portfolios are messy. They demand intimate and often frighteningly subjective talk with students. Portfolios are work. Teachers who ask students to read their own progress in the 'footprints' of their work have to coax and bicker with individuals who are used to being assessed [in more traditional ways]" (p. 37).

Sample 3: Class Overview

[In a minilesson or group meeting, teachers ask students to report on their activities and on their daily progress. Statements made on one day may lead to probing questions to keep students on task throughout the week.]

Reported Literacy Activities

Names	Monday	Tuesday	Wednesday	Thursday	Friday

(ETC....,...)

At their best, a major advantage of portfolios is that they allow teachers to manage their observations and collections of students' work in a systematic way and to periodically evaluate and tally artifacts that document students' progress. The purpose for which students keep portfolios and students' developmental levels will determine the minimum contents of each compilation. Table 9.2 lists some of the evidence that might be included in an elementary student's portfolio. Teacher-kept records and standardized test scores might or might not also be included. if such documentation is not directly included in a portfolio, then it can be factored into any grade or score determined by evaluating the contents of the portfolio itself. Their inclusion is often determined by the purpose and audience of a portfolio and the extent to which each student's portfolio will be accessible to the public.

Unfortunately but understandably, it is often easy for teachers to become caught up in the movement to sweep away standardized measures and end up with portfolios full of lots and lots of stuff that at best makes fuzzy sense to them and to the students who produced it. Keeping track of all the work samples, observations, and other pieces of paper is a challenge, especially if these highly individualistic, context-dependent, and often idiosyncratic artifacts are to be collated, aggregated, and reported on for valid, fair assessment decisions. This means that establishing a portfolio approach to assessment is not as easy as it might initially seem. Teachers must have a

Table 9.2.   Possible Entries for Literacy Portfolio

Portfolio contents should reflect the work students have been doing in their literacy classrooms. There should be a balance between evidence required by the teacher and that selected by the student. "Wild cards" include any extra evidence that students want to share with the readers of their portfolios.

1. Writing samples:
    Prewriting used to generate ideas
    Functional, expository, and imaginative writing efforts
    Graphic organizers
    Writing done outside of class
    Examples of writing in content area
2. Evidence of use of drafting and revision in writing
3. Responses to literature, including excerpts form learning logs
4. Dictation in lieu of authoring
5. Learning log and journal entries
6. Artwork, with or without writing
7. Tape recordings
    Students reading what they have written
    Oral reading samples
8. Nonstandard responses to reading, such as pictures or reports of dramatizations, puppet plays, and so foth
9. Data about reading habits and attitudes, often as checklists
10. Self-analysis and reflection, to the extent children can accomplish these tasks
11. Standardized measures, such as test scores
12. Wild cards: any example of students' literacy learning that they want to include in the portfolio once they have met the stated criteria for what to include

clear sense of the purpose the portfolios will serve for them and must then communicate this purpose and procedures to their students. Without student involvement and ownership, portfolios will be less beneficial than they should be.

INTRODUCING PORTFOLIOS TO STUDENTS

How children are first introduced to the idea of portfolios is crucial to the success of the approach. Portfolios must make sense to the children whose work they document. The classroom climate and students' expectations for literacy instruction and practice are also important factors. The climate must communicate to students that development is ongoing and gradual, full of starts and stops, successes, and frustration; students must feel comfortable taking risks. In such a climate, students view accumulations of work-in-progress differently than do those students in whose classes primary value is placed on getting right answers.

Literacy instruction and practice activities are also important. Students accustomed to real reading and real writing activities in meaningful contexts learn to talk and think about their work. They develop a vocabulary and a perspective that enable them to evaluate their work honestly and purposefully. The idea of selecting their best work to include in a portfolio and of reflecting upon that work will make sense to them.

Obviously the way to begin to keep portfolios is to keep work folders. To expand students' ideas about what should be included in work folders, teachers can introduce record keeping forms on which students track their activities. Such forms may be used to record the books students are reading, the pieces they are writing, and the strategies they have mastered in their pursuit of literacy. As students complete these records of their work, they also begin to learn to reflect upon what they are doing and to evaluate their efforts. Because portfolios require students to cull their work folders for their best or most representative work, they must learn to cast an evaluative eye on what they have been doing. In a subtle and nonthreatening fashion, forms to be completed daily or several times a week encourage reflection and evaluation. Samples are presented in Figure 9.2.

Keeping logs also contributes to students' understanding of the merit of looking at their work longitudinally, Entries from logs—whether they are specific learning logs or daily journals—can be excellent pieces to include in a portfolio.

Figure 9.2. Sample Student Record-Keeping Forms*

Sample 1: Reading Record

[Students should be encouraged to make daily entries to keep track of their reading. Sample space should be left in the columns so that students will write comments about their reading.]

Name _____

Date	Title and Author of what I am reading	Genre	What I think about the book or story

(ETC.......)

---

*Keeping daily, weekly, or periodic records of their literacy work increases students' metacognition, strengthens their ability to reflect on their accomplishments, and provides documents to use in assembling a portfolio of work for assessment.

Sample 2: Writing Record

[Students keep track of works-in-draft and their progress. They might use a star of other symbol to indicate when a work has been completed.]

Name _____

Date	Working Title	Status of the Work	Writing I did today	What else is needed

(ETC.......)

Sample 3: Strategies List

[Students should be encouraged to reflect on the reading and writing strategies they are mastering and state them in their own words. This kind of listing will strengthen their metacognition. While students do not have to fill in such a form daily, they should review and update it at regular intervals. The form can serve as a good starting point for a teacher/ student conference.]

Name _____

Date	What I can do as a reader and writer	Why these strategies are useful to me OR When I use these strategies

(ETC.......)

IMPLEMENTING A PORTFOLIO APPROACH TO ASSESSMENT

Once students understand the general value and purpose of portfolios, teachers must help them understand the criteria for selecting what to include in the portfolio and how the work will be evaluated. It is essential that work samples and observations will eventually be translated into some format that documents students' progress in descriptive, qualitative, and possibly even quantitative ways, and that students understand why and how this translation occurs. Additionally, teachers must communicate to students in an understandable and truthful manner what the criteria for judging work actually are. Essentially, this means letting students in on the secrets of evaluation in ways that can never happen with standardized testing. The sorts of "testwiseness" strategies that are often taught may indeed be helpful, but little can substitute for really knowing and understanding evaluation criteria. Dyson (1986, 1988) cites many student monologues and dialogues that give ample proof that, in an appropriate environment, even young learners can reflect on and critically discuss individual pieces of work and their growth and change as readers/writers and thinkers/learners. Understanding the qualitative differences between various pieces of evidence is the root of self-evaluation, but steps to build this understanding are frequently overlooked as portfolios are introduced.

To help students understand evaluation criteria, teachers need to talk about both literacy processes and products and need to encourage students to voice their own opinions about the efficacy of what they do. Such discussions must be well planned because the whole idea of evaluating and possibly ranking one's own work may seem strange to youngsters who are just beginning to feel competent as literacy users. Yet there is ample evidence that children who are used to their role in the process of constructing meaning through reading and writing can extend their energies to evaluation. Helping students identify and be able to speak about their own cognition—guiding them to become metacognitive—is part of what teachers must do to help students evaluate their own work.

The understanding that there are standards against which work is compared, and that there are definite, positive rationales for judging work, makes students more viable stakeholders in their learning. They sense that their daily work is part of an ongoing, cumulative, developmental process, propelled forward by their own efforts and energy. Learning does not happen because the teacher *does* something but because of the interaction between teachers, students, and the context of instruction and practice. As students see themselves as stakeholders in their learning process and as active participants in assessment, the idea of keeping portfolios will become very attractive to them.

Fortunately, there are ways to help even young students learn appropriate evaluation strategies. Individual and small group conferences, whole class minilessons and discussions, and written correspondence on student work and in journals can all serve to build these understandings. Discussions about text production decisions during group dictation sessions provide models for students to think about and evaluate their own efforts (Salinger, 1988). Using "neutral" pieces of work done by children from previous years' classes provides a focus to discussions and teaches students to concentrate their criticisms on work samples rather than on individuals.

Group or individual discussions must be conducted as open, nonjudgmental dialogue within the risk-free literacy community established in the classroom. It may seem contradictory to say that students will learn to evaluate their work through nonjudgmental dialogue, but this is in fact true. Judgment, as in the traditional testing methodology, seems to preclude growth and development; yet evaluation should acknowledge and spur development by focusing students' attention, not on what they have not yet achieved or mastered, but rather on what they have accomplished and how they can make their work better.

PUTTING THE PORTFOLIOS TOGETHER

If students have been keeping folders of their work, listing the books they have read, writing in journals, possibly audiotaping some of their oral reading, and reflecting on the strategies they use in reading and writing, they have ample raw material from which to assemble an assessment portfolio of their best and most representative work. Additionally, if they have begun to understand the criteria by which their work will be evaluated, they should be ready for their first "selection day." Table 9.3 suggests procedures for this first selection day.

To be practical and useful, portfolios must represent a culling of the accumulated work from any given period of time during the school year. That period may coincide with a marking term or may extend over even longer amounts of time. The process of culling or selecting work to include in the portfolio is the key to successful use of portfolios for assessment. Three major criteria must be met in the selection process.

1. Students must be involved in the process so that they feel ownership of the means by which they will be evaluated;
2. The work must be truly representative of what each student has done throughout the assessment period; and
3. The work must be truly representative of all the objectives, goals, and accomplishments upon which students will be evaluated during the period.

Students' involvement in selecting the contents of the portfolio intensifies their understandings of why they are learning certain things, why they are doing the practice activities they are doing, and the methods by which they will be evaluated. These understandings create a loop that cycles throughout the year: Ownership in the evaluation process motivates greater involvement in the learning process in general.

Table 9.3.   Steps for Initiating and Evaluating a Portfolio Assessment

These are general procedures to use to initiate a portfolio assessment approach in a single class or across several classes.

1. Decide what you *want* to see physically and qualitatively and make a tentative list. This should be based on the curricular scope of a particular period and on awareness of what students have been doing to master relevant content. Thus, the list will include categories of work samples along with indicators of quality of the evidence students will present. An individual teacher initiating a portfolio approach would make this list alone, based on knowledge of goals and objectives for the academic year. It is even better if a group of teachers decide to use portfolios and use this first step in evaluating portfolios as an opportunity to mutually review their curriculum and develop a common language for discussing students' activities and accomplishments.

2. Help students understand the criteria for selecting entries for the portfolio.

3. Schedule selection day(s) for students to cull work form their cumulative work folders.

4. Let the students make selections, discuss choices with them, and allow them time to assemble their portfolios. They may make annotations to contextualize their work and should also prepare a "Dear Reader" letter that discusses personal criteria for selection and their perceptions of themselves as literacy users.

5. If portfolios are to be used by teachers for grading and accountability, other evidence of students' work may be included as well. Teacher observation sheets, reports on teacher-student conferences, or test scores could all supplement the work sample students select.

6. Read through a sample of the portfolios to see what students actually selected; make notes about:
   a. the kinds of work samples students selected, such as essays, graphic organizers, lists of ideas, and so forth, and
   b. the reading and writing behaviors they have demonstrated, such as thinking and writing about what they have read, attempting to explore different "voices" in their writing, adopting a different point of view in examining an historical event, and so forth.

   If two or more teachers are using the approach, two readers should examine each portfolio and discuss any discrepancies they may have in their evaluation.

7. Compare this list with the list generated in Step 1 to determine the kinds of information actually available for evaluating students' progress.

8. Tally work samples and/or evidence of reading and writing behavior to evaluate the effectiveness of the first selection day as a measure of students' progress. If the information does not seem adequate to evaluate students' growth, restructure the selection process so that more specific kinds of work samples are included.

The organization of each portfolio should reflect the curricular scope of the literacy work students have performed both individually and as a class.[1] This important point is easy to misunderstand. It does *not* mean that students are given total freedom to select what to include, nor does it mean that teachers dictate exactly which work samples students must cull from

---

[1] For example, if portfolios are kept primarily for a language arts class in which instruction has stressed writing, contents should highlight the many kinds of writing students have attempted. If they are kept in a reading class, the contents will stress reading work. Of course, the best situation is for portfolios to be kept in a class which stresses the interactive nature of all language arts.

their work folder. The statement does mean that there is a middle ground: Teachers can (and should) specify the kinds of evidence needed for assessment purposes, and students can (and should) be allowed to determine what constitutes that evidence (Paulson & Paulson, 1990; Salinger, 1990). This freedom to select within broad curricular guidelines will work when students understand the underlying intent and purpose of the work they have been doing. Such understanding emerges over time when students are asked to perform purposeful, authentic reading and writing tasks rather than meaningless drill and practice. It develops as teachers talk about the work they ask students to do and as students talk and collaborate with peers. Such understanding becomes part of students' processes of metacognition.

To make this work, teachers specify the broad categories of work samples they want to see in portfolios and stress to students that they themselves will be responsible for determining what kinds of work will represent most accurately their work within each category. Teachers might, for example, state that students should select evidence to show their ability to draft and revise narrative writing; students must then go into their work folders to select a rough draft and its revised final form. Teachers may make even broader requests, such as asking for evidence of students' thoughts about something they have read. Students could then include and excerpt from a literacy log, a book report, or merely some jottings or drawings about a book they have liked. Any of these pieces of evidence would be acceptable so long as students' thinking is reflected in enough depth to serve as a source of information for the evaluator.

Teachers must also suggest the range of sources for evidence of accomplishment so that students do not limit themselves to paper-and-pencil efforts. Table 9.2 lists conventional and less conventional sources of evidence. The particular curricular approach and range of student activities would determine how many of these sources would be available for students.

Teachers may also ask students to include certain of the forms and checklists discussed above and shown in Figure 9.2. These documents help students chronicle reading and writing activities and list strategies they feel they have mastered. They give a sense of the breadth of the activities students have been engaged in, provide initial opportunities for reflection on accomplishments, and remind students what they have been doing so that they can better annotate their portfolio entries.

As students make selections about what should go into a personal portfolio, they should be reflecting on the growth that their work represents. They may want to accompany some entries with specific notes to tell the readers of their portfolio what a particular piece means or why it merited selection for the portfolio. Giving students "Post-It" notes to add comments to their work can be efficient. Students should also be required to summarize their thinking in a "Dear Reader" letter that presents an overview of the contents of the portfolio and a brief description of how each student views himself or herself as a literacy user. At first, such a letter will probably not show great depth of reflection, but its purpose is to have students focus their thinking toward the processes and meaning of their work rather than attending primarily to the actual products. As students became more accustomed to the portfolio process, they will realize that the "Dear Reader" letter can intensify their role as stakeholders in their own assessment.

MAKING SENSE OF THE PORTFOLIO CONTENTS

With time and thoughtful instruction, students will learn about portfolio assessment, can actually make selections from their comprehensive work folders, and will be able to reflect upon what the contents of their portfolios mean. Then the difficult, time-consuming work for teachers begins, for the contents of each portfolio must be analyzed and evaluated, data must be aggregated into some meaningful form, and results must be reported. Data aggregated from a portfolio must serve multiple purposes and communicate to several audiences, including the students themselves, teachers, parents, and administrators.

Figure 9.3. Teacher Worksheet for Evaluating Portfolio*

Names	Categories of Evidence	Categories of Skills/ Aspects of process	Indicators of Quality
	This colum records the number of pieces of evidence students have included in the portfolio. Students must meet a minimum number that has been stated by the teacher.		
		This column records the points (or other numerical accounting) that represents students' mastery of specific aspects of the literacy curriculum.	
			This column records teacher's qualitative judgment about students' work and is tied to a descriptive rubric or inventory.

* As teachers evaluate the contents of portfolios, they use a worksheet such as this to record quantitative and qualitative assessment of students' work. Their own observation records and notes can be used to cross reference this kind of recording sheet.

Depending on the purpose of the portfolio, teachers may select from numerous ways to evaluate contents. Table 9.3 provides for basic procedures for evaluating portfolio contents; procedures would be modified as needed to suit individual needs. As has been stated previously, teachers must have some predetermined reason for evaluation, some criteria against which contents will be evaluated, and some plan for keeping track of their observations of what students have elected to include. Many teachers develop a checklist of the kinds of work samples they want to see and the relative quality of the documents in each portfolio. A sample record-keeping form is presented in Figure 9.3 and explained in detail below. Such a checklist should be accompanied by descriptive entries that tie together the entirety of each student's work. Although it will take longer to keep both kinds of records, one record-keeping system without the other would not be enough. By using both a checklist and a descriptive chronicling, teachers are able to keep tract of the completeness and the caliber of the portfolios without effacing the richness of the evidence they present about individual learners. A sample scoring rubric for evaluating students' portfolios is presented in Table 9.4; it includes sample descriptors for reading, writing, and content area learning.

Table 9.4.   Rubric for Evaluating Literacy Portfolios

Using knowledge of curriculum, student activities, students' developmental level, and realistic expectations, teachers can develop a rubric that describes the range of work that might be included in a portfolio as evidence in reading, writing, and content area learning. The rubric is held as a standard against which the content of each portfolio is individually judged.

Outstanding Accomplishment

Writing in these portfolios exhibits the following characteristics:[a]
- real issues are presented and dealt with
- writing shows an authentic "voice" and sense of audience
- varied, competent writing strategies are demonstrated
- few errors in mechanics are evident
- strong thinking skills are evident in drafts and final pieces
- students considered topics and ideas in depth

Evidence of reading behaviors in these portfolios indicate the following:
- students read widely or have a clear, purposeful focus in their reading
- writing about literature shows high levels of comprehension
- students seem to be integrating what they read in various sources
- running records or tape recordings indicate fluency and inclination to self-correct errors
- running records, surveys, and other devices show awareness of multiple reading strategies and inclination to use them appropriately

References to content area learning in these portfolios indicate the following:
- students understand and use appropriate terminology
- students have grasped and can use necessary concepts
- students integrate information from texts and other sources and offer elaborated discussions of content areas
- students can interact with content material in appropriate ways, as in assuming different perspectives in writing about social studies or literature, explaining science experiences, and so forth

Commendable Accomplishment
Writing in these portfolios exhibits the following characteristics:
  • topics are treated in a thoughtful manner
  • evidence of thinking to some depth is present
  • varied, skilled writing strategies are evident
  • there is a clear voice, but not as strong as in papers above
  • there is a sense of audience
  • mechanical errors are infrequent and relatively minor
Evidence of reading behaviors in these portfolios indicates the following:
  • documentation about wide reading behaviors is presented, but it is not as strong as above
  • evidence of oral reading indicates fluency, ability to use numerous strategies, and inclination to self-correct
  • responses to literature show high levels of comprehension but less inclination to integrate reading and to refer to personal experiences
References to content area learning in these portfolios indicate the following:
  • terminology is used correctly
  • concepts have clearly been understood
  • there is less evidence of integration and elaboration than above

Adequate Accomplishment
Writing in these portfolios exhibits the following characteristics:
  • papers show competent treatment of and thinking about topics and issues but lack the elaboration and depth of papers in two top categories
  • students have clearly attempted to vary their writing strategies and have achieved adequate success in doing so
  • there are occasional errors in mechanics
Evidence of reading behaviors in these portfolios indicates the following:
  • an adequate range of independent reading is shown
  • there is indication of fluency, use of strategies, and self-correction
  • there is evidence of adequate comprehension
References to content area learning in these portfolios indicate the following:
  • grasp of content knowledge, concepts, and terminology is adequate but not elaborated.

Some Evidence of Accomplishment
Writing in these portfolios exhibits the following characteristics:
  • papers to not show deep or purposeful examination of topics, although there is evidence of competent thinking about topics
  • writing strategies are somewhat varied and used with some effect but errors in conventions are frequent
Evidence of reading behaviors in these portfolios indicates the following:
  • documentation of reading indicates a narrow range of interests and choices
  • discussions of literature, if present, are superficial
  • demonstrations of fluency show narrow range of strategies and disinclination to self-correct.
Reference to content area learning in these portfolios indicate the following:
  • content area understandings are less well developed, and gaps, incorrect ideas, and misuse of terminology may be present

Little Evidence of Accomplishment[b]
Writing in these portfolios exhibits the following characteristics:
  • examinations of topics and issues may be superficial; evidence of thinking lacks clarity and may be flawed

• writing strategies are not varied or are used inappropriately
• lack of control of writing conventions is evident
Evidence of reading behaviors in these portfolios indicates the following:
  • evidence of independent reading, if present, shows narrow range of interests
  • few indications are present of ability to access and use varied reading strategies to gain comprehension or decode unfamiliar words
  • disinclination to self-correct
References to content area learning in these portfolios indicate the following:
  • weak understanding of basic concepts, terminology, or information
  • inability or disinclination to integrate information

Minimal Evidence of Accomplishment
Writing in these portfolios exhibits the following characteristics:
  • treatment of topics, if present, is flawed, sketchy, insubstantial
  • mechanical errors impede reading of papers
  • serious handwriting flaws impede reading of papers
Evidence of reading behaviors in these portfolios indicates the following:
  • student does not engage in much independent reading
  • comprehension is seriously flawed
  •student does not have battery of strategies to use in oral or silent reading
References to content area learning in these portfolios indicate the following:
  • basic terminology, concepts, and issues have not been understood

---

[a]Characteristics presented are generic; grade and students' developmental levels will determine how many of the characteristics teachers can expect to see in portfolios at each level of the rubric.

[b]Distinctions between "Some Evidence" and "Little Evidence" may be difficult to identify, especially at the lower grades. Six distinct categories are presented here as a guide, but categories can easily be collapsed to better reflect the realities of individual classes' performance.

Another useful strategy for portfolio evaluation is to pose specific questions about the students' work, almost as advance organizers to guide teachers and other readers through the portfolio contents. As the list of such questions presented in Table 9.5 suggests, the questions will be quite holistic rather than stating specific enabling skills. They may well be overall goals for the literacy program. Teachers should look for answers to these questions about individual students and about the class as a whole. By looking for answers to these questions over time, teachers can develop both individual and class profiles. For example, during one portfolio period, teachers might notice a decline in students' correct use of the mechanics of writing but also a marked increase in their writing fluency and their willingness to take risks with new authoring techniques. The two pieces of information work together to communicate something significant about students' growth and also signal the teacher to observe carefully that, as students continue to expand their fluency, they also regain mechanical accuracy. If a balance is not achieved between fluent writing and mechanical accuracy, the teacher has a clear directive on how and where to fine-tune instruction.

Portfolios are often used in single classrooms to inform students (and

Table 9.5.   A Preliminary List of Questions to Guide Readers of Elementary Students' Portfolios

Teachers can devise a list of questions to guide their reading of students' portfolios. The questions focus on holistic aspects of students' reading and writing work, and answers to the questions are compared over time to gain a sense of the progress of both individuals and classes as a whole.

What evidence do the portfolios present that students can do the following:
1. integrate literacy activities into all their work?
2. use reading and writing as tools for learning?
3. select forms of reading and writing for different purposes and goals? For example, do they seem to know the difference between recreational and study reading?
4. demonstrate a wide range of strategies for use in reading and writing?
5. select the appropriate strategy to use in particular reading and writing activities?
6. use different writing styles and forms appropriately?
7. guide, monitor, and reflect upon their work?

How well are students gaining control of word identification, vocabulary, and comprehension skills and strategies? What growth is seen over time?

How well are students gaining control of the phases of the writing process? What evidence is there to indicate growth in ability to draft, edit, and revise their work?

How well are students gaining control of the mechanical aspects of writing? To what extent are students becoming more competent spellers? What progress is shown over given periods of time?

How are students demonstrating abilities and inclinations to self-correct in reading and writing?

To what extent are students becoming more fluent as readers and writers? What progress is shown over time?

---

possibly their parents) about individuals' progress and to gauge the effectiveness of instruction. In such cases, it is probably enough that the classroom teacher is the only portfolio reader, so long as she or he is very careful to blend hard-nosed evaluative objectivity with knowledge of the context of the classrooms and of the personalities and learning styles of the students whose work is being evaluated. While single-classroom use can be highly beneficial on a small scale, portfolios can be more advantageously used by several teachers working together, by all the teachers on a grade level, or by an entire school. When the use is more widespread, more teachers and students come to understand the approach, and its utility as a true alternative to standardized measures can take firmer grip on the fabric of a school.

When several classrooms use portfolios, teachers can share the task of reading and evaluating portfolio content; that is, each portfolio can be read by the classroom teacher and by one other teacher who is familiar with the scope of work that the portfolio is supposed to represent. As is the case with scoring procedures for writing samples, having two portfolio readers increases the objectivity and reliability of the assessment process. This makes the use of portfolio assessment seem more "serious" to skeptics who would want to cling to more traditional methods. Two readers can yield demonstrations of interrater reliability and thereby validate any grades or scores assigned to the portfolio content.

Being able to ensure valid, objective assessments of portfolio contents is only one advantage of having more than one reader. When teachers work together to establish a portfolio approach and then to share responsibility for evaluating contents, they must initiate dialogue and negotiation about what they think is important to teach and what constitutes evidence that students have mastered the objectives for each year. By talking about these issues and by collaborating upon criteria to evaluate students' work, teachers intensify their understanding of the content they teach, their skills for observing and evaluating students, and their strategies for fine-tuning instruction. They grow in their sense of community and professionalism.

ASSIGNING A GRADE

If portfolios of teacher observations and students work are to be taken seriously as assessment mechanism, the data they contain must be aggregated in ways that make sense to the many audiences interested in students' progress. This often means assigning the portfolio a grade or score. Aggregation of data in this kind of assessment is vastly different from the process of adding up grades in a marking book, taking an average, and assigning a letter or score. Grades that teachers derive from portfolios should in many ways be both holistic and analytic. They must acknowledge students' striving toward excellence and mastery, as well as the actual products presented as evidence of student work. This means that grades must be calculated through careful consideration of both the evidence presented in a portfolio and the contextual evidence teachers have accumulated through their assessment observations. It also means that grades alone are not enough to communicate assessment results and that descriptive, narrative feedback must also be prepared. Recognizing the intense amount of work the aggregation process can represent often makes teachers shy away from using portfolios as assessment mechanisms. In making these decisions, they miss the opportunity to move their assessment forward in meaningful ways.

There is no formula for converting a checklist or descriptive inventory about a portfolio to a numerical or letter grade. Many aspects of students' work must be considered, and the process is going to take work. A rubric such as the sample suggested in Table 9.4 can provide a guide against which teachers compare students' work to gain a holistic measure of accomplishment, but no rubric will automatically equate to letter grades. Teacher should look for other, analytic evidence to complement their evaluation.

Atwell (1987), p. 120) suggests assigning weights to the various aspects of students' literacy work and calculating grades according to the weights. For example, she divides a total of 100 points for writing work as follows: 20% for content, 20% for clarity, 20% for mechanics, 15% for focus, 15% for commitment (use of time, conferencing, and so forth), and 10% for taking risks with new techniques, modes, or topics. What is significant about Atwell's scheme is not the weighting per se, but that the categories and weights are aligned with her objectives and are easy to communicate to students. What is also significant is that the scheme quantifies aspects of students' work without reducing assessment to mere tallies on a checklist.

Atwell's six-part weighting scheme was developed for middle school English/language arts instruction. Teachers in lower grades or different teaching situation would be advised to think through a similar scheme to accompany their particular curricular goals and objectives and to reflect developmentally appropriate activities for their students. The scheme can be expanded to include evidence of reading achievement as well, but including categories for the accuracy of students' comprehension, their breadth of independent reading, their knowledge of reading strategies, and other components of students' reading behaviors.

The observation sheets or notes that teachers have kept as they have sought assessment opportunities within the fabric of their classrooms should be the final component of any grading decisions. Such notes help teachers contextualize other data as they attempt to understand and fully appreciate the processes and products of each student during a given period of time. Further, this information helps teachers provide the supplementary descriptive feedback that must accompany letter or numerical grades assigned to students on the basis of portfolio contents.

The vast array of data—holistic, analytic, and contextual—may seem overpowering. Teachers might use a graphic organizer such as the one presented in Figure 9.3 to control the data they collect. The first column indicates the answer to the first important questions about students' portfolios: Have the required pieces of evidence been presented? Such a representation can become a worksheet for determining grades, providing feedback to students, communicating with parents, and presenting a summary of students' accomplishments to supervisors and administrators. By itself, it does not communicate the richness of the data collected through observations and accumulations of work samples; but it does make the task of processing rich, individualistic data manageable. Without some management strategy, portfolios can never become true assessment devices.

SUMMARY

Because standardized tests serve very important purposes when used correctly, it is unlikely that classroom-based assessment approaches will ever

fully replace traditional testing methods. But the increased use of nontradi-
tional methods such as those discussed in this chapter offers teachers and
students real opportunities to play more active roles in assessment, align
assessment and instruction in productive ways, and grow in their ability to
think and talk about learning.

REFERENCES

Atwell, N. (1987). *In the middle.* Portsmouth, NY: Heinemann.

Chittenden, E. (1990, April). *Authentic assessment, evaluation, and documentation of student performance.* Presented at the California ASCD Invitational Symposia, San Jose, Riverside.

Dyson, A.H. (1986). Transitions and tensions: Interrelationships between the drawing, talking, and dictating of young children. *Research in the Teaching of English, 20,* 379–409.

Dyson, A.H. (1988). Negotiating among multiple worlds: The space/time dimension of young children's composing. *Research in the Teaching of English, 22,* 355–390.

Engle, B. (1990, October). *Literacy evaluation in the primary grades: A question of audience.* Presented at Alternatives in Statewide Educational Assessment for Early Grades: A Conference on Performance Assessments, sponsored by Delaware State Department of Public Instruction/University of Delaware, Wilmington.

Goodman, &. (Ed.). (1990). *How children construct literacy.* Newark, DE: International Reading Association.

Paulson, F.L., & Paulson, P.R. (1990, August). *How do portfolios measure up: A cognitive model for assessing portfolios.* Presented at Aggregating Portfolio Data, Northwest Evaluation Association, Union, WA.

Salinger, T. (1988). *Language arts and literacy for young children.* Columbus, OH: Merrill

Salinger, T. (1990, October). *Maximizing the potential of alternative assessment methodologies.* Presented at Alternatives in Statewide Educational Assessment for Early Grades: A Conference on Performance Assessments, sponsored by Delaware State Department of Public Instruction/University of Delaware, Wilmington.

Valencia, S.W., McGinley, W., & Pearson, P.D. (1990). In G.G. Duffy (Ed.), *Reading in the middle school* (2nd ed., pp. 124–153). Newark, DE; International Reading Association.

Wolf, D.P. (1989). Portfolio assessment: Sampling student work. *Educational Leadership, 46*(7), 35–40.

Chapter 10

Story Retelling: Combining Instruction and Assessment

Dorothy Feldman
Patricia A. Antonacci

INTRODUCTION

The goals of reading programs reflect the culture of society. As parents and educators we want our children to appreciate the gifts that literature bestows on them. To heighten that level of appreciation for stories, there is a need to emphasize children's literature in our reading programs at all grade levels.

For the classroom teacher, this means that story comprehension should take a lead role in reading instruction. Teachers know that such an appreciation of literature cannot be achieved through discussion alone. Enhanced understanding and appreciation for stories demand instructional and assessment strategies that engage students in increased story reading and enriching story activities.

Story retelling is a powerful strategy that can be combined as an assessment and instructional technique. As an assessment technique, story retelling goes beyond the restrictive standardized tests. This natural assessment technique provides the teacher with documentation of the student's level of development with respect to story understanding or story concept. As an instructional strategy, it provides the student with a structure to recall the important elements of the story. The combination of assessment and instruction permits the teacher to determine literacy growth in real and natural contexts using authentic literacy events. Thus the purpose of this chapter is to explore the potentials for story retelling in the elementary classroom.

Story Retelling

Story retelling has been gaining ground as a tool for assessing story comprehension, and to some degree it is being used in classrooms for instructional purposes. The procedures for story retelling may differ slightly, because the procedure itself will take the form of the retelling activity that is being used. In any case, the students simply retell the story or story part that they have listened to or read.

Using Story Grammar to Talk About Story Schemata

After we read or listen to a story, we are able to remember the important parts; we are also able to make comparisons of story parts to real-world events. We can go beyond that point and reconstruct a story the way we want it to end, and even more than that, we can write and tell our own stories. What explanation is offered for such complex thought abilities in the human organism? Two decades of research have led to a demonstration of how blueprints for prototypical stories continue to develop within young people, which enables them to respond to stories in numerous ways. The term often used is *story schema*. This research began with story grammar, a system for defining narrative text. Story grammar research led to important implications for classroom assessment and instruction as outlined below.

Story Schema: The Mind's Blueprint for Stories. Stories are not just a simple set of story events. Rather they are comprised of interrelated sets of events or actions that mirror real-world happenings, some not so real. One assumption that is used to explain how we comprehend stories is the development of a schema or a concept for story. This explanation rests on the notion that, since stories are well-developed, interrelated sets of events, readers need an internalized blueprint of the way stories are constructed—a mental organization for stories—to help them sustain the logic of the story events as they read. So readers use their story schema, a developing set of expectations for stories, which guide the readers as they organize story events into a whole.

When Do Children Develop a Schema for Story? Children develop and use story schema to recall and to understand stories at a very young age. Stein and Glenn (1979) demonstrated that even 5-year-olds use story schema to recall well-formed stories. Many people have implicit knowledge of story structure (Applebee, 1978; Whaley, 1981a). Further research supports the notion that story schema changes: Applebee (1978) noted developmental differences between younger and older children's story schemas. McConaughy's (1980) study clearly defines age differences found in story schema. She explained that, when kindergarteners were asked to retell a story, they included the beginning and ending components of the story, focusing their efforts on a literal interpretation. Children in the fifth grade, however, began to make inferences and supply the missing information that might fit into story. These same children also supplied explanations to account for actions and events. Finally, older children derived the theme independently.

Just how children acquire story schema is not clear. While Eckhoff (1984) reported that many children become sensitive to the structures of stories through either reading or listening to stories, research on the impact of direct instruction of story grammar on the development of story grammar differs. It is thought that rather than teaching story parts, much the same way as analyzing sentences for their grammatical parts, it is more effective to engage children in story experiences (Moffett, 1983; Schmitt & O'Brien, 1986).

Story Grammar: A Systematic Method for Parsing Stories. Initial research in story grammar began with the construction of a variety of procedures for categorizing story elements and for describing their relationships. The major approaches used to describe a simply story, such as a folk tale, have been developed by Kintsch (1977), Mandler and Johnson (1977), Rumelhart (1975), Stein and Glenn (1979), and Thorndyke (1977).

Story grammar may be described as an "idealized internal representation of the parts of typical story and the relationship among those parts" (Mandler & Johnson, 1977, p. 111). It is a procedure that consists of a set of rules that defines a text's structure in terms of its elements and their relationships, very similarly to the way sentences are defined by grammarians. People possess a knowledge about the structure of a prototypical story, story schema, or concept for story, and this changes or develops as they read, hear, or even see more stories. Researchers suggest that, when the reader's or listener's schema is similar to the story organization, which can be defined by story grammar, story comprehension is aided.

One procedure that is frequently used for parsing simple stories has been developed by Stein and Glenn (1979). According to their system, a story consists of two major parts, the *setting* and the *episode*. These are explained below.

> *Setting:* The setting consists of the main character or the protagonist, the time, place, and context in which the story takes place.
>
> *Episode*: The episode is the second major part of the story, which includes five categories. Very simple stories, such as fables, may be comprised of one episode, whereas more complex stories consist of several episodes. The five following categories are included in the episode:

The initiating event: This action or event sets the story motion and causes the main character to respond in some manner.

The internal response: is the main character's reaction to the initiating event, which results in the establishment of the story's goal that motivates subsequent behavior.

The attempt: This category is comprised of an action or a series of actions to achieve the goal.

The consequence: In this story part, there is goal attainment or failure by the protagonists to fulfill the goal.

The reaction: The final category of the episode reveals how the main character reacted to the consequence.

While simple stories contain one or two episodes with few characters, more complex stories contain numerous interrelated episodes. Figure 10.1 shows how the *Mrs. Cow* story has been parsed using the procedure discussed above.

Figure 10.1.   The Parts of *The Mrs. Cow Story**

Setting	One day Mrs. Cow was walking around the barnyard on Mr. Brown's farm.
Initiating Event	All of a sudden she spied Mr. Brown's garden, just outside the barnyard fence. The garden was full of ripe cabbages, tender green beans, juicy melons, and delicious squash.
Internal Response	Mrs. Cow said to herself, "My, those vegetables and fruits are very tempting. And I am sooooo hungry."
Goal	Mrs. Cow decided to get into the garden somehow.
Attempt	So she trotted all the way back across the barnyard, until she was as far away from the garden fence as she could get. Then she lowered her head and ran as fast as she could right at the fence. Wham! She hit the fence hard.
Consequence	The fence was old and it broke into 100 pieces. Mrs. Cow smiled in satisfaction and stepped daintily over the shattered fence, into the garden.
Reaction	Mr. Brown, of course, was not very pleased, and tied Mrs. Cow up in the barn for 3 days as a punishment. But Mrs. Cow was sure that it had been worth it!

**The Mrs. Cow Story* was analyzed by Spiegel and Fitzgerald (1986, p. 679). The same labels for the story elements were not used.

Story Retelling as an Assessment Strategy. The use of story retelling as a tool for assessing story comprehension makes sense. As a natural approach to assessment, it is holistic in nature. That is, it is unlike many of the formal tests of reading achievement where students are asked several unrelated questions about a short story constructed on a few paragraphs.

Conversely, when students are asked to retell a story, they must organize all of the events in the story to make a whole. The assumption is that "comprehension is organized and that the closer the reader's organization is to that of the text, the greater the comprehension is likely to be" (Marshall, 1983, p. 616). Further, as reading teachers, we are aware that fluent students have mastered those unrelated skills tested by reading achievement tests. However, it does not mean that comprehension is the sum of the parts; in other words, mastery of all the isolated skills does not insure story comprehension. As a tool to determine whether a student has acquired an understanding for story, "retelling is the most straight-forward assessment" tool (Johnston, 1983, p. 54).

While running records, or *informal reading inventories* (IRIs), are excellent measures for assessing a student's process strategies, there are indeed several limitations. For one, this assessment technique relies on a small portion of text that a student reads orally. Story retelling as an assessment strategy should complement the informal reading inventory, resulting in a more reliable judgment of a student's reading ability.

Analysis of a student's retelling "reveals which events in the selection are more memorable to them because of their interpretation" (McNeil, 1984, p. 12). What this means to us as teachers is that, as an assessment technique, story retellings bring us beyond the product of comprehension. It offers us valuable insights into how children are interacting with the text, using their prior knowledge and experiences to interpret the story. What it means to the child is that there are many ways to interpret events in a story; there does not have to be just "one correct answer."

Another obvious advantage of using story retelling as an assessment tool is that comprehension is being measured in a natural environment. The very nature of standardized tests is their objectivity and reliability. To achieve these characteristics, natural contexts are at best minimized. So children's performance on story comprehension is not measured in natural contexts when tested with a standardized test. According to Marshall (1984), this lack of ecological reliability is considered a serious limitation of formal measures.

To provide a natural environment to assess story comprehension, it is important to move from a clinical approach, as story retelling is commonly used in research and where a number of controls are likely to exist. To achieve a natural condition would be to place story retellings in the classroom part of the instructional activities that engage students daily. Therefore, it is suggested to assess students' story comprehension during instruction.

Figure 10.2. Record of Story Retellings

+ RECALLED   -   DID NOT RECALL

✓ RECALLED WITH PROMPT   ____   RECALLED AN INFERENCE

S E T T I N G   D A T E

MAIN CHARACTER(S)						
TIME						
PLACE						

E P I S O D E

INITIATING EVENT						
GOAL						
INTERNAL RESPONSE						
ATTEMPTS						
CONSEQUENCE						
RESOLUTION						

NAME _____

A Procedure for Assessing Story Retellings

The following procedure for evaluating student retellings has been suggested by Marshall (1983):

1. Select an appropriate story for the individual student. While kindergarteners can retell very short stories that they listen to, children who are in the fourth grade may be able to retell longer, more complex stories that they read.
2. Use regular reading instructional time. After children have read or heard the story, have one student retell the story while you record his or her responses on a checklist (see Figure 10.2).
3. If the student mentions the story element, record a plus (+) in the appropriate box; if he or she fails to mention the story element, use a prompt question to help his or her recall. If the student responds correctly to the prompt questions, record a check (✔) in the related box; if he or she fails in his second attempt, record a minus (−) in that box. To develop a prompt question, use the generic questions (Antonacci, 1988) listed in Figure 10.3 below.
4. Students retell the story individually. However, the variety of instruc-

tional activities in which assessment may be used are many; consequently, the type of activity will determine procedure modification.

5. Some stories do not contain all story parts; they are implicitly stated. For example, the reaction and the goal are often implicit story parts, but some students are capable of inferring story parts that have been omitted (Whaley, 1981b). To recall implicit text, students need to make inferences, which create greater demands on their comprehension processes. This type of recall should be given recognition. Therefore, code implicit story elements in the following manner: Underscore the plus (+), the check (✔), or the minus (−) for the recall of implicit story parts.

INTRODUCING STORY RETELLING

Teacher Modeling and Story Retelling

Teacher modeling is an effective method to introduce story retelling to students. Many young children who have had no experience with story retelling, and older children who are not proficient readers, could benefit most from the teacher modeling process. Children possessing a story schema that is not well developed use the teacher's retelling as a scaffold until they are ready to engage in own retellings. Since children tend to respond to familiar stories (Martinez & Roser, 1985), it follows that, when we introduce the strategy of retelling, we should use stories that were read on several occasions.

Procedure for Teacher Modeling with Story Frames. The process of story retelling may be introduced to beginning or reluctant readers by using the following procedure:

Figure 10.3.   Generic Questions Used to Develop Prompt Questions

Setting

Character: Who is the main character? What is s/he like?
Time: When does the story take place?
Place: Where does the story take place?

Episode

Initiating event: What happens at the beginning of the story to set it in motion?
Internal response: How does _____ realize s/he had a problem?
Goal: What is _____'s problem?
Attempt: What does _____ to solve the problem?
Consequence: Does it work?
Reaction: What happens to _____? How does _____ feel at the end of the story?

Figure 10.4. Story Frame

At the beginning of this story, the problem starts when _____

_____. Then _____

_____. After that, _____

Next, _____

_____. The problem in this

story is solved when _____

At the ending of the story, _____

1. Read an interesting story that contains a simple plot to a small group of students.
2. Show the story frame that is outlined below, in Figure 10.4, on the overhead and point to the different parts of the story, explaining each.
3. Tell the children that you will retell the story as they listen once again.
4. Using the story frame, fill in the missing parts by retelling the story.

Below is an example of a story frame that may be used with this technique.

The following are additional considerations in using this strategy:

1. While engaged in retelling the story, make a concerted effort to use descriptive language, bring in relevant details, make interpretations of story parts, and show personal reactions where appropriate.
2. During the modeling process, encourage students to add relevant information.
3. From the story frame, develop a checklist with the children of "Story Parts to Include in Story Retellings." Students may use this checklist as a self-assessment guide for subsequent story retellings.

Procedure for Teacher Modeling with the Flannel Board. Another method of introducing story retelling to young children in the early primary grades is through the use of the flannel board. This technique provides a graphic representation of story elements that will facilitate story recall. The set of props is especially useful to the young child who is just developing a sense of story. The procedure that follows may be used by the teacher in modeling the process of story retelling with the flannel board:

1. Draw or copy pictures of the main character(s), places, and major events of the story.
2. Mount them on oaktag and paste a flannel strip on the reverse side.

3. If pictures from the book were copied, use magic markers to color them.
4. After reading the story to the students, explain that you will tell the story once again using the pictures.
5. Using the prepared flannel board cutouts to support each story part, retell the story.
6. Having retold the story, invite the children to come up to retell the story or a certain part of the story using the flannel board cutouts.

The cutouts can then be placed in a large sturdy envelope along with the book. This packet can be used for follow-up activities by the students who will read the book and retell the story independently.

Procedure for Teacher Modeling and Story Mapping. The story map is another interesting activity to introduce story retelling to students. This is another graphic representation which depicts the story parts and may be used to structure the story as the teacher retells it. Because the students visualize the unfolding of the story as they hear it being retold, it may serve as a prop for the students' retellings.

To use the story map during retellings, the teacher displays the map. While the teacher tells that part of the story, he or she simply points to it. The students may use the story map, as outlined below in Figure 10.5, to

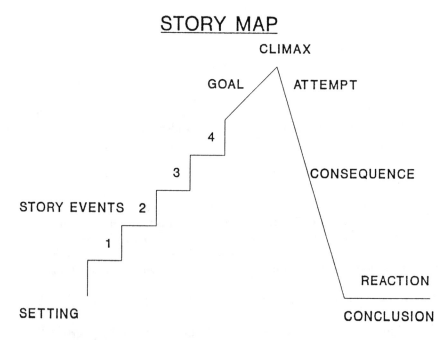

STORY MAP

Figure 10.6.   A Story Map for *The Mrs. Cow Story*

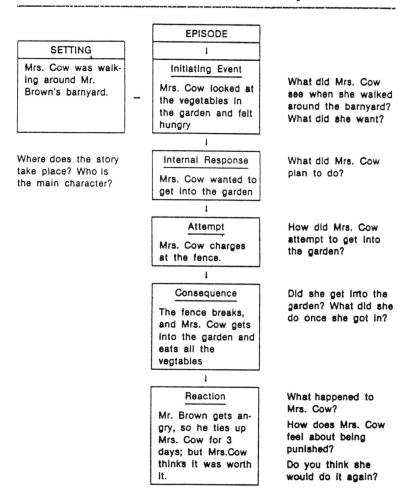

organize the story elements while they retell the story. They may also create their own kinds of story maps, filling in story elements as they are engaged in retelling the story. Another example of the story map that has been used with the "Mrs. Cow" story (Antonacci, 1988, p. 169) is found in Figure 10.6.

STRATEGIES TO DEVELOP STORY SCHEMA

We expect children to listen or to read a story and understand it. The extent to which they comprehend stories is largely dependent upon their story schema. As discussed at the beginning of this chapter, story schema is the mind's blueprint of a story. It allows the reader to have certain expectations for story events, to make predictions, to help the author solve problems in the story. However, story schema is not dispensed as the child enters school. Like other concepts, story schema develops with exposure to stories and active involvement with stories.

Story Retelling Through Questioning. There are a number of instructional strategies that will promote the students' involvement in stories. Retelling may be facilitated by focusing questions around story elements. Generic questions related to Setting, Story Events, Plot, and Theme will help students to structure the story as they read or retell the story. The kinds of questions offered in Figure 10.3 will, in many cases, help students becomes actively involved in the whole story rather than cause them to focus on specific details as most workbook type questions demand.

Teachers should not be the only ones asking questions; students may be trained to ask questions which focus on the story elements. Research demonstrated that, when students asked their own story grammar questions, there was increased comprehension for stories (Nolte & Singer, 1985). Using the patterned questions, children can be trained to ask themselves questions before, during, and after reading a story. This practice should lead to increased story comprehension.

Similarly, story frames which provide a narrative structure to record understandings in print may be used as a basis for story retelling. The generic story frame in Figure 10.4 will serve our purposes very well.

Story Retelling and Drawing. In the same way that writing after reading often leads to expanding insights, supplying clarifications, and signaling understandings, "Sketch to Stretch" (Siegel, 1984) encourages students to draw their interpretations of what they have read as a way to stretch their understanding. Although it is not a retelling strategy, it complements the process. For reluctant writers who are willing to use drawing to express themselves, these drawings become the basis for their first retellings. While students may initially draw scenes or events from a passage, the objective is to lead them to discuss their motivations behind their drawings. Rather than reporting on what they have read, students go one step further by bringing their own artistic interpretations to the story.

Collaborative Story Retelling Strategies. Reluctant readers who are not sure about their responses can benefit through collaborative story retellings. After students have read the story, discussion about the story follows. Instead of having one student engage in story retelling, the small collaborative group may engage in a "round robin" story retelling. Here each member is responsible for a story part that they have decided upon and rehearsed as a group. Another format is found in paired story retelling. Here a pair of students take turns to tell the story. One of the most obvious advantages of these collaborative learning techniques is that it promotes active involvement among all students during the entire reading activity.

SUMMARY

In this chapter we have discussed story retelling both as an instructional and an assessment strategy. What we have emphasized throughout this chapter is the powerful nature of story retelling for instruction and evaluation. While we have dealt with story retelling for instruction and assessment separately, it was not our intent to consider them apart from each other within the classroom. Rather, their separation was solely to provide further clarification. Natural assessment advocates monitoring literacy growth during real events in natural environments, and story retelling permits the teacher to do just that.

REFERENCES

Antonacci, P. (1988). Comprehension strategies for special learners. In C. Hedley & J. Hicks (Eds.), *Reading and the special learner* (pp. 155-176). Norwood, NJ: Ablex Publishing Corp.

Applebee, A.N. (1978). *A child's concept of story*. Chicago: University of Chicago Press.

Eckhoff, B. (1984). How reading affects children's writing. In J.M. Jensen (Ed.), *Composing and comprehending*. Urbana, IL: National Conference on Research in English.

Johnston, P.H. (1983). *Reading comprehension assessment: A cognitive basis*. Newark, DE: International Reading Association.

Kintsch, W. (1977). On comprehending stories. In J. Just & P. Carpenter (Eds.), *Cognitive processes in comprehension*. Hillsdale, NJ: Erlbaum.

Mandler, J.M., & Johnson, N.S. (1977). Remembrance of things parsed: Story structure and recall. *Cognitive Psychology, 9*, 111-151.

Marshall, N. (1983). Using story grammar to assess reading comprehension. *The Reading Teacher, 36*, 616-620.

Marshall, N. (1984). Discourse analysis as a guide for informal assessment of comprehension. In J. Flood (Ed.), *Promoting reading comprehension*. Newark, DE: International Reading Association.

Martinez, M., & Roser, N. (1985). Read it again. The value of repeated readings during storytime. *The Reading Teacher, 39*, 782-786.

McConaughy, S.H. (1980). Using story in the classroom. *Language Arts, 57*, 157-165.

McNeil, J.D. (1984). *Reading comprehension: New directions for classroom practice*. Glenview, IL: Scott, Foresman & Company.

Moffett, J. (1983). *Teaching the universe of discourse*. Boston: Houghton Mifflin.

Nolte, R.Y., & Singer, H. (1985). Active comprehension: Teaching a process of reading comprehension and its effect on reading achievement. *The Reading Teacher, 39*, 24-31.

Rumelhart, D.E. (1975). Notes on a schema for stories. In D.G. Bobrow & A.M. Collins (Eds.), *Representation and understanding: Studies in cognitive science*. New York: Academic Press.

Schmitt, M.C., & O'Brien, D. (1986). Story grammars: Some cautions about the translation of research into practice. *Reading Research and Instruction, 36*, 180-184.

Siegel, M.G. (1984). *Reading as signification*. Doctoral dissertation, Indiana University, Bloomington, IN.

Spiegel, D.L., & Fitzgerald, J. (1986). Improving reading comprehension through instruction about story parts. *The Reading Teacher, 39*, 676-682.

Stein, N.L., & Glenn, C.G. (1979). An analysis of story comprehension in elementary school children. In R.O. Freedle (Ed.), *Discourse processing: Multidisciplinary perspective*. Norwood, NJ: Ablex Publishing Corp.

Thorndyke, P. (1977). Cognitive structures in comprehension and memory of narrative discourse. *Cognitive Psychology, 9*, 9-110.

Whaley, J.F. (1981a). Readers' expectations for story structure. *Reading Research Quarterly, 16*, 90-114.

Whaley, J.F. (1981b). Story grammars and reading instruction. *The Reading Teacher, 34*, 762-771.

Chapter 11

The Four Ps of Context-Based Assessment: Evaluating Literacy Across the Curriculum

Denise Stavis Levine

With recent curriculum trends focusing on processes and strategies, interdisciplinary thematic teaching units, whole language instruction, writing across the curriculum, and collaborative learning, many teachers and researchers have begun to rethink the standardized objective examinations currently flooding our schools. (See, for example, Camp, 1990; Howard, 1990; Salinger, this volume; Weinbaum, 1991.) These machine-scorable instruments, which often drive instruction, assess only basic, lower level skills and factual knowledge, or those aspects of learning that are easiest to measure (Wiggins, 1989). They reduce thinking and learning to rote memorization, drill, and practice.

Thus, the challenge for us is to develop alternative assessment strategies that are more in line with new thinking about curriculum and new modes of instruction. We are seeking measures that are sensitive to the context in which learning occurs, and that take into account students' creativity, problem-solving strategies, and higher level thinking skills. To this end, I would like to suggest we examine literacy across the curriculum through use of the four Ps: performances, projects, publications, and portfolios.

While performances, projects, and publications are a part of student life in many schools and classrooms, they are often relegated to "enrichment," "extracurricular," or "extra credit" activity status. In actuality, these authentic, contextualized demonstrations of literacy and learning can tell us a great deal about a student's development over time. Let me offer some specific examples, beginning with performances as assessment.

It seems no more than common sense to assess learning in the performing arts—drama, vocal and instrumental music, dance, storytelling—through the use of student performances, and I know of at least two creative performing arts teachers who do just that. Both involve their students in writing and maintaining performance logs or journals in which they reflect on their performances before, during, and after the experience. Students' journal entries document changes in thinking over time, provide opportunities to explore feelings and emotions connected with performing publicly, and facilitate self-assessment.

For students in these teachers' classes, writing about their performances gives them a way to hold on to the experience in order to examine it, make sense of it, and evaluate it. (Heathcote, the grand dame of drama education, maintained that only through this reflective writing can we really learn from experience and make it our own.) Both teachers are also apt to document performances with photographs, slides, and/or videotapes. Like the logs, photos, slides, and tapes allow students and teachers to look back on performances, to evaluate progress from one performance to the next, and to set new goals.

What I propose is that using performances and their artifacts (photos, slides, tapes) to assess student learning not be limited to teachers of the performing arts. If, as Gardner (1983) has theorized, there are multiple intelligences, including musical intelligence, body-kinesthetic intelligence, and interpersonal intelligence, perhaps we need to allow students who wish to do so to utilize the performing arts to demonstrate learning in other curricular areas as well. History, for example, might lend itself to reenactment of significant events from various perspectives or viewpoints; or it might be possible for students to speculate about, and act out, other scenarios for historic incidents. Rather than focusing attention on recall of specific facts, such an assessment might focus teachers' and students' attentions on analyzing the motives of historic figures and synthesizing causal relationships. Furthermore, performances allow students the opportunity to demonstrate an ability to work together and to negotiate differences and conflicts, skills that are highly prized in the workplace.

Projects represent opportunities to assess how students organize their time, access and apply information from primary and secondary sources, solve problems, and communicate their findings. No standardized objective measure can do all that. I have had several direct experiences with using projects to assess students' learning; two were notable. One occurred in my middle school science class, the other in my architecture elective. In each class, students were required to prepare final projects and oral presentations of their findings for the class.

Many science teachers ask students to create science fair projects. I was no exception. Early in the term, my students brainstormed ideas for projects and investigations. The nature of the projects was open ended. While some students decided on classic science experiments (e.g., What is the effect of alcohol on mealworms?), others conducted and analyzed results of opinion polls about switching to the metric system, or developing nuclear power to meet our energy needs (see Gemma DiGrazia's, 1987, piece in James Moffett's *Active Voices II*). Six to seven months later, we began hearing oral presentations of what students had learned from their projects. Everyone was expected to submit an observational log and a written account of their initial question, modes of inquiry or procedures, results, conclusions, as well as problems encountered along the way.

Ricky was an eighth-grade student who clearly profited from this experience. I have told Ricky's story before (see Levine, 1986), but this time I want to focus on the project, an experiment on the effects of temperature on lima bean growth, as a way of assessing Ricky's scientific understanding and his growth in self-awareness. At the end of Ricky's oral presentation, a lively discussion of scientific research methods ensued. Some students took exception to the fact that one of the sites selected for its cold temperature (the refrigerator) also received less light than the other site (the desk in Ricky's bedroom). "So," one student explained, "you had an extra variable. You can't say for sure if it was the cold temperature or the lack of light in the refrigerator that killed the lima beans." Students brainstormed other sites in Ricky's home where only the temperature, and nothing else, would vary.

Another student was concerned about the fact that Ricky did not know the exact temperature of the refrigerator. They discussed refrigerator thermometers, where to buy them, and why these were necessary data for replicating the experiment. After the discussion, Ricky went home to reflect in writing about his science project and what he had learned. This is what he wrote:

5/9/85

   My project was the effect of room and low temperature on lima beans. My procedure was first I put the lima beans in separate cups then I put one cup in my refrigerator and the other in my room. Then I started a log week by week and when my project was finished I had a poster and a log. My log increased my reliability because it states what happened each week. My validity could have been higher if no sun would have gotten to the lima beans in my room, which was pointed out by Alan, or if I knew the temperature in my refrigerator. I learned a lot about doing projects and I am now not afraid to go up in front of the class anymore. (Levine, 1986, p. 146)

This is what Ricky demonstrated to me through his science project and his related writings:

- an ability to organize his time effectively by meeting all project-related deadlines;
- an ability to articulate a problem and develop a plan for investigating it;

- an understanding of the need for accurate record keeping in scientific investigation, as indicated by his observational log;
- an understanding that a relationship exists between accurate record keeping and the concept of experimental reliability; and that there is also a connection between controlling variables and validity;
- an ability to communicate and present findings, orally and in writing;
- an ability to accept feedback and use it to revise thinking, another of those areas that has broad implications for success in the workplace and in life.

This kind of organic assessment, which emerges from the classroom context and is closely tied to instruction and learning, provides far greater opportunity for "evaluating what we value, and valuing what we evaluate" (Wiggins, 1990) than do the more objective, standardized tests.

The architecture projects yielded similar kinds of demonstrations. However, where students embarked upon projects involving actual constructions, an even greater range of problem-solving strategies was indicated and exhibited. One such problem involved the construction of a working elevator for a model high-rise apartment building. The oral presentation by a team of two students, who were also best friends, was initially a litany of their trial and error failures and frustrations. Finally, though, they spoke of their successful solution, which involved a mechanized pulley system. (At the time, the eighth-grade physics curriculum was focusing on mechanical advantage and simple machines, including the pulley.)

Perseverance was in abundance here, maybe because friends were able to urge each other on. Perseverance was also the quality that marked Edison's quest for the electric light. Yet, while perseverance is an asset in work and life, it is rarely assessed by standardized tests. In fact, since most standardized measures are timed, students are often encouraged not to persevere, or not to dwell on any one question. "Just answer it and move on," comes the advice. Thus, the habit of persevering is neither valued nor evaluated.

As Eliot Wigginton has discovered in his two decades of work with *Foxfire*, publications may be one of the best vehicles students and teachers have for demonstrating and assessing learning and literacy. Publishing also provides real audiences for students' writings, and with them, real reasons for careful attention to spelling, grammar, and syntax. Finally, there is a reason to edit and proofread carefully. This establishes another link between curriculum and assessment.

Furthermore, publications may be used in any curriculum area and should not be thought of as a "frill" or "extra." I know a dance teacher whose students utilize class time to regularly publish a dance newsletter, a social studies teacher who created a publication of her seventh graders' colonial diaries, and science and mathematics teachers in an urban school district whose students published a math-and-science quarterly and used class time to develop articles, puzzles, and challenging problems.

My own experiences with publications have convinced me that they provide valuable assessment data for my students and me. As a federally funded reading teacher, working with ninth graders who were below grade level in reading, I used the daily newspaper as the course "text." After exploring the parts of a newspaper and the differences between news/facts and editorial/opinion, the students compared the New York dailies and contrasted the traditional format of the *New York Times* with that of the tabloids (*Daily News, Newsday, El Diario*).

Throughout this early work, students were writing and discussing their own reactions to issues emerging from their reading. Finally, near the Christmas holiday, one student suggested the class begin publishing its own newspaper after the break, with news and columns, "like for real!" he exclaimed. For the next five months, these students with limited English proficiency and low reading scores worked diligently on writing, editing, publishing, and distributing their own newspaper. They even produced special editorial "Extras," whenever they were especially concerned or felt some urgency about an issue.

In addition to the obvious content knowledge demonstrated in their newspaper (e.g., differentiating fact from opinion, knowing the parts of a newspaper, using and interpreting proofreading symbols), students also demonstrated the following skills and abilities:

- ability to organize and synthesize information in writing;
- ability to reflect on an experience or event and react to it in writing;
- ability to evaluate an experience or event in writing;
- ability to access information through interviews and to communicate findings in a cohesively written article;
- ability to develop an argument and support your point of view with facts;
- increased ability in proofreading and editing skills, and perhaps more importantly, an understanding of why this is necessary;
- understanding and development of layout and graphic arts skills;
- ability to organize time and meet deadlines;
- ability to handle and keep track of money and a budget;
- ability to work with others on a cooperative project.

A similar list of outcomes could be compiled for the intergenerational project I embarked on with Kerry Weinbaum, a middle school English teacher, and her eighth-grade students. But Kerry's students added a new twist. When she and I suggested producing an oral history publication to tell the stories of the senior citizens we had interviewed, some of her students decided they wanted to put together a "Student Interviewing

Handbook" as well. The students felt they had learned a great deal about conducting effective interviews and they wanted to share what they had learned about the process with their peers. Kerry, the kids, and I came to think of this as a demonstration of process and product, and we had separate publications for assessing students' progress in each phase of the project.

All of which brings us to our fourth and final "p" of context-based assessment—portfolios. Portfolios can best be thought of as envelopes that contain the documentation and evidence of learning associated with the performances, projects, and publications. Portfolios work best when they are embedded in the classroom or school context, when they represent the entire range of students' abilities (including evidence of processes and strategies), and when students are involved in the reflection and selection processes inherent in portfolio development. When these conditions exist, portfolios serve learning as well as assessment goals.

It is important to remember, however, that, since portfolios are meant to grow from the educational context, there is no one model, no one right way to develop or interpret portfolios. Instead, students, teachers, and supervisors need to begin a dialogue which focuses on what students need to learn, how best to facilitate that learning, how to provide evidence of learning, and how to evaluate learning. In these discussions, community values and criteria for assessment are established (see Camp, 1990). This is a necessary step in validating contextualized assessment. Nowhere is the educative power of this process driven home to me more forcefully than in the portfolios of my graduate education students, most of whom are teachers.

Each semester, I ask the students to create portfolios of their work for the course. Although specifics change with the focus of the course and the needs of the students, some things are constant. Portfolios need to reflect the range of reading and writing done for the course, as well as turning points in the student's learning process. Each portfolio must also contain a cover letter, reflecting on what was learned in the course, how it was learned, and how the contents of the portfolio provide evidence of learning. What has been most exciting for me has been the very different and individual ways people have found to demonstrate what they have learned and how they have learned it.

For example, last term one student selected excerpts from the journal she kept to reflect on class discussions, her readings, and her research for the final project. For each entry selected, she wrote a reflective note explaining how and why her thinking had evolved since the original piece was written. These notes demonstrated insight into her own thinking and learning processes. In the same class, another student photocopied pages of texts she had annotated, many of which included connections she made to experiences she had had or to other texts she had read. If *learning* is defined as making connections between the new and the known (Mayher, Lester, &

Pradl, 1984), then surely these text annotations must be a valid way of demonstrating how learning actually occurred. No objective measure can assess that kind of metacognitive process.

Semester after semester, though, whether I am teaching third graders, eighth graders, or teachers, the most significant assessment data are generally found in the reflective portfolio cover letters. In these cover letters students exhibit the critical thinking and metacognitive awareness necessary for assessing one's own learning, regardless of one's stage in life. Some examples from teachers' cover letters demonstrate this point. First, this excerpt from a secondary teacher:

> Until your class I never considered writing to have any greater purpose than to communicate... you had us write in order to realize our own literacy. I moved to an understanding of an assumption that teachers make. I noticed how I "heard" in my head the dialect of *The Last Hurrah*...I have always been a good reader... I expect my students to hear what I hear, and maybe they can't.

For this teacher, insight into his own reading and writing processes allowed him to connect to his students' processes. His new understanding stands in contrast to his prior "assumption" that his students heard what he heard in a given text.

A primary teacher focused her portfolio letter on "significant changes" in her teaching, which resulted from her work in the course. The changes included "spend[ing] more time simply observing [students] and... adapt[ing] classroom activities to collaborative learning." I agreed with her assessment that these were "significant changes" in teaching. It is easy to see how portfolios, as selections of representative works, can offer a window on thinking and learning processes.

So where does all this leave us? If standardized tests are on the increase, then we need to downplay their importance by providing our context-based assessment data, portfolios full of writings, papers, journals, process logs, photographs and slides, illustrations, publications, and audio and videotapes alongside the standardized test data. Furthermore, if testing continues to drive instruction for many teachers and students, then context-based assessment can at least drive it in the direction of 21st-century needs: accessing, interpreting, and applying information to explore and solve complex problems.

Those in the workplace have helped us to understand that this will require people to work cooperatively, to be able to accept new information or insights and revise their thinking accordingly, to persevere, to be able to communicate their ideas orally and in writing. To assess these skills and abilities, which transcend curricular lines, we will need to utilize more than objective examinations; we will want the four p's of context-based assessment to help us do the job.

REFERENCES

Camp, R. (1990, Spring). Thinking together about portfolios. *The Quarterly of the National Writing Project and the Center for the Study of Writing*. Berkeley, CA: Center for the Study of Writing

DiGrazia, G. (1987). A poll on nuclear energy. In J. Moffett (Ed.), *Active voices II*. Portsmouth, NY: Boynton Cook.

Gardner, H. (1983). *Frames of mind: The theory of multiple intelligences*. New York: Basic Books.

Howard, K. (1990, Spring). Making the writing portfolio real. *The Quarterly of the National Writing Project and the Center for the Study of Writing*. Berkeley, CA: Center for the Study of Writing.

Levine, D. (1986). Exposing the edge of thought. In J. Golub (Ed.), *Activities to promote critical thinking*. Urbana, IL: National Council of Teachers of English.

Mayher, J., Lester, N., & Pradl, G. (1984). *Writing to learn/learning to write*. Portsmouth, NH: Boynton Cook.

Weinbaum, K. (in press). Portfolios as a vehicle for student empowerment and teacher change. In P. Belanoff & M. Dixon (Eds.), *Portfolio grading: Process and product*. Portsmouth, NH: Boynton Cook.

Wiggins, G. (1989, May). A true test: Toward more authentic and equitable assessment. *Phi Delta Kappan, 70*(9).

Wiggins, G. (1990, December). *Performance-based assessment*. Presentation at the Association of Supervision and Curriculum Development's Miniconference, "Redesigning Assessment," Washington, DC.

PART IV

STORIES AND THE CURRICULUM

Chapter 12

Multicultural Literature and the Curriculum

Steven Tribus
Carolyn N. Hedley

One of the purposes of this chapter is to expand the canon of literature that has been the basis of our curriculum. Our society and our schools have experienced a great proportional change in the nature of their populations, in addition to seeing an increase in the variety of cultures and countries represented by the students in our classes. Women, racial minorities, religious groups, various social and cultural groups, such as the homeless, the handicapped, the disenfranchised, the poor, the young, the old, and those who are "different" have not been heard; these groups are each demanding a representation in the literature and learning of the country.

The changes in our student population demand that we examine our present literature lists and look to expand them to include works from countries, cultures, and societies hitherto unrepresented in our courses or represented in a meager and superficial way. To put this in perspective, consider these facts (Ornstein, 1989):

1. In 1951, only 11 percent of all immigrants came from Latin America, Asia, and Africa; by 1976, 79 percent came from these areas. In 1951, 89 percent of all immigrants were from Europe and the rest of the world; in 1976, only 21 percent came from these areas.
2. In 1986, about 50 million, or 21 percent, of America's 240 million people were of Hispanic, Asian, or Afro-American descent; "shortly after the year 2000 one out of three Americans will be nonwhite."
3. In 1950, all but one of the nation's 25 largest city school systems had a

white student majority. By 1980, all but two had a majority of minorities.

4. "The Hispanic population should reach 30 million in the year 2000 (10.8% of the total population) and 46 million in 2020 (14.7%) surpassing the U.S. black population (14%) as the largest minority group. . . . The Asian population is expected to total 12 million in 2000 (4.3%) and 20 million in 2020 (6.4%) compared to four million (2.0%) in 1980" (Ornstein & Levine, 1989, p. 486).

These statistics, while they pertain to only a few of the more than 300 ethnic groups, should bring educators to notice that changes in attitude and curriculum are necessary for teachers and supervisors of all subjects.

DEFINITIONS: MULTICULTURAL TEACHING AND LITERATURE

Multicultural literature may be seen to include both works that are about people in multicultural societies, and about people in specific countries and cultures, where the story told contains basic understandings about that group. These kinds of works provide us with models for understanding how other cultures work and help us to understand how the multicultural society can function. The National Council for the Teachers of English *Guidelines for the Preparation of Teachers* (1986) states that teachers of English need to know about an "extensive body of literature and literary types in English and in translations, that is, a literature by people of many countries, cultures, racial, and ethnic groups, and by authors from many countries and cultures" (p. 14). The Guidelines stress the issue of teacher attitudes, specifically a "desire to use the language arts curriculum for helping students become familiar with diverse peoples and cultures" stating the following:

> In a multicultural society, teachers must be able to help students achieve cross-cultural understanding and appreciation. Teachers must be willing to seek and to use materials which represent linguistic and artistic perspectives. In such diverse cultural contexts, students explore their own perceptions and values. (*NCTE Guidelines*, 1986, p. 14)

Multicultural education, which uses multicultural literature as a basis of information, should affect instruction of all students and implies changes in instructional methodology and program development in all subjects. Multicultural education is interdisciplinary and cannot be taught in isolation from other instruction. It differs from multiethnic education which focuses on ethnicity and its origins in terms of the American cultural characteristics for these groups. While this concept is useful, it is too limiting for our needs and does not deal with the development of morality, attitudes, and values in the realm of multicultural education. Further, multicultural education is not global education which tends to emphasize the nature of different countries around the world and the ethnic groups in those countries. According to Tiedt and Tiedt (1986) the following features characterize a sound multicultural education program at any level of schooling:

1. Students are taught to accept themselves with all their strengths and weaknesses.
2. Students learn to see other people as having equal worth and dignity regardless of their diverse backgrounds.
3. Instructional materials are free of bias and stereotyping and clearly demonstrate the positive aspects of our pluralistic society. All groups are represented and both text and illustrations tend to break down stereotyped thinking about career and social roles.
4. Instructional strategies promote student self-esteem and teach specific concepts related to the universality of human needs, feelings, and desires, as well as the positive aspects of diversity. Evaluation reflects respect for the individual and realistic expectations for each student.
5. Concepts permeate the total curriculum for all students in all subjects (Tiedt & Tiedt, 1986, p. 3).

Implications

We must consider changes in the literature used in our schools. Some twenty years ago, educational institutions began to rethink their attitudes about the content and practices in the literary offerings of our schools, making them more culturally broad-based, socially sensitive and congenial, and linguistically considerate. The bulk of literary works that was, and in many schools, still is, the staple of the language arts curriculum was almost exclusively Eurocentric. While this focus provided students with important experiences with some of the best fiction and nonfiction ever written, it did not allow the children in our schools to experience or even know of the existence of the wealth of outstanding literature that was written by or was primarily about cultural or ethnic groups that represent many of the minorities in our country. With the rapidly changing nature of our society and the presence of many new immigrants from around the world, it is clear that our schools' curriculum in language arts must change to reflect this social change. In addition, many groups who have been citizens of this country since its inception have not had their appropriate place in the curriculum: African Americans and Native Americans being prominent among these groups. There is clearly a need, therefore, for school systems throughout the country to reevaluate their language arts curricula in order to make it more reflective of the nation's population as well as to reflect more accurately the scope of excellent literature with which our students should be familiar.

As another issue, literature in English is an increasingly international phenomenon; English has become the *lingua franca*, of the world. With the international news networks, the many international businesses, the daily growth in international dependence, one language was bound to emerge as the language of the marketplace and that language is English. If we are to keep faith with the international community, we must broaden our literary perspectives. Writers and speakers from all over the world are finding it necessary to communicate in English: The Pacific Rim nations, Asia, Africa, and the West Indies, use English as a medium for communicating their lives in fiction, exposition, and poetry. One consequence is that literature in English has become increasingly multicultural, therefore creating a readership which includes many other cultures.

This chapter will focus on responding to four central issues related to making the scope of the literature used in our language arts curriculum truly multicultural:

- An approach to multicultural education
- A literary approach to multicultural education
- The literature of multiculturalism
- Issues and concerns

AN APPROACH TO MULTICULTURAL EDUCATION

James A. Banks, the noted educator whose work in the area of multicultural education has informed the development of numerous school systems' efforts to engender a multicultural approach to education, argues that it is not enough to add a piece of minority literature here and one new historical perspective there in an effort to broaden the focus of the curriculum. Rather, he posits that we must look at the total school environment if we are to make a legitimate approach to creating a truly multicultural school system.

Probably one of the best ways to use literature in a multicultural way across the curriculum is through the use of the theme unit (see Figure 12.1). By using a book, or passage, or even a theme, such as good manners in the Eskimo culture, as a focus for discussion, one can apply the understanding gained to other curricular areas. By devising activities and literary events that, for example, can be included in the social studies, the performing arts, or storytelling, teachers and students can expand their knowledge to other disciplines. Thus, the educator integrates not only the multicultural con-

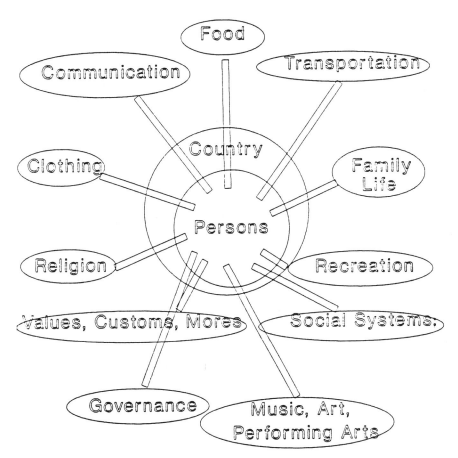

Figure 12.1. Literature webbing across the multicultural curriculum. Think of ways to integrate cultural activities from your reading into the content areas of the curriculum.

cepts, but the communication arts (listening, speaking, reading, writing and thinking) and the other content areas in the curriculum.

Following this line of thinking the New York City Public Schools have embarked on an overall approach to making its curriculum and its school environments multicultural. The two major goals of this effort support this approach:

1. To ensure equal educational opportunity to attain educational proficiency for all students regardless of their gender or socioeconomic background; their ethnic, racial, or cultural characteristics; and regardless of their special learning styles.

2. To promote an appreciation of ethnic, cultural, racial, and linguistic diversity, and in so doing to enhance the self-respect and self-worth of the entire school community.

Such an approach, particularly that embodied in the second goal, helps give students an important sense of their own importance and ability to succeed, a basic need for every fulfilled human being. While the various approaches to creating a multicultural education program may utilize numerous methods and foci, it seems clear that one essential and effective way to move toward the achievement of the two goals listed above is through the use of multicultural literature.

Self-Esteem

A student-centered multicultural literature program rightfully begins with a focus on individual self-esteem, a sense of the inner self. Strategies for teaching should allow for interaction and an exchange of ideas, should be hands-on, and should help students come to value themselves. To become more sensitive to students' values, attitudes, and feelings, it is prudent to develop the curriculum in a participatory manner. In English class, for example, reading a book, *Sumi and the Goat and the Tokyo Express*, by Yoshiko Uchida, for social studies understanding might include these activities:

- Keep a learning log summarizing their day's reading.
- Identify stereotypes associated with characters in discussion.
- List and discuss their personal strengths and understandings in the content of the social studies.
- Recognize the necessity to make some generalizations based on facts without stereotyping.
- Work cooperatively in group situations. Practice greetings in other languages (Japanese, in this instance).
- Act out the story related to cultural understandings of country or characters in the story.
- Discuss the contributions made by diverse groups in the society.

There are activities that one can use that reinforce the *self-esteem* fostered by the family. Name activities, introductions, taking care of yourself, class directories, all about me collages, personal histories, "bragging sessions," genealogies, and the like can be used to bring out these personal relationships. Self-esteem as an approach to literacy, especially writing about one's self, one's family and personal feelings, foster such feelings. Self-esteem is frequently found in family relationship and students should be encouraged to talk about helpful family members. But the result of sharing in the

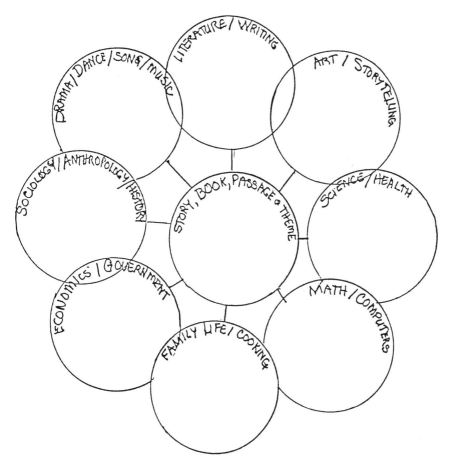

Figure 12.2.   Multicultural Education
What can you tell about the cultural concepts above based on the story you have just read?

multicultural classroom should be a sense of connectedness to the class and to the community. Books that lend themselves to such ideas are: *Conversation Club, A Father Like That, Leo, the Late Bloomer, Mufaro's Beautiful Daughters, And Now Miguel, Stevie,* and many, many others. As an example of how discussion might be covered, Figure 12.2 demonstrates that based on a story or film such as *Dances with Wolves* (both a book and a film), one could discuss the nature of persons (that is individual Souix), the country, and such aspects of the Souix culture as revealed in the film as food, communication, transport, religion, social system, housing, governance, and the arts. A literary experience can develop cultural understanding.

The Value of Diversity

As self-esteem and a sense of connectedness is being established as a goal for the multicultural literacy and learning program (through talking about common problems, such as sadness, fear, dealing and talking with others, or social relationships, such as dating), students come to understand the value of diversity. Creating a classroom environment that fosters acceptance and cooperation among students, would include talking about how individuals are unique, and how stereotypes are developed. They should understand that everyone has a name, a surname, a family, and an identity linked to a government; we all belong to many groups, such as being a girl, Chinese, a 12-year-old, a member of the class, a member of a religion, and so on; we identify with these groups to varying degrees. From these groupings we develop an identity, and often we develop positive images as well as unfortunate stereotypes. We need to examine books for positive images of women, men, aged persons, ethnic groups, racial groups, and elite/nonelite paradigms. Encouragement for working with others can be gained by discussing arguments, sharing problems, role-playing, cooperative learning, and discussing proverbs and cartoons from various cultures. Food and cooking projects, menus, recipes, snacks, and customs analyses can be used to elicit understandings of diversity. Through these activities the understandings below may be developed:

- People of all groups have a contribution to make.
- People are more alike than they are different.
- Differences in customs and attitudes are an asset to society.
- Prejudice and stereotyping are usually based on a lack of information.
- Understanding others will enrich our own lives (Tiedt & Tiedt, 1986, p. 65).

We are a nation of immigrants, with various national origins and different religions; we must focus on developing groups and on being part of the global village. Communications and travel systems are confirming that we can no longer exist with negative stereotypes and prejudices. To function in a multinational world successfully, one must simply understand and get along with others.

A LITERARY APPROACH TO MULTICULTURAL EDUCATION

Recent research has shown that two major foci in organizing an effective language arts program stand out from the variety of ways to organize what is an inherently amorphous subject:

1. An approach that integrates listening, speaking, reading, writing, and thinking within language arts instruction as well as in all content areas. This approach is clearly reflected in the principles which underlie the whole language philosophy.
2. An organization of instruction which is based on the use of quality literature, not only in language arts but in content area programs as well.

The first statement holds that separating the various communication components that comprise language arts may make the organization of instruction neater and easier to put together, but such an approach does not support the ways in which we learn and use language in the real world. To use such an approach, therefore may satisfy a management need but it does not satisfy the needs of the student and that is where our focus should remain. It is clear that putting together an integrated language arts program may be more complicated initially because it requires teachers and administrators confronting such issues as selecting appropriate materials, putting instruction into a logical sequence, and determining the best methods and activities for each particular student, class, and lesson. The results of such efforts, however, are well worth the initial extra effort since students will acquire and use language skills more readily and with a greater sense of interest and joy. As a corollary result, teachers will not only be more effective, they will have a good time in the process; this is *not* an insignificant change.

Our linguistic heritage needs to be recognized in our literary programs. We have always spoken English as a primary language, but as the different national and language groups came, we incorporated their words into the American English; the roots of our language reside in borrowed languages. We need to study comparative languages, note the similarities of one to the other and the cognate words. Students should be aware of the varieties of English—the dialects of region, of occupation, of sex, of class, of register, and of racial groups.

Students have a need to retain their native language and to be proud of its origins. Moreover, students should be encouraged to learn a second language if they speak only one language. Our TESOL (Teaching English to Speakers of Other Languages) programs must be supported and enriched to reach children who have not mastered English during their time in bilingual programs.

Thus, we need to become more sensitive to the language needs of others; once we become more sensitive to cultural and group needs, it should be a small step to developing considerable language experiences for our students. Teachers and administrators need to convince themselves that prepackaged programs, whether as basal reading systems, or textbooks, cannot substitute for teachers' judgments about what to teach, what materials to use, and what methodology to employ for their students' benefits. It is also clear that as teachers organize their instructional programs, the use of literature, particularly literature that reflects the multicultural nature of our schools' populations, will serve as a major medium to engage students in meaningful instructional activities while allowing them to enjoy the benefits that good literature can provide for them.

THE LITERATURE OF MULTICULTURALISM

There are probably very few educators who have not had the following experience or one similar to it: You are reading a book. The dog barks and attacks your cat, a car squeals to a halt outside, someone in your house or apartment calls your name... yet you hear nothing. You are lost in whatever locale or situation your book has taken you to. You are riveted to its words, the feelings it has evoked, the ideas it has sent reeling through your brain.

If you have had such an experience, then you know firsthand of the power and magic that literature contains. Unfortunately, far too many of our students have not had such an experience. Too many of the children in our schools have not been allowed to read or listen to good literature because of a prevailing attitude in too many classrooms that they haven't mastered all the necessary skills yet, and until they do, they can't read whole books, or for that matter, good literature. Instead, too many of them are fed a steady and stultifying diet of short paragraphs with questions at the end or "drill and kill" sheets in the belief that once they master these they can move on to what they should have been exposed to all along: good books, chosen carefully for their age and grade appropriateness and integrated into all that they need to learn.

In addition to the dearth of good literature, what the students do get to read is frequently so narrowly focused that many of them never see a face in a picture book or read about a family that resembles their family. These students almost never get to see people like themselves engaged in the situations which confront the myriad of literary characters who populate the books that are in their classrooms and libraries. It is clearly time for this to change. Those teachers and administrators who are responsible for organizing and implementing language arts and content area programs from pre-kindergarten through high school need to make every effort to base these programs on a solid foundation of quality literature and to ensure that the literature selected reflects a multicultural spectrum of authors and characters.

What groups should immediately be included in the literature of the classroom? First, it makes real sense to discover some of the groups that exist in the community, school, and classroom and put offerings about those cultures in your classroom library (e.g., African, Puerto Rican, Chinese).

Within specific ethnic groups Asian Americans include the Chinese, Japanese, Korean, Thai, and Vietnamese. Extensive lists regarding the children's books developed within these countries and cultures can be readily found in children's literature anthologies and bookstores. The Chinese, Japanese, Vietnamese, and their American counterparts among others have written numerous books which help youngsters develop a sense of pride, such as *Angel Child, Dragon Child* (Surat, 1983). In addition, there are many folktales, non-fiction books, newspapers, poetry, and general background information books for adults (see Tiedt & Tiedt, 1986). Likewise, Korean Americans and Philipino-Americans have produced much good literature.

Black Americans have a vast literature. Some books dealing with the past describe such a depressing history of slavery and oppression that they can seem demeaning without intending to do so. For example, *Nettie's Trip South* (Turner, 1987) describes such hard times, that some Black students may be angry to have Black persons portrayed in that manner. Good intentions may not be enough. Those who select literature must be sensitive to students' feelings and concerns.

A wide array of literature exists for Hispanics, if one considers that we deal not only with Mexican Americans, but a large number of other Spanish speaking populations, such as Cuban, Puerto Rican, and Spanish Americans, deriving from Spain. The schools that deal with these divergent Hispanic groups usually focus on one or two depending on who has settled in their community. It is wise to ascertain the literature of the predominant groups in your schools. In general, however, we should not limit students' experiences with literature to their own cultures, but give all students opportunities to experiences a wide variety of books. Mexican Americans have a huge literature, found in the various texts on multicultural teaching. Puerto Rican literature is becoming more and more available in English.

The Indo-Chinese, like the Vietnamese, have not been here long enough to have developed their version of Indochina-American literature. Recently, there has been a influx of Pakistanis and Indians to our country. These peoples who have a rich cultural history, much of which was translated by the English when they were colonialists, has not been brought into our literature yet. We need to work on this aspect of multiculturalism.

Native Americans have a great volume of books, folklore, and stories. Unfortunately, not enough of this work has been written by the American Indian, but may have been written in a rather patronizing way by others, who are sympathetic to the plight of the Indian. Unlike the Blacks and Hispanics, and to some degree, the Chinese and Indo-chinese, Native American literature does not seem to have claimed its deserved place in our literary offerings. It is a situation that needs rectifying. However, the oral history and folklore that we do use are beautiful.

In a sense, especially now, we are all minorities since no one ethnic group forms a majority in most of our major cities.

ISSUES AND CONCERNS

With these approaches, however, these are a number of issues and considerations which those implementing such a program need to study. Some of these issues are: What kind of staff development activities are needed to develop a sound multicultural education and literary program? What are easy and natural ways for incorporating literature into the other subject areas? Who selects this literature? Can we be sensitive enough to cultural nuances? Are we using language presentations that are considerate of our students? Are we using all the media available to us to develop the notion of multiculturalism in schools?

There are not easy answers to these questions except as they raise issues that are sustained in specific situated learning environments. There are many sensitivities that exist in each cultural and ethnic group; we need to bring these groups into our schools and encourage them to develop our awareness and our knowledge. We need to know about their stories. If they are not written down, then now is the time to do it (and to see that they are published). We need staff development programs that stress this kind of involvement. When we recognize that we are one world, integrating strategies for teaching multicultural literature can only serve us in the future and enrich our cultural heritage.

In many ways, we are in a kind of experiment in this country. If we cannot bring people into the community in harmony, around specified educational goals, then we cannot provide a model that is sorely needed today. In our world, we have nationalism based on racial and ethnic identity, rather than on self-worth, community values, and the accceptance of diversity in a world that is in a time and space warp in terms of needing to work together. If we are willing to read enough, to immerse ourselves in multicultural environments and literature, to engage in discussion with many others, and to make their literary traditions an integral part of our curriculum, then the benefits to our students will be immeasurable, both personally and in the knowledge that their lives and literatures benefit us all.

REFERENCES

Banks, J. (1977). *Multiethnic education: Practices and promises*. Bloomington, IN: Phi Delta Kappan.
Kraus, R. (1987). *Leo the late bloomer*. New York: Harper & Row Junior Books.
Krumgold, J. (1987). *And now Miguel*. New York: Harper & Row Junior Books.

National Council for the Teachers of English. (1986). *Guidelines for preparing teachers.* Urbana, IL: NCTE Press.

Shane, H.G. (1981). *Educating for a new millium.* Bloomington, IN: Phi Delta Kappa.

Stanley, D. (1983). *Conversation club.* New York: Macmillan.

Steptoe, J. (1986). *Stevie.* New York: Harper & Row Junior Books.

Steptoe, J. (1987). *Mufaro's beautiful daughters: An African tale.* New York: Lothrop, Lee & Shepard Books.

Surat, M.M., pictures by Mai, V.-D. (1983). *Angel child, dragon child.* New York: Scholastic Inc.

Tiedt, P.L., & Tiedt, I.R. (1986). *Multicultural teaching.* Boston: Allyn & Bacon.

Turner, A. (1987). *Nettie's trip south.* New York: Macmillan.

Tye, K. (Ed.). (1991). *Global education.* Alexandria, VA: Association for Curriculum Development.

Uchida, Y. (1969). *Sumi and the goat and the Tokyo Express.* New York: Scribner's.

Zolotow, C. (1971). *A father like that.* New York: Harper & Row Junior Books.

Chapter 13

Storytelling and the Drama Connection

Bob Barton

Rainbow Crow, Nancy VanLaan's (1989) retelling of a beautiful Lenape story, has provided the teachers and children I work with many stimulating story adventures in recent weeks. It is another of the familiar "coming of fire" stories, but this one seems to have worked wonderful magic on us all. Like all good stories, it begets dozens more, and I would like to share some of these with you.

For the 4-year-olds in a junior kindergarten, the coming of fire was of less interest than the coming of the first winter in which the animals of the world were buried in never-ending snow, thus necessitating the search for fire. The opportunity to play with the possibilities of a world under the snow was central to their response to the story.

Another class, of 5-year-olds, became intrigued with the powerful "Sky Spirit" who gave Rainbow Crow the gift of fire to warm the earth and rescue his friends. They returned to this part of the story again and again trying on the roles of both powerful spirit and humble crow.

Some 6-year-olds were deeply moved by the great personal loss suffered by Rainbow Crow in bringing fire to earth. The long journey back from the Sky Spirit caused the flames to turn his beautiful rainbow feathers to ashes and soot, but even worse, his once beautiful singing voice was altered forever to a hoarse, cracked *caw*! To these children, the story became one of "giftness," and they invented and presented suitable gifts for Crow to help make up for his sacrifice.

A class of 7-year-olds found the power of the fire awesome and determined that it might be a mixed blessing for the earth creatures. In order to practice gaining mastery over fire, they invented a drama about the first volcano, a safe place, they reckoned, to contain fire when it wasn't required.

A staff of teachers during an in-service workshop anticipated the loss of fire by the animal kingdom to humankind. They developed a new story to explain how fire changed hands and separated for all time the animal and human kingdoms.

In all of the incidents cited, the story quickly put everyone in touch with each other and got them all talking and sharing. In each instance, the story also took the participants in directions they hadn't anticipated.

In all of the incidents cited, drama was the medium used to allow the story to grow in the minds of the participants and to permit them to extend their language and thinking through the making and changing of the shared story.

It is indeed important to find stories to take into our classrooms which appeal to and stretch the imaginations of our students. It is equally important to listen to what the story has meant to them and to join them as co-explorer, open to the discoveries that can be made together.

When I think about story telling and drama in the classroom, I envision children engaged in powerful composing experiences, making, remaking, and changing stories in every conceivable way as they find the meanings the story holds for them.

Let's return for a moment to those anecdotes about the children's responses to *Rainbow Crow*.

The 4-year-olds borrowed from the tale. They borrowed snow and then invented their own story about it. An alert teacher, noticing their concern about animals getting buried in snow, took them to the school gymnasium and used movement work to allow the children to work out their concerns and ideas. Playing with the imaginative material of the story is familiar territory for most young children if they are encouraged and supported in their efforts.

The 5-year-olds retold the part of the story when Crow visited the powerful Sky Spirit. By means of interviewing "the expert," they were able to see both sides of the issue through their questioning. In so doing they explored their interpretations of a moment that they were curious about.

The 6- and 7-year-olds built on the story. Until they had extended it to incorporate their concerns the story remained unfinished.

In the case of the 7-year-olds, the story didn't tell how the animals handled fire once they received it. They only know from Rainbow Crow's experience that fire was deadly dangerous. Their work elaborated and elucidated a moment charged with significance.

In their new stories about the loss of fire by the animals to the "two-legged" (humans), the teachers invented a sequel.

In each of the examples drama made it possible to revisit the story in order to examine thoughts and feelings.

It is this aspect of drama I would like to stress. Doing the story is not all that important but going back to the story is, for it is in approaching it from many perspectives that our students can claim the story for themselves by finding in it something of their own life whether that be memories, fantasies, feelings, thoughts, viewpoints, or associations.

Many teachers shy away from drama work because they feel that they lack sufficient training to work successfully. More often I think they feel uncomfortable not knowing where a situation is going to take them. The beauty of combining storytelling and drama is that the story provides an anchor for us; there is no way we can become hopelessly lost.

Among the easiest ways to bring stories and drama together in the classroom is to encourage students to listen for the imagined voice of the story teller in a text and then attempt to recreate it. Short dialogue pieces from nursery rhyme and other collections make good sources; for example,

> What's your name?
> Mary Jane.
> Where do you live?
> Cabbage lane.
> What's your number?
> Bread and cucumber.

The question–and–answer structure is a good clue to follow; the selection can be divided into two speaking parts for whole–class or partner work. Students can explore the text by adapting opposite emotions (student A is a confident inquisitor; student B a nervous respondent) or physical states (student A is standing on one end of a circus high wire; student B is at the other end), or by speaking in opposite roles (student A is a powerful sorcerer; student B is a nervous apprentice), and so on. As they read it aloud many ways, many scenarios begin to emerge.

With selections such as the following, there is opportunity to create a rich texture of solo and chorus voices as well as sound effects and music. First speak the selection together several times. Decide which lines could be solo parts and which lines could be the chorus. Ask the students to try and figure out the overall mood so that it can be decided how the words are to be spoken. When these arrangements have been worked out, explore the possibilities for sound effects or perhaps a work song which could be whistled or hummed in the background. Put the entire piece together, perhaps building the layers as you go. With practice, students soon become quite skillful and inventive at lifting the sound of a text from the page.

This old hammer

This old hammer.
Shine like silver,
Shine like gold, boys.
Shine like gold.

Well, don't you hear that
Hammer ringing?
Drivin' in steel, boys,
Drivin' in steel.

Can't find a hammer
On this old mountain.
Rings like mine, boys.
Rings like mine.

I've been working
On this old mountain
Seven long years, boys,
Seven long years.

I'm going back to
Swannanoa Town-o,
That's my home, boys,
That's my home.

Take this hammer.
Give it to the captain.
Tell him I'm gone, boys,
Tell him I'm gone. (Traditional American)

As students gain more experience and confidence in recreating the "voice" of a text, try to find short texts that yield fewer clues about the identity of the speaker's voice and consequently demand greater inferencing on the reader's part. Nursery rhyme collections again are an excellent source for such material. For example:

Baby and I
Were baked in a pie
The gravy was wonderful hot
We had nothing to pay to the baker that day
So we crept out of the pot. (Anonymous)

Beneath these lines lies the rich subtext of our imagined stories, if we are willing to think about them. I like to challenge students to make bold educated guesses about who they think is telling the story, to whom it is being told, and why. The reading challenge will be to create a context for the words that, when read aloud, will tip off the listeners to the possible identity of the storyteller.

Often students identify the voice of the speaker in this example as that of children engaged in some sort of game. Once a group of children decided that this was one of the "four and twenty blackbirds baked in a pie" from another famous selection, and croaked out the lines in their best bird voices. Other guesses have included skipping and ball bouncing rhymes, wind-up toys involved in a kitchen accident, and a magic experiment gone awry.

Once the versions have been heard, ask the students to think of all the questions they would like to ask about the selection. For example:

- Who is the speaker?
- How did they get into this difficulty?
- Were they rescued by someone?
- Did they get out on their own?
- How did they get inside the pie in the first place?
- Is this something that happens a lot to those characters?
- Are they troublemakers?
- Are we in a land of giants?
- Are we in a land of midgets?
- Is this a funny story?
- Is this an adventure story?
- What should we be thinking about this?
- Are there other stories that are like this?

The posing of questions, especially after they have struggled to develop a scenario for the voices, usually generates a great many ideas for the possible stories that this incident represents. Now we can use our natural ability as story tellers to project into the tale:

1. We can form storytelling circles and create a new story by stepping into the mind of one of the story characters and retelling the incident as we know it in the first person. As the story travels around the circle each participant adds what he or she can; thus no one participant is burdened with the responsibility.

2. The participants can adopt the role of an observer who was not in the original story but who has additional information about one of the characters. Each person then shares in turn an imagined memory of that character.

3. The participants can form pairs. One can take the role of reporter, the other a story character. An in-depth interview can be conducted about a story's direction or outcome and that character's part in it. Reconvene the large group and have the reporters tell what they have discovered.

It also helps to try and think of other stories that are like the one we are exploring. A search of the folktale section of the school or public library might turn up stories that are similar to the ones the participants have invented. One class was delighted when they discovered Kevin Crossley-Holland's (1987, pp. 160-162) spirited retelling of this Tom Thumb incident in *British Folktales: New Versions*★:

One day, for fear of losing him, she locked him in a cupboard; next day she anchored him to a brick with a stout piece of twine in case the wind should blow him away; and on the third day she put Tom in her breast pocket and told him to stay there and fastened it securely. But for all this, Tom soon got involved in another scrape, and a much more dangerous one than ever before.

One morning in January, Tom asked his mother if he could go with her to milk the cows. "If I don't watch," he said, "how can I learn? And I don't even go to school now!"

"All right!" said Tom's mother.

So she scooped her little son into her milk pail, and carried him to the hill-pasture where a herd of cows were grazing—her own amongst them.

"It's not warm," said Tom's mother drawing her own cloak around her. "You'd best take shelter under this thistle. You can watch from here."

Tom's mother sat down on her three-legged stool and started to milk her cow. And while her back was turned, a red cow ambled up, and with one mouthful swallowed Tom Thumb, the thistle and all. The cow didn't bother to chew her mouthful, and Tom slid down into her stomach as easily as if he had been a dock leaf.

When her pail was full and foaming, Tom's mother stood up and stretched and looked round for her son. "Come on, Tom!" she called. But long as she looked for Tom, she was unable to see him, or the thistle either. "Tom!" she cried. "Come on, Tom!"

Tom's mother got no reply. She was cold and now she was worried. She put down her pail and began to weave her way through the herd of cattle. "Where are you, Tom! Where are you?" she cried. "Are you all right?"

"Here!" cried Tom. "Here! Can you hear me?"

"Where?" called Tom's mother.

"In the red cow! Inside the red cow!"

When Tom's mother finally made out where the muffled voice was coming from, she clapped one hand to her forehead. "Wait!" she shouted.

"I've no choice," cried the voice. But if poor Tom was in a pitiful state, the red cow was even worse, what with Tom shouting and dancing a jig inside her stomach.

Tom's mother ran back to her cottage, and returned in a few minutes with some powerful medicine. At once she pried open the cow's mouth and poured it down her throat. The cow gave Tom's mother a dim look and blinked.

★ From the selection "The History of Tom Thumb," in *British Folk Tales New Versions*, by Kevin Crossley-Holland. Copyright © 1987 by Kevin Crossley-Holland. Reprinted with permission by the publisher, Orchard Books, a division of Franklin Watts, Inc.

So Tom was delivered back into the world in a cow turd. Smeared from head to toe, and smelling none too good, he padded home beside his mother and, as soon as they got back to their little cottage, she washed Tom with sweet water from the well.

In the activities described, the students have been encouraged to listen for the potential voices of the storyteller and to explore them out loud. They have also slipped between the lines of the story to look for the implied stories and the possible voices which can tell those stories.

When working with longer and fully developed stories, it is often when an incident or the behavior of a fictional character is brought under close scrutiny that the links with life as the children know it are forged. Identification with the story by the reader is often at the subconscious level only. Conversation about the story is needed to bring insights about the story forward into consciousness. In the following anecdote, deeper reading, increased literary insights, wide use of oral language, and increased interest in the story were the results of extended talk.

A group of 10-year-olds had listened to a reading by their teacher about a seal woman who had come ashore to dance on midsummer's eve. Like the other seal creatures with her, she had shed her sealskins and taken her human form. A passing fisherman had fallen madly in love with the women. In order to get her to follow him he had stolen her sealskin and hidden it. Years later, the woman found her skin hidden under a haystack. This is quite a tense moment in the story, for she puts it back under the stack and turns back to her cottage. In that instant of turning, a light breeze bearing the sounds of the sea causes her to whirl about, snatch up her skin, and race toward the ocean. She is pursued by husband and children to no avail. She plunges into the sea, resurfaces in her sealskin, then dives "to the fairy places deep beneath the waves."

At the conclusion of the story, the teacher asked if the children could recall any pictures of the story which flickered through their minds as they listened.

For some, the dance of the seal creatures on the moonlit beach was quite vivid.

"I watched the fisherman's shadow interrupt the dance," one child reported.

Another described the seal woman as a translucent figure about 40 centimeters high.

Almost everyone could remember something distinctly or at least had an impression of character or place. For the most part, the children were mildly curious about the perceived images of their classmates. Then suddenly there was a change.

"Had anyone pictured the moment when the woman found the skin under the haystack, put it back, then grabbed it up?" the teacher asked.

Every hand shot up. For the next few minutes, blow-by-blow accounts were given, movements were recreated, unspoken thoughts of the woman were voiced. As they probed deeper into the seal woman's dilemma at that moment, it suddenly occurred to some that her decision to return to the sea world was a foolish one.

"What if she is no longer recognized and rejected by the seals?" suggested one voice. "She might even be put to death!" suggested another.

"She has no choice," observed one boy. "She was taken by force in the first place. She must return to her natural state."

The children, seeing the complications of the seal woman's situation, were quick to support the opportunity to play out some possible scenarios of the woman's return to her people.

Discussions with children about why they have selected a particular book to read quickly reveal how each individual's special interests, differing expectations, and unique concerns govern what they select. So, too, children will require the broadest scope for reflecting on their thinking, pursuing special interests and expressing themselves in the manner best suited for them.

Drama and storytelling offer us unique opportunities for all of the children to come together around stories shared in common for the purposes of encouraging reflection on and recreation of the story. Through such work children come to know and appreciate the unique viewpoints of their peers, extend their sense of story, and develop a deeper appreciation for specific works.

REFERENCES

Alderson, B. (1974). *Cakes and custard*. Portsmouth, NH: Heinemann.

Barton, B. (1986). *Tell me another*. Portsmouth, NH: Heinemann.

Barton, B., & Booth, D. (1990). *Stories in the classroom*. Portsmouth, NH: Heinemann.

Crossley-Holland, K. (1987). *British folktales: New Versions*. London: Orchard.

Crossley-Holland, K. (1985). *Folktales of the British Isles*. London: Faber.

VanLaan, N. (1989). *Rainbow crow*. New York: Knopf.

Chapter 14

If You Love Me, Read Me a Story

Patricia Hermes

Since I am by profession a storyteller, I would like to begin with a story—a true story. While visiting a school in North Dakota, I was talking about a book I've written called *You Shouldn't Have to Say Good-Bye*.

It's a book about a mother who is dying and her warm, loving relationship with her daughter, Sarah. In the book, the mother dies in the final chapter, and there is an epilogue, written by Sarah, about her feelings after her mother's death. While I was speaking to these children, a young boy, Tyrone, raised his hand. "Are you going to write another book about Sarah?" Tyrone asked. "Are you going to tell us how she did after her mother died?"

"No," I replied. "I don't think I am."

"Well, you should," Tyrone said. "You really, really should. People need to know how Sarah is."

"No," I said again. "I think the book is finished. I already know how Sarah is after her mother's death. Don't you think she's okay?"

Tyrone shrugged.

The other children in the audience chimed in, that yes, they thought that Sarah was okay after her mother died, that she was probably very sad, but she was okay. As proof of this, being thoughtful, fine readers, they brought out facts from the book to support their thinking: Sarah's mother had given her lots of love while she was alive, they said. Sarah had her dad and her best friend, Robin, they said. She was going to be all right. All the children seemed to agree on that. All but Tyrone.

Tyrone silently shook his head, folded his arms across his thin little chest. "I want," he said, "to READ it. I want to know how she will do."

After the session with the children was over, I sought out Tyrone's teacher to see if I could find out something more about him.

"Oh, Tyrone," said his teacher with a sigh. "His mom's a drug addict, and she's almost killed herself twice so far this year."

Now, I don't think it takes a genius to understand why Tyrone was so insistent on knowing how Sarah made out after her mother's death. I believe Tyrone was looking for a story to help him understand and make sense of his own life. He was looking for reassurance. And hope.

In her book, *The White Album*, the author Joan Didion says, "We tell ourselves stories in order to live." I think that is perhaps a more sophisticated way of saying what Tyrone was saying unconsciously—that we need stories in order to try to make sense of our own lives, to help us understand, to make some sense of the real life story of his real life mother and her coming death.

Nor do I think Tyrone is unique in wanting a story that will help him understand and cope with his life. I believe that all children, and possibly adults too, if we are honest enough to admit it, might agree that we need stories to help us understand our own lives.

But who will bring the stories to the children? And what stories will they bring? I believe children need not only parents to read to them., but they need teachers, educators, those who have the children in their care many hours a day—those are the ones who must bring the stories to the children. They must bring the stories that bring nurturing and support to the children's lives. And they must bring the stories now because our children are in desperate need.

But I imagine a murmur of opposition here. One has only to read the daily papers to know of the uproar about reading and the need for the "return to the basics." Isn't what I am saying too esoteric a philosophy for a school—that reading to a child will help him understand his life? Should schools not concentrate instead on helping a child to decode the words, helping a child to read the signs, to fill out job applications, to learn to read and understand the news? Isn't that what the real business of education in reading is all about? It seems to me that these are important questions to ask, because there is an uproar going on in the press about the failure in our schools to teach the basics, and there is an equally loud clamor going on among those who believe in allowing children in school to read real books.

So what is the answer? What is the real business of education in reading?

In her book, *The Gates of Excellence*, Katherine Peterson says, "Don't we want (for our children) more than just the ability to decode? Don't we want for them the life and growth and refreshment that only the full richness of our language can give?" She goes on to quote Joan Didion, that we fail the children if all we give them are the platitudes, the cliches, the slogans of our society, which we throw out whole to keep from having to think or feel too deeply.

It is hardly a curious or provocative statement—that we want from books much more than just the information they contain. Yet to some, it is not only provocative; it is foolish.

Of course not everyone feels this way. There are those who believe in the value of stories for themselves. But even for those of us who believe it is the job of the school to bring understanding to young lives through books, it can sometimes seem almost impossible to put that belief into practice. We can believe in the value of the written word as read to the children, and we can still end up by bringing them books that are little more than the platitudes and cliches of our society. Why? Because we do not always know what children want or what they need. We do not know just what is suitable. Sometimes, too, I think, we are afraid to make the choice because we are afraid of those who will second guess our choices, those who seem to know more than we. So how *do* we choose? How do we learn to trust our instincts when choosing which books to read to the children? And what kind of books *are* appropriate?

I am asked these questions about once a week in my travels around the country, speaking in schools. I am asked specifically the question—"What kinds of books are appropriate?"—not only about the books I recommend we read to children, but especially about the books I write for children. Yet it is strange to me because the person asking that question is often asking only about certain of my books. I am asked about *You Shouldn't Have to Say Good-Bye* or *Nobody's Fault*, both of which deal with death, or *A Time to Listen*, which deals with youth suicide. It strikes me as strange that I am not ever asked about my books, *A Place for Jeremy*, or *Kevin Corbett Eats Flies, Be Still My Heart*, or *I Hate Being Gifted*, books that are lighter and funnier. I am never asked if *those* books are appropriate for children. So it seems to me that there is an assumption on the part of the questioner, is there not? The assumption is that certain books are appropriate for young people, and other books are not. And so the question perhaps is not what books are appropriate for children, but rather whether *those* stories—stories of pain and illness and death—are really appropriate for children?

Many people who ask me that question have an answer. They suggest that we bring bland, light stories to the children, stories that deal with life's funnier moments. Others say that we must choose light stories, but insist that they be wonderfully rich stories, such as the ones by Beverly Cleary. There are those who insist that we should only choose the classics, that pain as expressed in the classics is permissible. Still others urge that we avoid *any* literature that is dark and filled with pain, as some in the Moral Majority would have us believe. And so, how does one decide? Shall we choose only the classics? Shall we choose stories only of fun and joy? Shall we exclude any books that deal with bathroom humor, with sex, with "dirty" words? Or should we allow in many stories, including ones that deal with death or the Holocaust, drug addiction, or pain? How does one choose, with all those around who are so sure they know what is good for the children, and what we should choose?

To answer that, I'd like to take a brief detour—but trust me for a moment, there is a purpose to my detour. And this is what I want to do. I would like to take just a moment to review some brief items I have taken from the press in recent months.

Item 1: At a welfare hotel in New York City, three young boys were playing pool. They were 11, 12, and 13 years old. Sweaty, tough talking, they were streetwise and hard—except that two of them were sucking their thumbs, and the 11 year old was holding a stuffed dog. When this child was asked what his hopes for a job were when he grew up, he said he wanted to be a street cleaner. "I don't want to feel dirty," he said. "Nobody wants to feel dirty." (A special mayoral commission has determined that these children are destined to become tomorrow's poor.)

Item 2: The gray light of winter's dusk settles over the tenement as a social worker finds a family she has been told to visit. It has been reported that the mother is a drug user, that she rarely feeds her children, and she has beaten them with a belt buckle. When the social worker opens the apartment door, she finds it almost empty of furniture, no electricity, and four burners on the stove providing the only heat. The three children are there, almost naked. Immediately the social worker decides that the children are not safe there and they will be placed, at least temporarily, in a foster home. As soon as she announces that, the little one begins to sob. "Sometimes," the counselor says, "later at night, when you're home in bed, you can still hear the crying."

Item 3: According to a study by researchers at Johns Hopkins Public School of Health, homicide is the leading cause of injury-related death among children under the age of one year. It accounts for 17% of injury deaths among children under one year of age.

And finally, from my own observations: Three small children were leaving school across the street from my home at three in the afternoon. Two of them were running ahead, hair flying, backpacks bumping against them, exuberant about getting out of school at last. Behind them, another child ran. "Wait up!" she called. "Wait up!"

They turned, looked at her, and then laughing, ran on.

The last child stopped running. Head lowered, she walked slowly, kicking her shoes against the sidewalk. And as she walked, she cried.

And now, at last, the point of this long detour—why do I tell of this? Because I want to pose a question, a question I often ask myself. What shall I write for these children? What shall we read to these children? What shall I write for the boy in the Welfare hotel, whose highest ambition is to be a street cleaner, to be clean? Shall I write him a story of kids in summer camp, of the use of his parents' cars and credit cards?

What shall I write for the little boy who is taken away sobbing from his abusive mother? What shall I write for the social worker that can ease the sounds of the crying in her dreams? Shall I write a nonsense book about separation where all things work out for the best?

And what shall I write for the little girl who walked home alone, crying?

What do these children need? What is fit for them? What shall I write for them? And what should we read to them?

It is a question I hear asked frequently. And it is one I ask myself. It is one to which I am not sure that there is a definitive answer.

However, not knowing answers does not prevent me from making some assumptions and some educated guesses. Because I have been educated in the writing world and the real world, educated by the kids to whom I talk, by the letters I receive, and yes, even by the awards I have won. In response to what do children want and need, what is fit to write for and read to children, this is what I think:

I do not pretend to know what children want or need. I know only one child well, the child I once was, and in many ways still am, the child who lived in me more than 50 years ago, and is still very much alive today. Because I *am* the child in the welfare hotel who still takes a stuffed toy to bed because she is so lonely. I *am* the child who sobs when taken away from his abusive mother, sobs because although the mother is abusive, she is all I have. I *am* the little girl who walks home alone crying, because her friends will not play with her today.

But it is important to note that I am also characters in other books, characters who have much more joy than sadness in their makeup because the world is not one-dimensional. The world is not, nor is the world of children. I am Mimi and Libby in *What if They Knew*, full of nonsense and mischief and prone to trouble and to fun. I am Kevin in *Kevin Corbett Eats Flies*, a smart, tough kid, wise in the way of the world, determined to be master of my fate. I am Bailey, a foster kid in *Heads I win*, tough, smart, who sees the world with no illusions, who fights for what she wants. And wins. I am KT in *I Hate Being Gifted*, who hates her status, not really because she is gifted, but because her gifted status makes her different and lonely.

But about the books that deal with pain—why do I take on the troubles of the world? Why do I write of my own pain and the pain I see in others? Because I live in the world and am part of the world, and sad and violent and troubled times produce sad and troubled books. Certainly these times are troubled, occasionally violent. But even more, I have lived through times of great personal pain—and which of us has not? No, my books are not autobiographical, and the things that happen in my books have not really happened. But all the *feelings* in the books are my own—positive feelings and the not-so-nice ones, too. Joy, fear, anger, hatred, jealousy—I am not a stranger to any of these emotions. I know them well, and so I believe, do most of the children know them. We owe it to the children to recognize those feelings, to recognize what they are living through, and to write them honest books. That is my responsibility.

But what about the teachers and librarians who pick and choose the books the children will read and have read to them? What are their responsibilities? Which books will they choose for the children?

I believe that the important thing to remember when talking about choosing literature is to view books in relation to our society, to view them as reflecting basic changes in our society, as Betsy Hearne (1982) has pointed out in an article called "Facts of Life in Children's Literature." Authors do not create divorce, poison gases and missiles, teenage pregnancy and drug addiction, homelessness and drug addicted infants. These are not phantoms of an author's fevered dreams. Authors reflect what goes on in society, in the world.

So, does that mean that I suggest that we expose our children to anything and everything? Am I suggesting that librarians, teachers, and educators should choose books of horror and hate because life is sometimes filled with horror and hate? Should we be permissive, without standards? Should we impose our own standards? Perhaps even we should try and control what young people read in an attempt to protect them.

No. I do not believe that permissiveness is the answer nor is censorship or force the answer. I believe that children want standards and limits and directions, and I think exploitive literature is as bad as exploitive anything— be it movies or television or whatever. But I also do not believe that the alternative to permissiveness is force, keeping out anything which repels us, anything that we fear.

How then do I suggest that we choose?

This is what I believe: I believe we must become involved in the real world, in the child's world, in *our* world. We need to know what kids are facing today. We need to know, really know, that they are facing some very, very difficult things. And I think that we must provide them with the kind of literature that deals with those issues. We can still pick and choose, and in fact, we must. But I think that teachers and educators, more than anyone else besides the authors, have an obligation to be educated about the world, and especially about the child's world. Issues, tough ones, must be faced honestly and without fear. And books that we might not like should not only be allowed, but accepted and encouraged. Why? Because children are helped by literature. Tyrone is helped by knowing how Sarah copes with her mother's death—a purely fictional death—but a real one to him.

But if we choose to keep out books we fear, we will get dishonest books. Yes, there are many books that are questioned with honest motives, but many more are being censored out of fear. And it is fear—fear of discomfort—that can be all too often disguised as outrage. And as Judy Blume (1982) has said, "Moral outrage can be intimidating."

It can. Can't it?

And that brings me to another point—because what I am really talking about here is not only *our* choice of books for children—but how other people will sometimes choose which books may or may not be read to children. In other words, censorship. It used to be that when we talked about censorship or about keeping books away from our children, we were talking about pornography. Today, good solid books are being banned.

The *Diary of Anne Frank* has been banned on the grounds that it perpetuates the myth that the Holocaust really happened, *The Grapes of Wrath* because it's un-American to discuss the plight of the farm worker, *Future Shock* because it describes the future and leaves open multiple options for lifestyles. *The Pigman, Of Mice and Men, To Kill a Mockingbird, The American Heritage Dictionary, Time* magazine, *Scholastic Scope,* and *Jesus Christ, Superstar*—all have been censored and removed from shelves.

Silly? Perhaps, but it has gone beyond that—and I am sometimes frightened. I was invited to speak to one school, and then the invitation taken back after a librarian discovered a dread word in one of my books. (The word was "mosquito ass.") I am frightened because someone else is deciding what our children can and cannot know. It is an important issue to me as a writer. I must write what is honest, or I should not write at all. Yet that is what seems to be demanded of me, that I shall not write about pain, drug addiction, street-wise kids, abortion, war—or death.

Many, in fact, all of my books deal with separation, and I explore it every time I sit down to write. Yet those who would take away books from children would force me to deny that most basic fact of my existence, and I believe, of the human condition. Those who remove books have succeeded in having *Charlotte's Web* taken from at least one library—because *Charlotte's Web* deals with death, the death of a spider. Absurd? Yes. But there are those who are asking me to change my vision of life—of at least, my *writing* about my inner visions. Even responsible journals have their say, demanding that in books, honesty and hope must be combined. And what if I do not believe in hope? (Now, it so happens that I do hold a vision of life and hope. But if I do not? And if I write as though I do? I will produce a dishonest book.)

Finally, I would like to end with this thought, something I asked before: Should we allow anything and everything? No, but I do believe that we have a responsibility. I think we have a responsibility to become involved in the world. I think we have an obligation to know what it is like for young people today, to face up to the hard truths that they are facing up to, as well as the goodness in the world today. Face it, know it, and then choose for the children the books the children need. Books we may not even like, but that we know are desperately needed.

Finally, I do not think we need to choose only those books that reflect life as it is. I think there are wonderful books out there that show life as it *can* be. I think that Martin Luther King's message, "I have a dream," is remembered today as much for its stirring content as for the words themselves. The words reflect a basic human truth as strong as the need for love, for support, for food, for intimacy, and independence. "I have a dream" hints at the fact that each of us has a vision, each of us knows that life is not only what it is—but life is what it can become.

Life for young people can become better. It can become different if all of us hold ourselves open to visions and dreams. And many of the best visions and dreams have first been dreamed in a book.

I hope we will take those books, reality as well as visions and dreams, and read them to our children.

REFERENCES

Blume, J. (1982, January). What kids want to read. *The Principal.*
Hearne, B. (1982, February). Facts of life in children's literature. *Learning Magazine.*

PART V

LITERACY ACROSS THE CURRICULUM

Chapter 15

Curriculum as Transformation: A Case for the Inclusion of Multiculturality

Clement B.G. London

If a man does not keep pace with his companions, perhaps it is because he hears a different drummer. Let him step to the music which he hears, however measured or far away.

Henry David Thoreau

THE PHENOMENON OF CHANGE

Change is in and of itself, a function of life. It is evolutionary and it has its paradoxes as well. New ideas, concepts, technologies, and developments may revitalize some systems, while they may make others obsolete. Change, therefore, both creates and destroys at the same time that it can become enabling or disabling.

Some periods of change are literally more intense than others. Our current era, for example, presents itself as an intense period of change. In part, it is characterized by technological innovations, scientific discoveries, gross income disparities, as well as abject social dissonance, a lack of tolerance, understanding, and ordinary human relationships.

In an engaging examination of the concept of change, Herbert I. London (1988), dean of the Gallatin Division of New York University and senior fellow of the Hudson Institute, identifies four specific change conditions serious attempts at reorganization must address. They are: respect for the past, an ability to adapt, confidence in the future, and recognition of the inevitability of change itself. Aside from these conditions, London reminds change agents of the prudence of reorganizing that much of change is derivative, and that the developments that have served as leaps of faith into the unknown or as strokes of brilliance that seem to transcend social evolution are the outcomes of efforts which examined the seemingly possible and, thereby, allowed for the uncovering of the possible. Indeed, when the future seems uncertain, the belief exists that something should be done also within the constraints of reality to affect change, because, in the final analysis, it remains that the extent to which the future is viewed as a challenge is, to some degree, the extent to which the control of destiny may derive some of its impetus.

EDUCATIONAL CHANGE: GOING BEYOND RHETORIC

There is a sense in which the responsibility for educational change must transcend mere rhetoric; it should find its figure and ground in the context of hard, realistic issues that call attention to those underpinnings and support systems that possess the wherewithal for conceptualizing, organizing, and facilitating guided evolutionary transformation. Agents of educational change must bring a seriousness and commitment to what is correctly perceived as intricate public "business" (Crews, 1990).

Educational systems by themselves cannot eliminate ignorance, nor can they singlehandedly overcome the dire effects of illiteracy, simply because they are only one set of players in a social system that has, in large measure, failed many of its most valuable and vulnerable members, its young. The making of substantial progress toward achieving our national goals for education, whatever these are, will require a national commitment that incorporates all of the plays for all of the young. Such national commitment must first find its underpinnings in moral responsibility. It is the pump that must now be primed for the national statements that grew out of the now famous Conference of the President and the Nation's Governors.

EDUCATIONAL RESPONSIBILITY MORALLY DEFINED

The issue of moral responsibility lies at the heart of American values. It is a fundamental issue in education (Locina, 1982). Brademas (1982) notes that, if education is to serve the people, the knowledgeable must be vigorously engaged in the shaping of public values. Teaching, therefore, becomes more precisely cogent because it presupposes that something of value is to be taught (Tom, 1980). Similarly, educating each individual citizen is inherently moral, because the inequality of status between teacher and student suggests that one has an obligation to promulgate the growth and development of the other through a system of relational procedures (Peters, 1965).

Philosophically, the equilibrating process requires strategies of educational initiation and determination that will facilitate access into the larger social domain in an educational rite of passage with adult rights and responsibilities. An initial step toward this approach would suggest that a consensus must be built around a set of goals and policies that are representative of all of the diverse groups within the polity. And in order that a consensus be built, there must be active and meaningful participation, which suggests that everyone is a part of what exists (Dumfree, 1979).

A healthy society has the responsibility for securing the future of its youth. The youth must develop the skills and the understanding of the accumulated wisdom, the civilization of what constitutes the rational life. But this cannot happen unless the nation acts as if it believes that all children are equally valuable as persons, whatever their circumstances. In other words, the nation must find ways to express the convictions of the meaningfulness of the moral, ethical values that are both implicit and explicit in the educational goods and services offered as part of a comprehensive curriculum in schools everywhere (Ryan, 1988; Wicks, 1982).

The curriculum offered at school is a major component of the orientation and socialization processes. Moreover, it is part of what constitutes the developmental process, for development is a vital issue of values, a reference of attitudes, life styles, understanding of the symbolic universe, frameworks, belief system, and networks of individuals and groups, all of which give due meaning to life (Goulet, 1971). In essence, these characteristics, these essentials, involve human attitudes and preferences, self-defined goals and criteria for determining tolerable costs associated with the act of change.

Educational institutions must receive the affirmation and support of the larger society in taking the initiative to exercise and teach moral judgment. Human conduct is conducive to good in the moral sense, because it carries values for individuals and also because it affects the human conditions as well as the common weal. To be moral, argues Raimo (1982), is to be social minded and intelligent in the venture of living. It implies the observance of wholesome living, and includes such universals as friendship, honesty, courage, justice, truth, and self-control. There is an order of things in the universe, and that order must be respected if the polity is to experience health, happiness, and human fulfillment.

Integrating moral judgment and responsibility with teaching is imperative. Morality in education provides rational bases which ultimately suggest what knowledge is of most worth. It is part of a larger dynamic that suggests the purpose of education and leads to curricular ideas in the context of their function. Morality helps to contextualize a curriculum; it affirms the unique qualities of the human being. Helping the individual to confront life situations through making ethical judgments and moral decisions must remain a responsibility of education and schooling. In cooperation with supporting institutions, schools taking their cue from the larger, national goals must exercise the initiative in preparing the young to make critical judgments derived from critical skills for use, both as survival and for posterity. Indeed, part of the awesome responsibility of schools is to help learners recognize values and ethical codes, to use the skills of decision making in both academic and nonacademic settings. They need to know how to think clearly, choose wisely, and act responsibly for their own individual, group, and societal good. They need to be helped in developing moral-ethical standards with which to evaluate problems and solutions that they will inevitably face as adults. National leadership must provide requisite moral affirmation.

A WORD ABOUT CURRICULUM THEORY

Whether the educational discourse places emphasis on the concerns of students, teachers, professors, parents, and community member-participants, the consensus seems always to be about what schools are and what they should teach. In short, all of these publics pay attention to the fundamental issue, curriculum. The curriculum is the heart of every school's program and, therefore, remains essentially the most critical concern of schooling (Ornstein, 1982).

Curriculum is a public issue. Because the general public uses the results of curricular processes, public policy issues cannot be avoided or obscured, since the compelling concerns question what is being taught, how well it is being taught, how well it is being learned, and what should be adopted, deleted, modified, or adapted. It follows that any approach to curricular design, in particular creative curriculum, must eschew haphazard, fragmentary approaches and, instead encompass systematic, developmental planning. Indeed, it would become virtually impossible for creative programs to command academic respect if their formulation ignores acceptable principles of design. Without this critical concern, the acceptability of curricular programs within educational communities is diminished considerably (Gay, 1979). Likewise, a systematic procedure of well-defined sequential steps should make the process generically and universally applicable.

Since one of the end-products of education involves passing on the social heritage along with the development of individual talents, a major concern should suggest a grounded theoretical import that aims to sharpen and clarify, rather than confuse. Theory of curriculum decisions inevitably involves conflicting ideals and values that require careful and logical dialogue for compromise and consensus.

Communication between and among participating groups is necessary.

Talking about theory permits persons to examine the theories they hold, and, eventually, this leads to further understanding. Each group's interpretation can be helpful in shedding light on problems of philosophy, conceptualization, organization, presentation, and evaluation procedures. A combination of views could be helpful in developing theories and positions which are grounded in practical realities and in promoting genuine improvement, not merely change. Because various persons have different theoretical expertise and perspectives, and because curriculum issues are complex and rarely clear or easy to solve, collaboration is a basic and logical course of action (McCutcheon, 1985).

Curriculum change requires energy and time, often scarce commodities in schools and universities. It also requires a certain level of commitment and security, which often precedes educational risks. Fear of the unknown, and the maintenance of the status quo, are factors that may impede curriculum change. Therefore, far from employing irrational and defensive rhetoric designed to stymie change efforts, there is need for orientation, compromise, openness, flexibility, and honest dialogue that will allow the issues to be fairly articulated. Then, growing out of these pertinent curricular acts should come meaningful, logical, and pragmatic adjustments made in consideration of the issues presented in light of reality. For as new disciplines become central in contemporary scholarly and scientific life, old foundational knowledge proves inadequate, and new foundations must be erected (McCutcheon, 1985).

HUMAN INTEREST IN CURRICULUM ISSUES

Questions of legitimacy are always important in curriculum decisions, in part because every epoch and every interest group has its view of what knowledge is of most worth for schools to translate. Bullough, Goldstein, and Holt (1984) provide some suggestions that are viewed as addressing specific cogent human interests. These, they believe, will attempt to:

a. Unravel the complex manner in which the institutional structures of schools that seek to form and reinforce a particular set of attitudes and beliefs; in a way of seeing the world that is hostile to human freedom and development;
b. Encourage the development of greater understanding; ensure and provide as an example, what may be called critical or philosophical-mindedness; and
c. Provide a statement of hope, in order to offset what remains as silence, a deafening silence, which ensures defeat (p. viii).

Guided by a concern for an enhancement of character and intellect, a broadening of knowledge and its relevance and grasp, and the fostering of a sense of commitment, Bullough et al. believe that a humanistic approach may be conceived in this context, especially given the power of technology in its apparent "reduction" of the size of the globe. At both national and international levels, new and telling human circumstances pose critical curricular questions. For example, local, regional, and world events have generated a large number of exigencies. In recent years, some of these exigencies have sent population segments fleeing from such manifestations as war, repression, hunger, famine, violence, natural disasters, and the fundamental and humane desire for economic, political, and religious freedom (London, 1989). As a consequence, dramatic population shifts have become a sequel of many national and international conflicts, thereby hastening traditional, peacetime migratory trends to the United States. As the "push" effects serve to exacerbate the outflow of groups of populations, the "pull" effects, serving as countervailing forces, attract those persons who join the ranks of immigrants to the United States.

Here, within this context, these immigrants, who come largely from Third World countries, provide a concomitant inflow of students who create demands on schools and school people alike for their accommodation, adjustment, and acculturation. In addition, other Western-oriented, highly developed nations continue their traditional migratory trends. Therefore, these new constituencies of different, cultural, ethnic, and linguistic characteristics pose new and differing problems that require the forging of new curricular modalities for addressing their largely nonwhite, non-European groups of "regular" immigrant students, while the nation struggles with itself and the students benefitting from traditional European-oriented educational offerings (London, 1990).

IMPLICATIONS FOR CURRICULAR ADJUSTMENTS

School problems affecting recent immigrants are pervasive, and they have their sources in many areas. Among these are the schools themselves, teachers, and the students. Such issues require a clear understanding of their nature and an initial recognition of their existence. Teachers, for instance, are often unfamiliar with the educational systems of the incoming students and the procedures by which they operate: their curricula, teaching methodologies, evaluative procedures, teaching aids, values emphasized, and parental participation in the teaching–learning transaction. In this way, many social, cultural, or emotional problems become difficult for teachers to comprehend, let alone address.

Endemic racial and ethnic hostilities in the United States spill over into hostility between majority and minority children; ethnic awareness and social distance among white and nonwhite children have been found as early as 4-year-olds (Goodman, 1952), prompting the idea that research (Canino, Early & Rogler, 1980; Dominguez, 1975; Greer, 1972; Henderson, 1979;

Ornstein, 1981; Rogler, 1972) should be incorporated with new and creative curricular conceptualizations for the improvement of educational and relationships, and the avoidance of confrontations with hatred, prejudice, and resultant violence against newcomers in United States public schools. Moreover, efforts to reduce hostility, ridicule, and prejudice should include the infusion of curriculum materials which place the new immigrants in a positive light by celebrating their own contributions and those of other minorities to the totality of the civilization. This need is even stronger for minorities already here.

Rivlin (1973) notes that having a diversity of cultures and ethnic groups to contend with at institutions of learning can be seen as a threat, an asset, or a problem. However, he avers that cultural pluralism, rather than cultural homogeneity, must be recognized and accepted within our educational institutions. It must be seen not as a necessary evil but as a strong positive force, because difference does not mean inferiority or superiority, just as sameness is not necessarily advantageous. To ignore these factors is to deprive the nation of the presence and contributions which can be made by each of the many groups that make up our country. What parents want for their children is, indeed, what the nation should want for all of its children.

CHANGE: A STRESSFUL ISSUE OF EDUCATIONAL TRANSFORMATION

All change is stressful for education, because schools are universal institutions charged with the service of children of those who want change and those who resist it. Educational theorists can therefore ignore these developments or accommodate them. At any rate, the highest educational duty demands that help be given to schools in order to make curricular change for our time. Reality sets us this challenge. It is what John Dewey, Horace Mann, and William James did in their time. Their best should be honored, but not simply by preserving the educational forms they created, but by following their example of helping to create forms best suited to our own and future times (Walker, 1985).

Curricula of institutions of education have traditionally been in a fundamental process of change in which new content has been added and some old materials have been modified or altogether discarded. But more often than not, many new programs, or portions thereof, have looked very much like their predecessors. At the same time, however, the gradual process of curriculum change has tended to reflect the relatively gradual evolution of society itself.

The launching of Sputnik in 1957 became a direct cause of vastly accelerated curriculum revision. A major educational movement was under way, most notably in mathematics and the physical sciences. But the first round of school curriculum reform, then, was a middle-class as well as an upper middle-class affair, primarily embracing college-bound students. The cry of the poor or disadvantaged ethnic minorities was as yet only a whisper (Goodlad, Stoephasius, & Klein, 1966). Today the tension within as well as between and among nations; the rapid political changes; the instability, economic, political, and social conditions; and the changing circumstances affecting the human condition, following technological advances and greater intolerance and understanding, have all heightened the need to change the emphasis on some aspects of curriculum theory, structure, content, and methodology in order to reflect an address of deepening human problems.

But to make such a dramatic change will involve implications of significant transformation. Doubtless a significance of transformation lies in its definition. Transformation itself can mean a change in the essential nature of something or a change in appearance only. Viewed in the context of education, transformation must mean substantive change, for example, a reconstruction of aspects of the educational order to include historically conscious and technically skilled persons, the integration and continuity of tested, relevant, and traditional practices and customs with new, sound theoretical and pedagogical concepts and ideas that anticipate the future and match the old with the new (London, 1990).

An assumption here is that transformation is considered as a social, economic, and political process, an act of faith which transcends the mere offering of basic literacy or the apparent appeasement of special interest groups. A purpose here is that of making the citizenry more cognizant, more culturally conscious, more socially understanding and tolerant, as well as more economically and politically mobile for the continuing thrust toward modernity.

Abiding faith of people the world over continues to place emphasis on the potential of education to transform their lives. Therefore educational expansion has long been viewed as an absolute essential ingredient for securing more equitable social and economic participation within the context of the democratic process (Hodgkinson, 1977; Hyman & Reed, 1975). Educational expansion that logically leads to transformation, according to Wiley (1990), should gravitate from a state of choice of options to the expansion of citizenship itself and the incorporation of citizens into the state with all the rights and responsibilities thereof.

THEORY OF CURRICULUM REFORM: A CRUCIBLE FOR CHANGE

Elliot Eisner (1971) observes that many theories are developed in noneducational settings, and that they are applied to educational practice in the hope that they will predict and control educational phenomena. Educational scholars such as Franklin Bobbitt, William Kilpatrick, W.W. Charters, Henry Morrison, Ralph Tyler, Hilda Taba, B.O. Smith, and John I. Goodlad have all contributed to the long line of participants in the field, clearly adding to the traditional, consistent quest for educational improvement, through constructive thinking, theory, and research (Eisner, 1990).

In light of current and future needs, it is believed that future citizens will require specific preparation for competition in the global marketplace. It also implies that knowing what as well as knowing how should become crucial factors for the next generation. Preparation for the 21st century would suggest a commitment to educational reform and restructure, logical action, and a doubling of all efforts toward our young. The challenge is perceived as a crucible for change and creativity (Apple, 1982).

Until now, many school systems continue to use curricula that owe their form and function to an earlier agrarian societal structure, which allowed for minimal schooling for the masses. Now that the nation has quantum-leaped into a cultural status of high technology, information processing, and a postindustrial context, citizens need for now and the foreseeable future curricula that approximate the needs of the times. Citizens must be able to process information and communicate with others in the immediate environment, nationally and internationally; they must know how to locate, organize, and use data in order to help solve problems; moreover, they must be able to understand people of various backgrounds, languages, cultures, philosophies, and persuasions, and to work cooperatively with others in different countries on common human problems. The nation needs humanely balanced curricula. This is literacy.

Such diverse needs and requirements would suggest exposure to an inclusive, innovative curriculum which would allow students opportunity to explore diversity, to study society by studying its parts, to foster respect, tolerance, and understanding in the practice of humanity (Sobol, 1990). They should reflect the experiential exposure of all the pieces of the nation's multiethnic mosaic in an appreciation of the value and function of diversity, and most assuredly of dealing with factors of the human condition.

MINORITY NEEDS BECOME MAJORITY CONCERNS

This chapter does not pretend to defend the authenticity of multiculturality and its corollary, the multicultural curriculum. In point of fact, many serious scholars (Banks, 1976, 1987, 1988; Banks & Banks, 1989; Bennett, 1981; Cross, Baker, & Stiles, 1977; Gold, Grant, & Rivlin, 1977; Longstreet, 1978) have defined and clarified the concept and its ramifications, thereby establishing its legitimacy as a worthwhile study of cultural pluralism within a body of knowledge that examines the variety of institutional, cognitive, and historical differences and similarities among ethnic groups.

These research-based efforts include knowledge of, and consequent appreciation for, all the ethnic groups that participate in the national life of the United States. They are, therefore, very well grounded.

Douglass (1991) notes that, in addition, the volumes developed from those research-based efforts have substantively treated concepts and themes as *diversity*: the manner in which individuals, groups, and cultures differ; *interdependence*: the way in which individuals, groups, and cultures depend on each other; *power*: the way in which individuals, groups, and cultures understand themselves and learn to get along in society; and *change*: the way individuals, technology, conflicts, and events have impact on society.

A very creditable contribution of this basic research is the creation of a precedent for serious attention to a critical and worthwhile issue. Moreover, there is not any need to present special courses on single issues such as ethnic diversity. There is already available a plethora of literature on this and other cogent themes. It is prudent to take these several tested and tried models and to incorporate them into comprehensive programmatic curricular designs that would reflect and strengthen their authenticity across educational spectra for Early Childhood, Elementary, Secondary , and Postsecondary schooling. Group needs should now telegraph and articulate societal responsibilities.

To bring about the inclusion of multicultural curricula into the mainstream is well justified. Research results show the positive impact on academic, cultural, and social development of all children, and this is certainly good for national and international understanding. That multicultural educational programs demonstrate that children derive a better understanding of and an appreciation for diverse groups remains a challenge for education in general to incorporate, adapt, and disseminate in public schools across the nation as part of national policy. Logic demands it.

But while it is argued that multicultural curricula should be included in mainstream education to foster individual and group understanding among the young, it is necessary to indicate that a sense of identity, race, and ethnicity are only small parts of the learning picture that is envisaged. It is further necessary to indicate that significant others do not misread the culture concept as the only barometer of what students should or can quite seriously do. Beyond these immediacies there are other concerns.

A professional sense of seriousness and commitment to education requires hard work, substantive curriculum conceptualization, teacher knowledge, and preparation, as well as parental participation in the ecology of their children's school. In essence, aside from media hype, governors' conferences, and presidential declarations, the actualization of school restructuring in the final analysis should be reflected in teachers and students becoming more motivated about doing well at school (DePalmer, 1990; Dervarics, 1990; Hale-Benson, 1989).

Institutions have a responsibility to provide the necessary support services so that students can succeed. Concerns about diversity must also extend beyond immediate classroom activities. Many progressive and creative educators are realizing that a bona fide push for multiculturality must mean a departure from business as usual. Goals must be committed to the development of society through the provision of support services like counseling, financial aid, tutorial, remedial, and developmental programs, a broadening of faculty representation, and a good-faith effort to carry the services to children as acts of logical intent in the dramatic accommodation of minority needs and concerns in education.

Our educators, merchants of hope, have a moral responsibility to take the challenges and circumstances beyond the gridlock of Eurocentric curricular and instructional practice, seeming hopelessness and despair, insensitivity, intolerance, and impatience with the ordinary dynamism of discourse and negotiation, and to translate them into acts of faith in our students, our population, our nation. Such acts must incorporate a vision that reaches beyond the 1990s. They should reflect the work that attempts to balance theory and practice with the need and will to engage the truth of our real human condition.

The culture of the United States owes it to itself to ensure that no one should be denied the opportunity to share in comprehensive curricular and instructional practices; practices that treat the understanding of the human condition, not necessarily as a chronological perspective of only economic, political, and military events; not simply using events that are articulated in textbooks driven by marketing and profit matrices, and not only events that feature a strictly Eurocentric grounding by white males who add insights to those economic, political, and military events, but a comprehensive set of offerings that reflect and benefit the concerns of all people (Apple, 1985).

The nation deserves an education that is shared in the context of keeping alive the philosophical commitment to a literate society. Literacy across the curriculum must mean more than segmented and disproportionate offerings. Parity and equity of service must serve the larger, national purpose.

However, Eisner (1985) warns that, if schools of today and the future are to provide realistic, productive idiosyncrasies for students, then it also follows that there must be an equally productive idiosyncratic change process for teachers, so that institutions of higher learning can provide them with preparation which fosters complementary qualities. Significant change in the ecological environment requires attention to systematic instructional factors recognizing that the propensity for stability of practice is deeply engrained in the structure of the educational system itself, and that these factors themselves must give cognizance to signals of compelling social issues of relationships, that is, human relationships of how people of diversity can get along together.

Whether efforts to induce people to get along better should emanate from recent racial acts of violence or from the logical, broad-based needs of the larger ecological environment, it is prudent to suggest that multicultural and multiethnic curricula must be included in those of the public schools in order to facilitate students' understanding of themselves and others. In history, curriculum must deal not only with Eurocentricity, for instance, but with all aspects of history; more special programs must be increased and included in the schools in order to lessen prejudice; and more black, Latino, and Asian principals, counselors, and teachers must be trained and hired to actualize the efforts. All publics must be significantly involved. Multiculturality suggests this.

An argument for meaningful and challenging curricula can draw sustenance from recent research and the examples of programs that convincingly demonstrate that children can learn all kinds of skills and ideas at much higher levels than have been previously expected. Creative schools have done just this. Creative schools are those in which all children, not just a few, are believed to be capable, where all are offered rich learning opportunities, held to rigorous intellectual standards, and are expected to succeed. In this instance, mental activities, rather than the aggregation of facts, enable students to turn their school experiences into knowledge they can remember as well as use.

CREATIVE SCHOOLS

The efficaciousness of Creative Schools is predicated on performance. Such performance is evidenced by the work of such educators as Jaime Escalante's advanced calculus students at Fairfield High School in East Los Angeles. There, students who have been frequently stereotyped as most unlikely to learn much of anything have confounded those negative perceptions by their performance. Evidence also comes from Westside Preparatory School in Chicago, where Marva Collins's students have demonstrated that they can indeed learn with great facility and also appreciate Shakespeare. From Central Park East in Harlem, New York City, Debbie Meier's students demonstrate that they can learn at much higher levels in all subjects at their school (Gardner, 1990).

Similarly, evidence comes from the model school in operation in the Shoreham-Wading River School District in Shoreham, New York, where many teachers are engaged in developing and delivering curricula from a Constructivist perspective as part of the school district's *cognitive level matching* (CLM) project (Grennon, 1984). These examples appear in what may be defined as "pockets of operation" across the nation: from public and private schools, rich and poor, urban and rural. In those institutions, students are learning things which parents and teachers often thought they were incapable of.

Envisaging the inclusion of multicultural curricula assumes the conceptualization and administration of the Creative School Model or something that approximates it. Essentially, this model incorporates certain specific characteristics. One characteristic, the enhancement of character and intellect, addresses specific personal traits considered nationally, as well as internationally, crucial. This characteristic should be fostered by schooling with complements of enthusiasm, contractual responsibility, and persistence.

A second characteristic, the broadness of knowledge, indicates that the curriculum contents should cultivate understanding of the interconnection among a wide variety of subjects, programs, events, and experiences. It implies that history as a historical grasp of the present should become a critical element in one's learning. It suggests that subject matter such as the physical, biological, and social sciences, mathematics, art, music, and literature must be well learned with the support of a philosophy that draws its essence from multiculturality in order to promulgate improved education as well as critical thinkers.

A third characteristic, commitment, refers to internalizing the standards and educational values one has learned in the context of expanding one's outlook, intentions, and activities. In this area there are skills, ideals, values, and ethics that will enable an individual to make important differences respecting one's identity and his or her relationship to others. From the standpoint of teaching, this assumes as well that teacher training will include preparation and the striving for the embodiment of the ideals in teaching activity. It also means in a very profound professional way the desired standards of excellence through a criterion of commitment, tacitly teaching and, by example, a master teacher model to be emulated as an ideal facilitator of a literate citizenry (Eisner, 1982).

This is a conceptualization of multiculturality that reflects the concern of ethnic gender diversity in its composition and implementation. It speaks to the inclusion of a multicultural curriculum. In many parts of the nation, particularly in large urban areas, there is a preponderance of nonwhite, multiethnic student groups. A concomitant disproportionate number of black and Latino dropouts is associated with this situation. There is also an underrepresentation of nonwhite faculty members. A curriculum of multiculturality that is included in a comprehensive mainstream package is a first attempt at striving to offer the combined input of the reflected diversity of the socially constructed communities of the United States.

Because of the history of racism in the nation, nonwhite people are present in fewer public school faculties, but in community organizations they are in far higher proportion than in colleges. What goes on at the precollege levels of education has a telling effect on the outcomes at the adult levels of society. One extension of this effect is that most academic positions and professional organizations have few nonwhite members. This situation reflects the fact that most professions, academic professions in particular, remain largely de facto segregated.

Both logic and experience indicate that change should no longer frustrate efforts to include multiculturality in traditional curricula. Therefore, the need to establish institutional reform should aim:

1. To help bring multicultural curriculum into the level of educational activity, through the removal of barriers, to greater inclusion and participation;
2. To promote existing use of multicultural studies, research, and other education-related activities, areas too often ignored by mainstream curriculum decision making, and to infuse these components into the larger scope and sequence; and
3. To move against the compartmentalization of the study of racial/ethnic studies, isolated from the majority, white-oriented curriculum and participation, and to promote an inclusive curriculum that is complex, encompassing, rigorous, and multicultural as requisite educational fare for all.

CURRICULUM AT THE CROSSROADS: LOOKING BEYOND THE 1990S

The great educational debate that is taking place around the issue of a *curriculum of inclusion* is part of a larger discourse that is attempting to critically examine the status of education in the United States, albeit with a view toward improvement. Caught in the ideological diatribe of "what knowledge is of most worth" for the nation, many of the issues have become mired in the rhetoric of political ideology, which often appears to cloud some of the pertinent ones. Unfortunately, within the context of ideological discourse, the prevailing democratic conception never quite achieves the dimension of political ideology, for it often fails to deal with the conflict and struggle, as well as the phenomenon of power which serves to resolve both.

But conflict over educational values is theoretically resolved by argument, discussion, scientific research, and intellectual agreement. Such are the factors that place curriculum at the crossroads in the United States today. Of course, such a resolution is both possible and desirable. However, it is in the realm of human action that decisions must be made, because social policy cannot await agreement from dissident groups. Unfortunately, educators, while refraining from discussions of power and politics, never-theless engage in the same as the reaction to criticisms and changes imposed on the field of curriculum suggest.

In addition, educators hide their mobilization for power under the seemingly legitimate but self-righteous concept of *professionalization*. Huebner (1965) warns against such a strategy, arguing that the bid for power and influence need not be so legitimized, because the search for professional status is too easily interpreted as a move for prestige rather than a desire to assume greater responsibility for educational change. These political machi-nations are seen even against the international challenge leveled at the United States. International competition has assumed dramatic fierceness.

In the face of both domestic and international challenges, such compel-ling urgencies, it would seem pertinent that caution should be exercised against oversimplification, against curriculum arguments and choices com-ing in matched pairs, one obviously right and the other clearly wrong. Instead, there should be a logical search for, and incorporation of, sound reorganization, and the adoption of cogent discourse directed toward rational decision making and commitment making rather than plati-tudinous, political rhetoric that leans toward seemingly easy solutions or the debunking of new ideas.

These participants in the dialogue about curriculum change have hard-ened their stances, but all in all, priority should be given to the voice of reason. Sound research and theoretical thought and postulations should lead to curricula that are designed to prepare each United States child for 21st-century challenges. So, too, they should foster the realization of the democratic meaning of equal opportunity and optimal growth, rather than as a mere attempt to keep a child in school, as important as this is.

In essence, the gap between the principles of equal opportunity and general educational practices must be bridged by infusing curricula with the consideration of the overriding, legitimate importance of the individual and the values that dignify and enhance all humanity. To do this requires the integration of combined inputs from educators, behavioral scientists, and academic specialists, together with lay and religious personnel, as well as the fullest and judicious employment of appropriate resources, including technology.

But Goodlad (1990) goes far beyond these thoughts by calling for something to be done structurally to arrest impediments and thus vastly improve on what is already available. It is an appeal which cautions against a "quick-fix mentality" and suggests, among other things, the inclusion of social strategies that carry the potential for reversing the drift toward a bipolar society in which the nation's inner cities have been abandoned to an underclass without hopes or prospects. It is further believed that all children must be prepared for responsible participation as citizens, and for critical dialogue in the human conversation, while pedagogy and stewardship should embrace all children in their charge, as well as the whole of the school's moral functioning in a social and political democracy.

MULTICULTURALITY AND EDUCATION

Multiculturality admits several definitions. The concept of multicultural education is described as an approach that promotes the appreciation of ethnic, cultural, racial, and linguistic diversity. This perspective turns on the assumption that it will enhance feelings of self-respect and self-worth within entire school communities and among administrations, teachers, students, and parents. A general philosophical view of multicultural education avers that ethnic diversity and cultural pluralism should become essential ingredients in the conceptualization of innovative education in the United States (Banks & Banks, 1989; Gold et al., 1977; Hale-Benson, 1988).

Another popular position describes multicultural education as concerned with the modificaiton of the total school environment, such that children from all ethnic groups may share in the equality of educational opportunity. This notion refers to its pluralistic possibilities; that the values instilled in a multicultural/pluralistic educational component will flourish when programs offer breadth of study that transcends the ordinary order of things. A dynamic perception of the mission of a multicultural education program is to promote the development and implementation of a structured, integrated, disciplinary curriculum that is designed to foster knowledge, understanding, and constructive intergroup relations among people of different cultural, linguistic, ethnic, and religious backgrounds. As a process it requires the full participation of school personnel, the family, and the community.

Multicultural education accepts cultural diversity as a valuable resource that should be extended and preserved. It incorporates the notion of equity with regard to gender, age, race, disability, or sexual orientation. It suggests the equitable distribution of knowledge, instructional resources, and financial school support, irrespective of school district tax bases. Indeed, multiculturality turns on the logical assumption that people living in a multiethnic society need to have a greater understanding of their own history and that of others; that shared knowledge will contribute to a more harmonious, patriotic, and committed polity; and that all persons in a nation's educational institution should have an opportunity to learn about the differing and unique contributions to the national heritage. It also includes modeling how individuals may keep their own identities and heritage yet live and work together in a collaborative manner.

However, as in any emerging field, there are some telling concerns which may confront the attempts of educators in their efforts to organize and implement sound programs in multicultural education. Some of them include: conceptual confusion, philosophical conflicts, as well as widespread disagreements about what should be the proper role of the public schools and institutions of higher learning in handling these innovative conceptualizations, especially in terms of the adaptation of programmatic packages in their own institutions. Educators and social scientists with diverse and conflicting ideological positions are now involved in proposing and promulgating a wide range of educational reforms and programs related to ethnic diversity (Banks, 1981). The debate rages on across the nation.

Thus, a curriculum comes into being when all interested and competent publics adopt a set of recurring responses to a set of recurring circumstances in schools (English, 1983). But quite apart from the complex, unceasing, and frustrating task of curriculum development, it becomes more difficult when a discipline or subject area is relatively new, still in the process of becoming, and whose philosophical articulation is not quite clearly definitive. Such is the case of multicultural education. It is clear, however, that discussion about what does, can, and should go on in public classrooms is fundamental to the nation's philosophic stance, its values, if you will.

CURRICULUM FOR INCLUSION AS LITERARY AND EDUCATIONAL TRANSFORMATION

It is not that it is right or wrong to have an inclusive curriculum, but there must be an appeal to a higher educational authority, an appeal to a higher wisdom, a higher philosophy of educational purpose, if you will; one which will not only transcend the immediate, but will set out to counter the serious impediments to relationships, impediments that nurture social dissonance. That a need exists for the development of greater appreciation among the various ethnic groups, the significant features of the nation's uniqueness, is paramount. Intolerance must be addressed as a serious human dynamic gone awry.

While an ideal or classical theory of curriculum design, organization, and treatment strongly suggests an overarching comprehensiveness, the pragmatics of such undertakings have always seemed to indicate the prudence of taking logical portions in manageable dimensions for completion in their own natural settings. Such piecemeal attention may suggest a temporary approach that promises a future escalation when the nation dares to undertake a more comprehensive restructuring of curricula to meet postindustrial needs.

The 1957 educational watershed witnessed, in the pantheon of curricular change, the most dramatic event in the nation. This was the era of Sputnik and the sequel that logically followed. It was a most dynamic change, the impact of which took the United States culture into a quantum leap to a postindustrial, high-technology, information-processing level of ascendancy. This dynamic shift enabled the nation to take charge of change in a manner that was not contemplated, or altogether planned, but that now reflects an ability to meet compelling exigencies head on; that a call to innovative exists is a mild assertion among contemporary realities. Indeed, educational change agents and change facilitators must now take up the challenge by taking charge of change.

A curriculum for inclusion of literacy and educational transformation will honor, and have far-reaching effects on, the national capability and will. For one telling factor, such a curriculum will honor societal diversity and will orient the citizenry to be better able to address the compelling issues of relationships that emanate as naturally existing curricular needs.

Through such incorporated curricular concerns, identified as needs and provided for through rational content, students can be prepared with materials, concepts, ideas, and experiences which can address current and future needs. They can then be prepared support systems and orientation which implicitly or explicitly clarify concerns of understanding, respect, tolerance, justice, and cooperation to be exercised for the common weal or good, not as a way of maintaining the "way things have always been" (Apple, 1990), but by a rational plan of departure, precisely because the truth of our history demands it (Sobol, 1990).

The time for chalk and talk about making substantive curriculum change and using such change for educational transformation is long past. We should be about the business of actualizing the outcomes of the numerous commissions, conferences, seminars, and meetings.

Curriculum has been interpreted throughout as a comprehensive undertaking, as the mechanism by which a culture performs the socialization of its young. It is the reason for education, schooling, and training. All that occurs reflects the philosophical position of a culture regarding the status of its people. Curriculum, then, must be comprehensive in scope and sequence. The necessity of inclusion derives its legitimacy from this perspective. The development of multiculturality and its inclusion are not going to be easy accomplishments. Educational history shows this to be traditional. But more than this, the difficulty is compounded by the fact that other impediments must be removed or attended to. There is the need for respectable knowledge of design as well as comprehensive understanding and preparation of teachers and administrators for schools and classrooms in which the climate can facilitate the implementation of curricular reforms that are designed to be responsive to the import of ethnic diversity and multiculturality.

Above all, despite the nature of the strategies employed in the conceptualization, design, and implementation of literacy across the curriculum, it remains essential that inclusion of curriculum should reflect generic curricular features such as establishing a rationale or philosophy of a curriculum of inclusion, assessing the needs, establishing the goals and objectives, selecting and organizing the contents and learning experiences, and evaluating student learning, and finally, utilizing the information that is yielded by the evaluative procedures to make adjustments in the ongoing programs with specific attention to their dramatic improvement.

We are engaged in a profound human quest, the efficacy of which lies essentially in the strength and vigor of the effort. In order to participate in, or share, degrees of accomplishment in the search for means of educational transformation, a culture must delight in the conscious husbanding of all its available resources, or as T.S. Eliot puts it in *Little Gidding*:

> We shall not cease from exploration
> And the end of all our exploring
> Will be to arrive where we started
> And know the place for the first time.

REFERENCES

Apple, M.W. (1982). *Ideology and curriculum* (2nd ed.). London: Routledge, Chapman, & Hall.

Apple, M.W. (1985). Making knowledge legitimate: Power, project and the textbook. In A. Molnar (Ed.), *Current thought on curriculum.* Alexandria, VA: ASCD.

Apple, M.W. (1990). *Ideology and curriculum* (rev. ed.). New York: Routledge.

Banks, J.A. (1976). *Curriculum guidelines in education.* Arlington, VA: NCSS.

Banks, J.A. (1981). *Multiethnic education: Theory and practice.* Boston: Allyn & Bacon.

Banks, J.A. (1987). *Teaching strategies for ethnic studies.* Newton, MA: Allyn & Bacon.

Banks, J.A. (1988). *Multiethnic education: Theory and practice* (2nd ed.). Boston: Allyn & Bacon.

Banks, J.A., & Banks, C. (1989). *Multicultural education: Issues and perspectives.* Boston: Allyn & Bacon.

Bennett, C. (1981). A case for pluralism in schools. *Phi Delta Kappan, 62,* 589-591.

Brademas, J. (1982). Higher education and the nation's future. *Educational Researcher, 11,* 6-13.

Bullough, R.V., Jr., Goldstein, S.L., & Holt, L. (1984). *Human interests in the curriculum.* New York: Teachers College Press.

Canino, I.A., Earley, B.F., & Rogler, L.H. (1980). *The Puerto Rican child in New York City: Stress and mental health* (Monograph No. 4). Bronx, NY: Hispanic Research Center, Fordham University.

Crews, A.C.L. (1990). Needed: Real agents for change. *Black issues in Higher Education, 7*(21), 72.

Cross, D.E., Baker, G.C., & Stiles, L.J. (Eds.). (1977). *Teaching in a multiethnic society: Perspectives and professional strategies.* New York: The Free Press.

DePalmer, A. (1990, November). The culture question. *The New York Times Education Supplement,* pp. 22-30.

Dervarics, C. (1990). Afro-centric program yield academic gains. *Black Issues in Higher Education, 7*(20), 1, 34.

Dominguez, V.R. (1975). *From neighbor to stranger: The dilemma of Caribbean peoples in the United States.* Boston: Yale University Press.

Douglass, M. (1991, January 5). Making a case for multicultural education. *The New York City Amsterdam News,* p. 13.

Dumfree, M. (1979). Unity with diversity: A common commitment. *Educational Leadership, 36,* 344-348.

Eisner, E.W. (Ed.). (1971). *Confronting curriculum reform.* Boston: Little, Brown, & Company.

Eisner, E.W. (1982). *Cognition and curriculum: A basis for deciding what to teach.* New York: Longman.

Eisner, E.W. (1985). *The educational imagination: On design and evaluation of school programs.* New York: Macmillan.

Eisner, E.W. (1990). A development agenda: Creative curriculum development and practice. *Journal of Curriculum and Supervision, 6,* 62-73.

English, F.W. (1983). *Fundamental curriculum decisions.* Alexandria, VA: ASCD.

Gardner, B. (1990). A crucible for change. *Education Week, 10*(4), 26.

Gay, G. (1979). Curriculum design for multicultural education. In C.A. Grant (Ed.), *Multicultural education: Commitment, issues, and applications.* Washington, DC: ASCD.

Gold, M.J., Grant, C.A., & Rivlin, H.N. (1977). *In praise of diversity: A resource book for multicultural education.* Washington, DC: Teacher Corps, ATE (Association of Teacher Educators).

Goodlad, J.I. (1990). Better teachers for the nation's schools. *Phi Delta Kappan, 72,* 185-194.

Goodlad, J.I., Stoephasius, R.V., & Klein, F.M. (1966). *The changing school curriculum.* New York: The Georgian Press.

Goodman, M.E. (1952). *Race awareness in young children.* Cambridge, MA: Addison-Wesley Press.

Goulet, D. (1971). An ethical model for the study of values. *Harvard Educational Review, 41,* 205-227.

Greer, C. (1972). *The great school legend.* New York: Basic Books.

Grennon, J. (1984). Making sense of student thinking. *Educational Leadership, 42,* 11-16.

Hale-Benson, J.E. (1988). *Black children: Their roots, culture and learning styles.* Baltimore, MD: Johns Hopkins University Press.

Hale-Benson, J.E. (1989). *Black children: Their race, culture, and learning styles* (rev. ed.). Baltimore, MD: Johns Hopkins University Press.

Henderson, G. (1979). *Understanding and counseling ethnic minorities.* Springfield, IL: Charles C. Thomas.

Hodgkinson, H.J. (1977). Education does make a difference. *Educational Leadership, 35,* 222-225.

Huehner, D. (1965). Politics and the curriculum. In H.A. Passow (Ed.), *Curriculum at the crossroads: Power, politics and precedents.* New York: Teachers College Press.

Hyman, C.W., & Reed, J. (1975). *Enduring effects of education.* Chicago: University of Chicago Press.

Locina, L.J. (1982). Three perspectives on the ethical considerations of moral education. *Education, 102*, 258-259.

London, C.B.G. (1989). Recent immigrant children in American schools: Are they lost? *The Journal of New York State Association for Bilingual Education* (SABE), *5*, 1-19.

London, C.B.G. (1990). Educating young new immigrants: How can the United States cope? *International Journal of Children and Youth, 2*(2), 81-100.

London, H.I. (1988). The phenomenon of change. *The Futurist, 22*(4), 64.

Longstreet, W.S. (1978). *Aspect of ethnicity: Understanding differences in pluralistic classrooms.* New York: Teachers College Press.

McCutcheon, G.M. (1985). Curriculum theory/curriculum practice: A gap on the Grand Canyon. In A. Molnar (Ed.), *Current thought on curriculum.* Alexandria, VA: ASCD.

Ornstein, A.C. (1981). The ethnic factor in education. *The High School Journal, 65*, 74-81.

Ornstein, A.C. (1982). Curriculum contrasts: A historical overview. *Phi Delta Kappan, 63*, 404-408.

Peters, R.S (1965). Education as initiation. In R.D. Archambault (Ed.), *Philosophical analysis of education.* New York: The Humanities Press.

Raimo, A.M. (1982). Moral education should permeate the total curriculum. *Kappa Delta Pi Record, 18*, 49-56.

Rogler, L. (1972). *Migrant in the city: The life of a Puerto Rican action group.* New York: Basic Books.

Rivlin, H.N. (1973). Cultural pluralism (Preface). In M.D. Stent, W.R. Hazard, & H.N. Rivlin (Eds.), *Cultural pluralism in education: A mandate for change.* New York: Appleton-Century-Crofts.

Ryan, K. (1988). Moral education in the life of the school. *Educational Leadership, 45*(8), 4-8.

Sobol, T. (1990). Understanding diversity. *Educational Leadership, 48*(3), 27-30.

Tom, A.R. (1980). Teaching as a moral craft: A metaphor for teaching and teacher education. *Curriculum Inquiry, 10*, 317-323.

Walker, D.F. (1985). Curriculum technology. In A. Molnar (Ed.), *Current thought in curriculum.* Alexandria, VA: ASCD Yearbook.

Wicks, R.S. (1982). *Morality and the schools* (Occasional paper 32). Washington, DC: Council for Basic Education.

Wiley, . (1990). How deep is the seated commitment to diversity? *Black Issues in Higher Education, 7*(21), 1, 6-7.

Chapter 16

What Should a Teacher Know About Social Studies? A Case for Geography

Salvatore J. Natoli

More than 30 years ago I was hired for my first college teaching job in a small college in a small town in northern Pennsylvania. Because there were only two townspeople for each college student, a newcomer in town was extremely visible. Early in the academic year I was going through the check-out counter in the local supermarket. The check-out person struck up a conversation, the gist of which went this way:

"You new in town?"

"Yes."

"Are you with the college?"

"Yes."

"Do you teach there?"

"Yes."

"What do you teach?"

"Geography."

"Geography! I always had trouble with that subject in school. I could never remember all those dates!"

If he had said, "I never could remember all those places," I probably would have found some consolation in the statement, but it still would have been far off the mark.

However extremely wrong the public perception of the field is, since that time I haven't heard anyone make that mistake again.

Over the years I have had many chance encounters with people on planes or in airline terminals who have given me some interesting responses when I told them I was à geographer. Here are a few:

"How is that different from geology?"

"Oh, do you work for the *National Geographic*; I get the magazine and they certainly publish some terrific photographs!"

"An urban geographer! Never heard of that one. Is it like urban sociology?"

"What's left for you to do? Outer space? The whole world's been discovered."

"What do you do with a Ph.D. in geography? The last geography course I had was in eighth grade!"

"My son majored in geography. He works for the CIA, so I have no idea what he's doing with it."

"So you're in the map-making business!"

"I could never figure out the difference between ecology and geography. Are they the same?"

After working for the Association of American Geographers for 18 years, I had become inured to the public misperceptions about geography and thought that, when I joined the National Council for the Social Studies, my defensive posture would get some respite. Little did I know how few people knew just what the social studies were!

GEOGRAPHY IN THE CONTEXT OF LEARNING ABOUT THE SOCIAL WORLD

Following are a few ideas about what geography *is* in the context of learning about our social world as well as what it *is not* and to address the important question: What should a teacher know about geography? or better yet, how and what do teachers teach when they teach geography? The end question is, how do you know you are teaching geography, and how will you know whether or not you have made an impression on your students? Also, how does geography inform and enrich the social studies?

One of the most prevailing myths in education is that anyone can teach geography. There are some obvious reasons for this. People find it hard to put their finger on the content of geography—it apparently includes information about the world or about a particular place. Other subjects taught in schools or referred to in the media have to do with something people can clearly identify, such as plants and animals—biology; the structure of the universe—astronomy; the idea of the universe—philosophy; money, banking, trade, business—probably economics or business and finance; social institutions—sociology; the culture of humankind—anthropology; and the past—history. But a geographer also studies these things—and even more. Because things may be obvious, we sometimes fail to grasp their significance or try to understand them. Whereas we can identify most other fields of study (with the exception of history and astronomy) by the objects or phenomena they study, geography contributes to knowledge by studying things or identifiable objects not for their own sake, but why these things or objects relate to places (and the spaces these places occupy) where we find them. Further, it tries to examine how events, issues, and processes relate to the *places* where they occur. One of the major organizing principles of geographical inquiry is that spaces or areas on the earth's surface have significance because of their locations, and why all manner of human activities that have occurred now occur, or might occur, on that space.

PERSONAL GEOGRAPHIES

A truism is that everyone has a personal as well as a social geography, uses some of its everyday language (sometimes in an offhand manner), affects and is affected by it throughout their lives. What most people do not realize is that they neither quite understand their personal or social geographies *as well as they might* nor appreciate why the multiple decisions they make create that geography. Every day we get up, we perform certain rituals and take certain routes to get from one place in our homes to another; we then proceed by a route to our automobile, public transit, or on foot to go to our places of work. When we arrive at those places, we follow certain routes to get exactly to the location of our work.

Consider also: Why do you live where you do? Probably most of the decisions you made about locating your home involved important geographical questions such as: *Where* do I want to live? *Where* can I afford to live? What are the *distinctive characteristics* of the neighborhood—both physical and cultural? How will I get to work? Are there good schools in the area, and where are they? If not, how long will it take to reach them? Will this alternative fit in with my own or my family's journey to work or does this school provide transportation? *Where* are the services I need in relationship to where I want to live—grocery, department, convenience stores, dry cleaners, banks, physicians, recreational sites, religious institutions, and so on? Will some of these services be equally accessible if they are near my home or my place of work?

Do hazards exist in the place where I live? Is it near heavily trafficked arteries, low-lying areas subject to flooding, hills that might become icy in the winter or slopes that might give way in heavy rains, near or on active fault lines? Is it downwind from a noxious industry, have chemical wastes entered the groundwater system, and so on? How has this area developed? What was the previous land use? What factors will preserve the characteristics I like about it or might change it? Will the open space remain open? Does the park that is so attractive by day attract undesirable or bothersome activities at night? What are the landscapes of fear that constrain not only our locational decision making but restrict our freedom of movement (Downs & Stea, 1977; Tuan, 1979)? Does it receive good public services, and how accessible are they? What necessary services are nearby—fire stations, hospitals, child care?

All of these are geographical questions, and we can ask these about any area of the world and at a variety of scales. But what most people lack is a systematic way of asking these geographical questions, or of making sense out of the alternative solutions that each of these questions raises.

MISUSE OF GEOGRAPHY IN THE CLASSROOM

Every day what might pass for geography occurs in many classrooms—a finger pointed casually at a map, a discussion about world events without any maps to describe their location, pop quizzes to see if students remember the names and location of states, major physical features, or the leading imports and exports of a particular place, mindless coloring of maps without addressing the characteristics of a good map and the meaning of the patterns created, or using maps as decorations in our classrooms because teachers may be uncomfortable in using them.

Too often what we observe as geography in the schools can be identified as a series of missed opportunities, poorly informed questions, or searches for precise answers when none exists.

RATIONALES FOR STUDYING GEOGRAPHY

How can we capitalize on these missed opportunities? First, geography is not, nor has it to be, boring. Second, it should not be trivial by expecting students to play endless games of recalling unrelated facts about the world, especially when the questions posed are not really geographical questions. Third, it is a challenging subject and can appeal to the most gifted subjects. Fourth, some of its basic ideas should and must be learned by the least gifted and can be presented in ways that will appeal not only to them but that they should find useful. Fifth, because it is such an eclectic subject, many geographical skills can enhance learning in other fields—some general, some specific, such as reading and comprehension, the scientific method, writing and drawing skills, observational skills, making real the sense of history, current affairs, or literature, sharpening critical thinking, improving mathematical skills, and enriching, enlivening, and giving the social studies a relationship to real world places. Sixth, and perhaps most important of all, it is there; it should satisfy our intellect by whetting curiosity about other places and temper attitudes and perceptions about other people, and, by developing a scientific knowledge about our environment, it should foster a sense of stewardship for the planet earth. In other words, no educated persons should suffer bewilderment about their world or disdain its value if they possess a deep knowledge of geography.

More practically, how much time do we lose on precious vacations by getting lost, by missing significant landscapes that lie off the beaten track, or confining ourselves to a few places in foreign countries because the unfamiliar might be threatening because we don't understand it?

Having just provided a litany of the benefits of studying geography, the initial question-—"What should a teacher know about geography in the social studies?"—becomes somewhat daunting, or it can take on new dimensions that can revitalize our social studies, history, or science courses.

The question: What should a teacher know about geography when he or she plans to enter a classroom? Many ideas, concepts, and teacher educators during the teacher formation period inform this question.

In an effort to focus the discussion rather than to try to answer the aforementioned questions completely, we can start by asking: "What shouldn't a geography teacher know"—or better phrased: What are some of the prevailing myths about teaching geography?

PREVAILING MYTHS ABOUT COMPETENT
GEOGRAPHIC EDUCATION

One of the major myths among educational administrators is that any teacher can teach geography given good materials and a good textbook. Another is: Any teacher can teach geography, because geography is really a collection of life experiences and materials derived from other subjects such as geology, meteorology, botany, sociology, anthropology, history, political science, psychology, and so on. True, there are many breeds of geographers, and like other practitioners, some are thoroughbreds, some hybrids, and others are mutants. Among them are geomorphologists, climatoligists, plant geographers, social geographers, cultural geographers, historical geographers, political geographers, behavioral geographers, communications geographers, cartographers, and so on. But the adjectives simply inform the nouns, *the geographers*, who are the actors—those who do geography rather than address the adjectives. Another prevailing myth, especially in the social studies and sciences, is that geography teaching and learning occur when you teach map skills. Saying this is like saying literature occurs when you teach the rules of grammar, or chemistry when you teach how electrons combine, or psychology when you teach about neutral synapses, or history when you fix an event in time. Another is that geography teaching and learning occur when you ask students to memorize the states of the U.S., their capital cities, chief products, longest rivers, highest elevations, extremes of temperature and precipitation, or their populations and areas. Or that geography teaching and learning occur when you study other parts of the world.

These are just some examples of half-truths and popular conceptions of geographic education. But what do we expect teachers to know about geography, and what do we expect them to teach when we ask them to do so? Most importantly, what do we want students to learn about geography or when does geographical learning occur?

THINKING GEOGRAPHICALLY

The best way to describe thinking geographically is to provide a few personal insights than attempt a facile answer. A high school geography teacher of long acquaintance perhaps summed it up best, about what she wanted her students to learn in her class, when she said, "I want my students to learn to think geographically." But that poses another and more important question: What do we mean by *thinking geographically*? The essence of understanding geography is to think about the world in ways that are different from art, literature, history, political science, geology, and sociology, but not unrelated to them. But what is that way? Richard Morrill (1985) gives a nice explanation in his article, "Some Important Geographic Questions": Geography exists because "*Space* exists, physical and social and social processes require *space* to operate (with respect to carrying on human activities), *space* (as the environment) varies in content and utility, and phenomena, including people, are *place-bound*—they cannot be everywhere at once? (p. 263).

> Given these facts it is possible to assert two "meta" theories which define the domain or the essential principles of geography.
> 1. *SPACE*, both in the form of extent and separation of "things," and in the form of differential environmental quality or content conditions physical and social activities and processes.
> 2. *Human activities* both alter and define or "create" the character of space (place) and the structure of space. (p. 263; emphasis added)

Within a few lines he adds: "What is geography?" Simply understanding HOW the landscape, physical and social, is differentiated and structured and how that character evolves, including how space, as separation and as content, both influences and is influenced by individual and collective activity" (p. 263).

In more simple and perhaps less elegant prose, but with just as deep meaning, Robert Morrill (personal communication, June 4, 1983), another geographer, said, "at the end of my course (in introductory college geography), I'd like my students to be able to look out this window and make sense out of what they see." Making sense of the world we see (or even hear about) is the beginning of thinking geographically. Just think of the consequences of some misperceptions! The world we live in, unless we can begin to think geographically (or can conjure a mental image of it) must be, according to Charles Gritzner (1981):

> little more than a confusing hodgepodge: places without location, quality or context; faceless people and cultures void of detail, character or meaning; vague physical features and environments for which terminology, mental images, causative agents and processes, and human patterns are lacking; temporal events that occur in a spatial vacuum; and a host of critical global (and local) problems for which (we) have no criteria on which to base analyses, judgments, or attempts at resolution. Such individuals are prisoners of their own ignorance or provincialism. (p. 264).

THINKING GEOGRAPHICALLY IN THE REAL WORLD

To give some real-world examples of how to go about thinking geographically, let us pose some questions about the New York City region or about any region in which you might be teaching (Figures 16.1 and 16.2). We might want to begin by asking some simple geographic questions of our students, and then expanding upon the ideas and concepts learned.

Why is New York located where it is? (*Location*). Where is it located with respect to other cities and places? (*Relative Location*). What are the distinctive characteristics of New York City that are similar and different from other places? (*Place*). What particular physical and cultural features influenced this city to grow and prosper and conversely, to begin to decline? (*Relationship within Places or Human/Environmental Relationships*). Why did it grow to such a large size and dominate a large area of the northeast, the Megalopolis, and for a time, even the world's finances and businesses? How did its connections with the rest of the U.S. and the world develop and how did they influence its growth and decline? (*Movement or Spatial Interaction*). What characteristics make the New York region distinctive? (*Regions: How they Form and Change*). The students' answers will begin to demonstrate that they

Figure 16.1.   The five boroughs of New York City.

are thinking geographically. They are trying to make sense out of a place called New York. If we analyze these questions, we can examine them according to variations on the five fundamental themes of geography (noted above) from *Guidelines for Geographic Education: Elementary and Secondary Schools* (Joint Committee on Geographic Education, Association of American Geographers, and National Council for Geographic Education, 1984). Restated, these interrelated themes are location, place, relationships between places or human environmental relationships, movement (relationships between or among places) or spatial interaction, and regions: how they form and change.

Further, how do these themes relate to a model of the scientific method that identifies the higher order thinking skills involved in each stage of the process: conceptualization—bringing together students' previous knowledge, text information, and context information to identify problems or issues; causality—developing cause–effect relationships such that, if "P" happens, then "Q" will happen; validity of explanations—derived from gathering, organizing, and evaluating information so that any causal claim or statement about an event, person, issue, or trend can be judged by degree

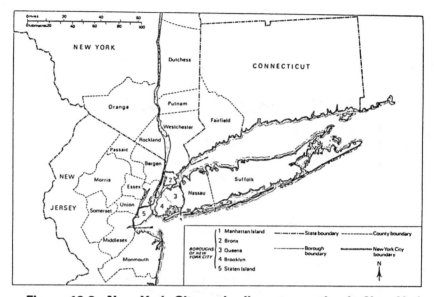

Figure 16.2   New York City and adjacent counties in New York, New Jersey, and Connecticut. These constitute the metropolitan region of New York City. For the specific boundaries of the New York City Consolidated Metropolitan Statistical Area of New York City (Bergen-Passaic, NJ; Bridgeport-Milford, CT; Danbury, CT; Jersey City, NJ; Middlesex-Somerset-Hunterdon, NJ; Monmouth-Ocean, NJ; Nassau-Suffolk, NY; New York, NY; Newark, NJ; Norwalk, CT; Orange County, NY; and Stamford, CT) consult the most recent volumes of the *U.S. Census of Population: New York*. Metropolitan regions are the areas under social, economic, communication, and transportation influences of the center city.

of accuracy, completeness, bias, or ideology; and creative extensions— involving the student's ability and the classroom setting, to bring a new issue, solution, or explanation to light (after Hartoonian, 1989). In addition, we can also examine these questions by applying midrange concepts used to describe, explain, and make predictions with which to understand the world: adaptation, system, change, resource allocation, conflict and competition, and decision making (based on "orienting concepts" of the *Project 2061 Social and Behavioral Sciences Panel Report* (1989, pp. 1–10). We can also examine their consistency with the National Council for the Social Studies Position Statement (1989), *Social Studies for Early Childhood and Elementary School Children Preparing for the 21st Century*, that describes the function of the social studies to direct and focus the natural characteristics of children to help them understand and function in their personal and social worlds, and permit them to participate effectively now in the groups to which they belong and to look to their future participation as adult citizens.

Perhaps even more important, in view of the current emphasis on teaching critical thinking skills, geographical inquiry is a natural vehicle to use with students to hone these skills. Students can develop such skills as a result of their encounters with geographical knowledge. The result is that both the teacher's understanding of the discipline and the student's perception of its worth would be enhanced.

CRITICAL THINKING ABOUT THE NEW YORK REGION

Let us examine a statement related to some of the questions we asked earlier about New York according to a general set of criteria used to define critical thinking: New York is the *primate city* of New York State and the United States. By *critical thinking* we mean the process of determining the authenticity, accuracy, and worth (value) of information or knowledge claims (on a subject). A variety of discrete skills can be used to determine such authenticity, accuracy, and worth. Rather than dwell on the skills and processes involved in critical thinking, because the educational literature is indeed substantial (and somewhat inconclusive), some examples might illustrate the process.

Conceptualism. First of all, what does *primate city* mean? Obviously it has to do with New York's singular importance among all the cities of the United States. *Primate* is a strong word: It refers to one (or an object) of first order or rank. Thus, there is an implicit assumption that there are other cities in the United States. (In geography, the word *city* means something very specific and therefore adds even more credence to the primacy of New York.) Yet a critical examination of this statement should bring forth many questions and objections centered around applying the adjective *primate* to New York. For example, primate for what? in industry? crime rates? concentration of wealth? quality of schools? quality of housing? environmental deterioration? population numbers? etc.? This should lead logically to the truth or fallacy in the statement or proving or disproving the statement or to qualifying it. In some of its characteristics, New York is the primate city; in others it is far from the mark.

Causality. Without a protracted discussion, we can, after considering various arguments, concede that because of a variety of factors-both geographical and others, New York grew to be the largest and most influential city in the state and continues to hold that position.

Validity of explanations. By arriving at that statement you can introduce and examine many other ideas—early in its history New York City capitalized on its good harbor, its later connections to the expanding Midwest via the Erie Canal, its central location along the Atlantic Seaboard, the skills of the many immigrants who landed there, the economic efficiency of its connections with the rest of the country, and its developing capabilities as financier to the country during the nation's great industrialization and transportation-building period.

Creative extensions. These could include ideas derived from comparing and constrasting New York with other cities in the state, in the region, the nation, and the world. It should produce some generalizations about the geographical factors that contributed to city growth (and decline) as well as supply increasing amounts of understanding that will fix more clearly in students' minds the realities of cities as unique geographical expressions in the spatial patterns of settlement.

To conclude this discussion and to amplify some basic notions about what a geography teacher should know, the following is the outline of an exercise I used in attempting to impress upon my introductory college geography students about the significance of *space* for human activities and why it was necessary for them to develop some systematic knowledge about it. Teachers should be able to derive a modified version of this for middle school students and even to impress upon early childhood students about spaces in different places that support their needs.

ON THE VALUES OF LEARNING ABOUT SPACE

Consider the following. The world's population today is estimated at 5 billion people (in 1975 in reached 4 billion—it took just about 12–15 years to add 1 billion people).[1] But it took from about the dawn of history to the year 1820 for the world's population to reach 1 billion. Two things are operating here—population is increasing, but the space available for habitation is relatively finite. At present about 131 million babies are born each year, and about 53 million people die (a net gain of about 78 million people per year). In general terms this means that, every year, the world adds as many people as live in Mexico today (Mexico has a population of about 30% of that of the U.S.). Or, we add, about 10 cities the size of New York. A critical question is: *Where* will all these people live? In a standing position, an individual occupies about 3 square feet of space, and each acre contains 43,560 square

---

[1] These data and those relating to principal city population and areas can be obtained from the *Statistical Abstract of the United States* (published annually and available in Washington, DC at the Bureau of the Census, U.S. Department of Commerce).

feet. If we divide 3 square feet into 43,560 square feet, then about 14,520 people can stand on one acre of land. An acre of land is about the size of a football field. New York City contains just over 301 square miles, or 192,640 acres, or 8,391,398,400 square feet. This means you can stand 2,797,132,800 people in New York City, and each square mile can hold 9,292,800 standing people. By extension, 12,796,185,600 could stand up comfortably in Long Island. The state of New York, with 49,108 square miles × 640 acres per square mile = 31,429,120 acres × 14,520 (people able to stand up in each acre with each occupying 3 square feet) could have room for 456,350,822,400 standing people, but not if they lie down. Consider the 2.7 billion people standing in New York City, and then ask them to lie down. To lie down would require about 25 square feet apiece so they could stretch out, but not very much.

Let us use some simple multipliers:

- 1 standing person occupies 3 square feet
- 1 lying down person occupies 25 square feet

A person needs 22 additional square feet to lie down, or 335,669,363 people could lie down in New York. Because we need so little space to stand or lie down, however, does not mean that 25 square feet is enough to support a single human being. If we use average standards of living we know that, even in the poorest nations, people need more than 25 square feet of living space.

To expand the issue, examine how we must multiply significant space requirements just to satisfy our basic needs. It might be a good idea to develop a matrix that lists human needs on one axis and the approximate space in acres required for each use on the other axis. The way people use land and allocate it for different uses varies considerably around the earth, depending upon land availability, fertility, cultural and religious values, climate, topography, land tenure systems, and a host of other physical and cultural factors.

SPECIAL NEEDS

We need some space on the earth to provide the materials to build homes—to grow timber, to manufacture the other building materials required for construction, to supply the fuels for heating, cooking, bathing, and washing clothes—and even space on highways and railroads to move these materials to our home sites. At the other extreme, we need space to bury our dead.

Because we wear clothes we need space to produce the materials, manufacture them, ship them, store them, retail them, and to carry them home plus provide dry cleaning space to clean them, as well as closets and drawers in which to store them.

What about our food? Again, we ask the same questions about space. Just an interesting fact for thought: Excellent pasture land in the humid eastern section of the United States will provide enough food for one cow on one acre of land (i.e., 43,560 square feet). In drier areas it might require 10 to 20 acres—about 10–20 football fields worth of space. An interesting example from U.S. history is that the Homestead Act (1862) permitted each person willing to settle government land 160 acres. In the humid East, such acreage would be sufficient, not only for subsistence production, but also for some surplus that could be marketed. In the semiarid West, such acreage might have enough natural pasture to carry only one cow, or five sheep, or seven goats. By 1910 individual states increased the acreage allotments to 320 acres, and then to 640 acres in Nebraska, to account for the dry conditions west of the 100th meridian. This is an example of how the legislators from the humid East, lacking geographical knowledge of the rest of the country, made a serious error in attempting to encourage the same type of agriculture possible only in the humid East in the semiarid to arid West.

Food, clothing, and shelter are basic needs; what about spaces for education, work, recreation, medical treatment, hospitalization, religious services, entertainment, banking, parking, voting, governing, law enforcing, criminal incarceration, pets, monuments, etc.? We also know that we can capitalize on the use of a piece of land by building several stories of use over the same space, but we also know that shared spaces may be suitable for residential, business, retail, wholesale, industrial, and even some transportation and agricultural uses such as double-deck highways or grain elevators.

Another way of compensating for limited land space is to permit multiple uses on the same parcel of land, such as recreation, lumbering, wildlife preserves, and watersheds. We know that it is difficult to share such spaces for most agricultural uses, many types of industrial uses, some types of transportation uses (e.g., airport runways), but seldom for water storage in reservoirs). We also know that we can combine surface and underground uses in mining, transportation, and storage. One result of such increasing densities for various types of land use is that they can result in overcrowding—especially in residential areas and in situations where uses seem incompatible with each other, e.g., solid waste disposal site near residential water supply watershed. It is also necessary to consider that the most desirable types of land—relatively level, well drained, and accessible to markets—induce severe competition among various potential users such as residential, agricultural, transportation, and industrial. Usually the user willing to pay the highest prices gets to use the land. As a result, some countries have established strict land use planning or zoning legislation.

Consider for a moment that the earth has 58,451,000 square miles of land area. Of these, large portions are too hot, too cold, too wet, too dry, or too

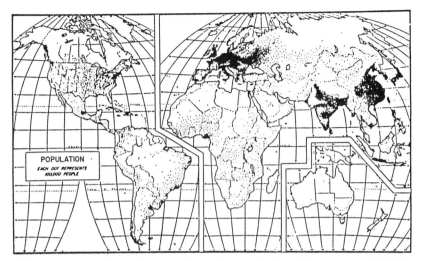

Figure 16.3.   Distribution of world population. The world's 5 billion people occupy less than half the world's land surface. The lands of densest population are all in the Northern Hemisphere. Note the three major centers: the intensively cultivated and emergent industrialized areas of eastern and southern Asia, the highly industrialized Western European and eastern Anglo-American regions. Major population growth centers are now in many of the developing nations of Central and South America, central and south Africa, and Indonesia. Most of the sparsely settled areas are either too hot, too cold, too wet, too dry, or too steep for human habitation (courtesy U.S. Department of Agriculture).

steep for people to live or support human activities without vast expenditures of capital (Figure 16.3). The current population density of the world is about 90 people per square mile; each person has about seven acres of land (about seven football fields) available to supply his or her needs. Subtracting the land that would not support people would narrow the margin of error.

Therefore, it appears that, in order for the human race to survive and prosper, we must be extremely concerned about how we use the most precious space resource we possess—our land.

CRITICAL SOLUTIONS

Despite these pessimistic projections, we might apply critical thinking to consider the optimal solutions for these problems. A conservationist would argue that we need even more space than we have now. A technologist might reply that innovations in agriculture, housing, biology, biochemistry, and work-reducing technology can compensate for the world's rapid population growth. On the other hand, some scientists are working on both the scenarios and technology for additional life space on orbiting stations in outer space, or even on the moon. Our ethical and moral values will question the implications this discussion has for population control and other restrictions to the use of space on earth. In any event, we are dealing with an eminently geographical problem and can apply critical geographical thinking to it. *Simply stated, geography deals with the study of the earth and its spaces. Because practically all human activities, and thus the social activities, take place on the earth's surface, it should be unthinkable to ignore the significance of land and space to the human equation.*

Everyday we play out our lives on the surface of the earth. Almost innumerable activities are occurring on earth, and each area contributes to and interacts with the others in vital ways for our daily survival.

What should a teacher know about geography and how these concepts relate to the social studies? A teacher should know that the spaces humans occupy and use have very special characteristics and functions, and that these spaces and uses are changing constantly. We should learn to know how to examine these spaces systematically, to make sense of them, and to involve our students in the thinking processes that examine that space. They will be living on the earth longer than we will, and they will have to share that space with many others, both near and far. How well they achieve this knowledge will condition and affect the quality of their lives and their children's lives.

REFERENCES

Downs, R., & Stea, D. (1977). *Maps in mind: Reflections on cognitive mapping.* New York: Harper & Row.

Gritzner, C.F. (1981). Geographic education—where have we failed? *Journal of Geography, 80,* 264.

Hartoonian, M. (1989). Social content and higher order thinking. In *Teaching complex thinking in school subjects.* Alexandria, VA: Association for Supervision and Curriculum Development.

Joint Committee on Geographic Education, Association of American Geographers (AAG), and National Council for Geographic Education (NCGE). (1984). *Guidelines for geographic education: Elementary and secondary schools.* Macomb, IL and Washington, DC: NCGE and AAG.

Morrill, R. (1985). Some important geographic questions. *The Professional Geographer, 37,* 263-270.

National Council for the Social Studies (NCSS) Position Statement. (1989). *Social studies for early childhood and elementary school children preparing for the 21st century.* Washington, DC: NCSS.

Project 2061 Social and Behavioral Sciences Panel report. (1989). Washington, DC: National Academy of Sciences/National Research Council.

Tuan, Y.-F. (1979). *Landscapes of fear.* New York: Pantheon Books.

Chapter 17
Communicating in Mathematics

Mark Driscoll
Arthur B. Powell

INTRODUCTION

This chapter will focus on the use of communication skills—reading, writing, listening, speaking—in the mathematics classroom. Our attention will be on forces that are bringing an enhanced role for communication skills in the mathematics classroom. In this regard, we will consider current research interests, current recommendations for change in curriculum and instruction, and some examples of how these recommendations are being implemented in actual instructional strategies and curriculum materials.

BACKGROUND

Research as a Force for Change

Ten years ago, one of us was part of a project designed to gather together findings from the education research literature that were relevant to mathematics teaching and to interpret them for mathematics teachers. The project produced a volume, *Research Within Reach: Secondary School Mathematics* (Driscoll, 1984). One of the chapters in the volume covered the topic of communication and mathematics and to see how substantially attention to the topic has changed in the past decade.

First, there has been a massive increase in attention to the topic of communication in mathematics: reading, writing, speaking, and listening. In the writing of the 1980 chapter, it was possible to locate only 20 or so references that focused centrally on the topic. Today, however, there appear to be hundreds of articles and papers on communication in mathematics.

Second, researchers' working perspectives on mathematics teaching and learning and on literacy and communication skills have changed significantly in the past 10 years. A decade ago, you would not have to dig very deeply into the writings of mathematics education researchers to gather that mathematics was perceived (perhaps not consciously) as a rather inert body of facts and techniques and that the primary function of mathematics instruction is to pass this body of facts and techniques on to students. Those researchers who addressed communication issues in mathematics education 10 years ago appear to have tied reading, writing, speaking, and listening almost entirely to the conveying of information to students or the translation of information by students. Thus, researchers were looking at issues such as:

- how students get confused by the differences between mathematical language and ordinary language—for example, "point" means many things in ordinary language, but has a single meaning within mathematics; or how students can be misled by the ordinary meaning of "multiplication" to conclude that mathematical multiplication "always makes bigger" (when, of course, multiplication by fractions can yield products that are smaller);
- how unfamiliar, strictly mathematical terms, like "polygon," can create problems for students;
- how to analyze the difficulties that plague many students when they try to translate from word problems to algebraic representations; for example, how word order influences student decision making;
- how much can teacher modeling (e.g., the use of logical constructions in classroom speech) positively affect student learning. For example, there is some evidence that such modeling of "if-then" constructions produce increases in students' use of such constructions. (Driscoll, 1984, p. 37)

With the exception of the last example, which points to the social nature of the process of learning mathematics, the communication-and-mathematics studies of a decade ago were narrow in focus. They concentrated on the role of language in delivering mathematical information. Even so, the studies were important. Indeed, many of them—especially in the area of algebra misconceptions—were pioneering studies that led to a large body of research throughout the decade.

The changes in the past decade have not been just quantitative—that is, it has been much more than a matter of increased attention and more publications. The perspectives of researchers on mathematics and communication have broadened to include the *processes* as well as the *products* of each. It is not uncommon now to see mathematics viewed by researchers as a *dynamic* body of knowledge; to see the process of learning mathematics identified with *doing* and *constructing* mathematics; and to find a broad representation of the point of view that reading, writing, speaking, and listening are tools in that constructive process. There are rapidly growing bodies of literature that look at a broad range of issues, including:

- to what extent can students' writing about their learning of mathematics improve their reflectiveness; what kind of writing assignments work best in this regard;
- how much can students' understanding of mathematical concepts be improved through their creation of word problems that represent the concept in a realistic setting;
- does learning improve in settings where student conjecture and student problem posing are used as regular parts of classroom instruction;
- how might student portfolios and oral presentations be used to assess mathematical learning more authentically than do current tests;
- how might the reading of mathematical stories in the classroom enhance students' understanding?

National Recommendations as a Force for Change

Education researchers who are attending more to the role of communication in the learning of mathematics are far from alone in their interest. As we shall illustrate, the interest has begun to influence developers of mathematics curriculum materials. Further, a new paradigm of mathematics assessment has been emerging in the past few years that incorporates student writing and speaking into assessment activities, as well as a much richer brand of reading activities than is traditional in testing.

As a political backdrop to all of this interest, a set of recommendations has appeared calling for sweeping changes. the call has come from a comprehensive cross-section of leaders representing mathematics interests in industry, schools, and academia. Central to their recommendations is a commitment to a dynamic perception of mathematics and a vision of mathematics instruction that is rich in the use of communication.

What Is Mathematics? The prevailing perceptions and beliefs about what mathematics is dictate the form that curriculum and assessment materials take; these perspectives shape classroom instruction and learning. If, for example, it is generally believed that mathematics is a rather static body of facts and techniques, then the educational system will respond (as it has responded) accordingly. If, on the other hand, we as a society should perceive mathematics to be dynamic and open ended, then mathematics schooling would look significantly different. The crux of the issue of reform in mathematics education is that people who use mathematics professionally perceive mathematics as dynamic and open ended and they recognize that perceptions and beliefs about mathematics have to change as well.

The Mathematics Sciences Education Board (MSEB), an emergent national leader in policy reform efforts affecting mathematics education, has made a forthright effort to redirect the popular definition of mathematics and the perceptions and beliefs about mathematics. In its recent publication *Reshaping School Mathematics*, MSEB recommends that all future changes in mathematics education be rooted in the definition of mathematics as "the language and science of patterns."

> If mathematics is a science and language of patterns, then to know mathematics is to investigate and express relationships among patterns: to be able to discern patterns in complex and obscure contexts; to understand and transform relations among patterns; to classify, encode, and describe patterns; to read and write in the language of patterns; and to employ knowledge of patterns for various practical purposes. (Mathematical Sciences Education Board, 1990, p. 12)

For the purposes of educational reform, the MSEB definition could prove to be strikingly effective in its elegant simplicity. In six short words—"the science and language of patterns"—it creates an image of mathematics as a subject area that is perpetually dynamic and tolerant of immense variation in the search for patterns, and it creates an imperative for paradigms of instruction and assessment that allow communication about patterns to be at the core of the learning experience.

Curriculum and Instructional Changes. MSEB's efforts are mostly at the policy level. The substantive counterpart—what specifically should change in the mathematics classroom—has been expressed by the National Council of Teachers of Mathematics (NCTM, 1989) in its *Curriculum and Evaluation Standards for School Mathematics*, a 200-page document that lays out the blueprint for change in K-12 mathematics education. The book's sections on curriculum are organized by grade level (K-4, 5–8, 9–12) and by content area standard (there are approximately 12 curriculum standards for each of the three grade levels). Of interest in this context, there is a "Mathematics as Communication" standard at each of the three grade levels. Here, for example, is how the 5–8 level communication standard looks.

MATHEMATICS AS COMMUNICATION

In grades 5–8, the study of mathematics should include opportunities to communicate so that students can:

- model situations using oral, written, concrete, pictorial, graphical, and algebraic methods;

- reflect on and clarify their own thinking about mathematical ideas and situations;
- develop common understandings of mathematical ideas, including the role of definitions;
- use the skills of reading, listening, and viewing to interpret and evaluate mathematical ideas;
- discuss mathematical ideas and make conjectures and convincing arguments;
- appreciate the value of mathematical notation and its role in the development of mathematical ideas.

Communication and the Quality of Mathematical Thinking

If curriculum materials and models of instruction are changed according to such recommendations, then mathematics classrooms will look very different. However, it must be stressed that the issue behind increasing the role of communication in school mathematics is the quality of mathematical thinking. The underlying conviction is that students can develop a more robust sort of mathematical thinking through reading, writing, speaking, and listening.

To illustrate, we offer an example based on the work of Powell. The examples reveal how the use of reading, writing, listening, and speaking in the mathematics classroom can alert teachers to divergent understandings among students and can enrich the quality of instruction and the quality of mathematical thinking among students.

Communicating in Mathematics

The quality of students' mathematical thinking and the richness of their mathematical meanings are correlated to the emphasis and extent to which communicating is supported in the curriculum. To augment appropriate communicating opportunities, we must deepen our understanding of the nature and role of communicating in learning mathematics. The use of writing as a communicative tool to learn mathematics has been documented by a number of educators for all levels of schooling (Borasi & Rose, 1989; Countryman, 1992; Frankenstein & Powell, 1989; Hoffman & Powell, 1989; Powell & López, 1989; and Sterrett, 1990). Recently, examining another vehicle for communicating in mathematics, some researchers have discussed the current state of research in the area of reading to learn mathematics (Borasi, Sheedy, & Siegel, 1990), presenting specific teaching interventions to support the role of reading in learning mathematics (Siegel, Borasi, & Smith, 1989). However, little work has been done in the area of reading textbooks, providing ways for helping students manage this task. It is important that four of the communicative processes—reading, talking, listening, and writing—become vehicles for students to generate meaning from text. Though the setting of the following is with college students, its implications are more widespread.

One of us teaches developmental mathematics to first- and second-year students at the Newark Campus of Rutgers University. In the context of teaching these courses, I have observed that many students either do not read textbooks or have difficulty comprehending them. What I have observed appears to have two principal sources. The first is that some students have experienced instructors who "talk" the textbook and, consequently, these students are in the habit of not needing to read it. The second source is more insidious in its origin, development, and effect. Students who have difficulty reading textbooks, and some who resist, often have negative beliefs about themselves as learners and low expectations about how thoroughly they can comprehend transactional text. These beliefs and expectations are psychological impediments and, in large part, engendered in students by authorities who opine that there is little, if any, room for differing interpretations of scientific or mathematical texts. I recall a college professor of mine who, when frustrated by incorrect, imprecise, or tentative responses, would declare to our class that "You cannot read a mathematics text the way you do a novel. You either understand it or you don't." That professor's dichotomous dictum finds support in the literature on reading transactional or technical texts. For instance, at the start of *Reading Technical Books*, Eisenberg defines scientific writing: "Language in science is special and particular. Each term has a very precise meaning. This is entirely different from the way language is used in everyday life" (quoted in Petersen, 1982, p. 108). For too many students, these opinions if not expressed as fact, precipitate self-fulfilling prophecies. Rarely do students or teacher question these taken-for-granted "facts."

As a teacher-researcher, I strive to better understand the nature of reading mathematics texts and to develop a teaching intervention that could mitigate against received opinion and help students deepen and enrich the quality of their mathematical thinking by reading texts. In the reading literature, few educators have attempted to demonstrate that prevailing conceptions of the nature of technical reading are too narrow. At his university, Petersen (1982), for example, analyzed the written responses of a number of humanities faculty to a nonmathematical passage in a *Scientific American* article. He instructed them to write what the passage meant to them. In his analysis, he found that the responses to the technical passage were similar to responses that he, an English professor, would expect from readers of aesthetic or poetic writing. That is, among his colleagues, he discovered that they differed considerably in the style and level of abstraction in which they wrote. Moreover, and contrary to received opinion, he documented that their written interpretations of the technical article were based in personal associations and uses of language. Their responses were not constrained, as conventional wisdom would have one expect, either by the "precision" of the text or by its transactional style.

As convincing as Petersen's experiment is, he involved a group of professionals, reading a nonmathematical text, containing no symbolic referents other than prose. I wondered whether similar findings result from a group of upper-level college students who are initiates to conventions of mathematical discourse. Further, I was interested in using a text with a high prose to symbol ratio. Specifically, I wanted to discover first whether conventional notions of processes involved in reading transactional writing were misleading and second, whether the efficacy of mathematics pedagogy benefits when students engage socially in oral and written responses to text.

The Experiment. My experiment involved six students at the Newark Campus of Rutgers University. At the time of the experiment, they were mathematics tutors; most were mathematics majors. All the tutors, except for one who had recently completed a semester of pre-calculus, had completed one or more semesters of calculus. I asked each tutor to read a three-paragraph passage on the Jordan curve theorem (Figure 17.1). In the passage, the writer defines a closed curve, motivates the question of how to determine whether a given point P has the topological property of existing inside or outside a closed curve, states the Jordan curve theorem, and uses its proof structure as a procedure for determining whether a given point is inside or outside a complex-looking, closed curve. I selected the passage since I was reasonably sure that none of the mathematics tutors was familiar with the theorem and since the mathematics in the passage was not beyond their background.

I gave the tutors as much time as they needed to read the passage and to write a response to the following question: What does this passage mean to you? Probably since English is a recent second language for two of the six tutors, the group spent roughly 45 minutes to complete the task. Below their responses, unedited, are identified by consecutive letters of the alphabet. As you read them, notice the styles, levels of abstraction, and uses of personal interests and language

Tutor A: A closed curve does not have its borders crossed at any point. Sometimes we may have a point and we may want to determine whether it is on the inside or outside. This may not always be obvious from inspection. If this is the case, then we use the Jordan curve theorem. This theorem requires that we connect the given point to another point on the outside of the closed curve with a line. If the curve in question is crossed an odd number of times, it is on the inside. If it is crossed an even number of times, it is on the outside.

Tutor B: The passage was interesting. It expressed specific topological theorems in a clear, concise manner which I found easy to follow. In fact, I can not

Figure 17.1. THE JORDAN CURVE THEOREM

A closed curve is one with an unbroken boundary such that by starting at any point on the boundary it is possible to return to that point by traversing the boundary in either direction. There is therefore a well-defined inside and outside to such a figure. The question may arise as to whether a given point P is on the inside or the outside of such a figure. If the figure is not complex, often the eye can determine the answer by examination. But the problem becomes more difficult for a figure such as on p. 229.

We could by trial and error work our way through such a maze to see if we could get from the given point to the outside. But we are saved the effort by an early theorem (a provably true proposition) in what has become known as the branch of mathematics called topology. The Jordan curve theorem states that if a point P is not on the boundary of a closed curve, it is either on the inside or outside, and to determine which is the case the following procedure

can be followed. Connect the given point P to any point Q on the outside of the closed curve by drawing a straight line from one point to the other. If the curve is crossed an even number of times, P is on the outside. If the curve is crossed an odd number of times, P is on the inside. In its most general form, the theorem states that to determine whether two points not on a closed curve are on the same side of that closed curve, they can be connected by a straight line. If the line crosses the curve an even number of times, the two points are on the same side of the curve. If the line crosses the curve an odd number of times, they are not on the same side of the curve. This general form is, of course, consistent with the first form, where to test whether a given point is on the inside or outside we always connect it with one on the outside.

We can apply this theorem to the example above by arbitrarily selecting some point that is clearly on the outside of the curve, connecting this point to the given point P with a straight line, and then counting the number of times the curve has been crossed.

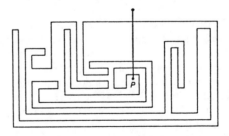

The curve is crossed four times by the straight line. Four is an even number, so the point P is on the outside of the closed curve (on the same side as Q, which is known to be on the outside).

Russell, D. (1979), *Mathematics: Ideas and Uses*, New York: Van Nostrand, pp. 228–9.

imagine giving a "summary" of this passage as it can not really be made more clear or concise.

Tutor C:

$$\text{even} \rightarrow \text{outside}$$
$$\text{odd} \rightarrow \text{outside}$$

Because the point placed outside can clearly be seen as being in the outside of the curve than the statement said can be easily tested. What is interesting is even and odd. Even is a nice number and the point is placed outside so the number of lines becomes even. If the point place is outside "Q" but "P" is inside then the lines are odd.

Tutor D: The passage saying that P is connecting to Q by a straight line which crosses the maze 4 times. Therefore according to Jordan curve theorem, P is outside and Q is outside.

Tutor E: The reading excerpt is introducing me to the branch of mathematics termed topology. It's briefly expounding upon the concept of a closed curve via the Jordan curve theorem. The excerpt also discloses a general formula for discerning whether a point "Q" connected to a given point "P" is on the outside or inside of a given curve.

Tutor F: Its a method to determine whether a point is inside or outside the complex curve. The method is to find the point *outside* the curve and we choose *outside* because its easier to determine the outside point than the inside point. Then connect the two points with a straight line, if the line intercept even number this means the two points are on the same side *outside* the curve.

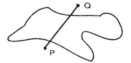

The straight line is from P to Q.
2 is even which means p is outside.
If it intercepts the curve at odd number, this means the points are at different sides and because Q is *outside* P should be *inside* in this case.

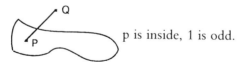 p is inside, 1 is odd.

Ignoring considerations of syntax, grammar, and accuracy, a striking feature of the six written responses is the variability of their length. They range from B's 43-word paragraph to F's sample with 119 words. The average response contains 71 words. In terms of the number of sentences, B's contains three while A contains seven. Four is the average number of sentences in a response. On average, the responses of the mathematics tutors correspond in word and sentence length to nonprofessional writers. In this sense, the above responses exemplify the writing of students in the developmental mathematical courses I teach.

There are other insights that those responses yield into how students initially respond to mathematics texts. In their attempt to connect with and comprehend the text selection, the tutors' responses display stylistic variations as well as differences in levels of abstraction and use of personal interests and language. Some tutors chose to explain the procedure for determining whether a given point is inside or outside of a closed curve. In so doing, some stayed close to the text, while others made generalizations and used language that was not in the text selection. Tutor E wrote a short, expressive summary of the passage, while Tutor B, in fewer words, evaluated the passage as "interesting," "clear, concise," and, for these reasons, he could not imagine a "summary" of it.

The written responses of these two tutors give us little evidence upon which to infer much about whether the passage evoked richer meanings. With varying styles and levels of abstraction, other tutors wrote about meanings that the passage evoked in them. Tutor A begins by stating in a transactional style, that a closed curve "does not have its borders crossed at any point." This seems to be an insight, new information, generated by confluence of his meanings and his perception of meanings of the writer of the text selection. Continuing, Tutor A informs us when to use the Jordan curve theorem and, in a special case, how to determine, knowing the parity of the number of times a straight line connecting the given point to a point outside the curve crosses a closed curve, whether a given point is inside or outside the curve. Tutor D and Tutor F also chose to explain the technical procedure of the passage. The former, focusing on the generalization of the procedure explained by Tutor A, introduces the word "maze" to describe his perception of the closed curve given in the passage. Tutor F, on the other hand, introduces new diagrams into his written response to explicate his understanding of the general procedure. In each of the above cases, the tutors decide to interpret the passage to incorporate new information, in personal ways, a distance away from the literal information in the text.

Still other tutors connected the text to their own affective and cognitive, *a priori* structures. Tutor C, as did Tutor D, connects information in the passage to prior knowledge. In this case, because of his apparent interest in the number theoretic properties of even and odd numbers, he focuses on, attends to, and explores in writing this feature of the Jordan curve theorem. It is worth noting that, in this sample of responses, there is an inverse relation to a student's mathematical background and the freedom with which a student explored his or her understanding in writing. The student with the greatest mathematical background, measured by the number of college mathematics courses taken, Tutor B, wrote the least about the passage on the Jordan curve theorem, while the student with the least mathematical background writes with delight at the connection between his interest in even and odd numbers and the appearance of these notions in the proof procedure 'of the Jordan curve theorem.

Finally, the responses give us information about the extent to which all readers of transactional text, at first, attend to the details and precision of the text. In each of the above samples, as an initial response, none of the students wrote unambiguous interpretations of the passage. Of these relatively sophisticated mathematics students, who, through lectures and other readers, are accustomed to the definition-theorem-example convention of mathematical discourse, none adhered to it in their interpretive responses. Further, none gave evidence that they used knowledge of this convention to comprehend the text. Finally, none of the tutors, the first time through, wrote "correct" interpretations of the passage.

The experiment included more than the written responses of the tutors. After writing, the tutors exchanged and read each other's responses. Then, in turn, each tutor read aloud his response and, after each reading, the group discussed the response and debated its contents. At the end of this process all the tutors articulated a richer, deeper, and more elaborated interpretation of the text. Their understanding of the passage evolved closer to my perception of the meaning of the passage.

From this experience, I draw several theoretical implications and have developed pedagogical activities for engaging students in constructing individual and then social interpretations of text.

Theoretical Implications. I have found that against the backdrop of the above experiment, we can examine prevailing myths about the nature of reading and the process of understanding mathematics texts. These myths manifest themselves in what is contained and not contained in instruction. Among the myths, three are salient: (a) reading and understanding of text occurs at once the first time through; (b) since the prose in mathematics text is precise and concise and mathematical symbols are unambiguous, they, therefore, leave little or no room for varying interpretations; and (c) in reading texts, one learns only about the author's meaning, not about one's self. Interestingly, these myths have led to frustrations when we realize that our students' interpretations are often quite different from either our own or from those of other students. Given the prevailing myths, it is problematical to explain why students interpret mathematics texts in various ways.

To better understand this problematic, I have found it necessary to shift my perspective from the text, as representative of or identifying the writer's meaning, to the perspective of the reader. From this perspective, apart from the enterprise of decoding, reading involves two major processes. When we read we infuse and extract meaning in both a dialectical and a dialogical process. We engage in a dialectical process of infusing into and extracting meaning from text. That is, we use our affective and cognitive experiences, expectations, and prior relation to and knowledge about the subject matter of the text to generalize from our perception of the content of the text. Each act of reading uniquely combines our past and present affective and cognitive associations of the perceived text. Reading also involves dialogue. Thinking occurs as we read and is often a dialogue between ourselves and text. In addition, as we search for meaning of text, reading involves us in dialogue with cultural precepts, conventions, and values as well as with those of other individuals. Reading is an ongoing communicative dialogue between ourselves and text and between ourselves and other individuals. The communicative dialogue occurs at different levels of abstraction and interpretation. Consequently, in interaction with the dialectical and dialogical processes, reading involves both individual and social acts.

Pedagogical Implications. As stated at the beginning of this section, not necessarily do students have effective ways of reading mathematical text. Some are not in the habit of using the text as a resource other than as a database of practice problems. Other students harbor feelings or beliefs and expectations about themselves and about the nature of reading transactional text that impede understanding. Furthermore, many do not explicitly engage in social forms of constructing and negotiating meaning and knowledge. Consequently, the efficacy of mathematics pedagogy benefits from activities that allow students to become aware of and develop individual and social means for interpreting text. For this purpose, an activity that I have developed usually contains three stages:

1. Students are asked to read and respond in writing to text. The text can be selected from their textbook or from other sources. The selected text may contain a discussion of a definition, a historical event, an algorithm, or an application. The reading and response writing can occur either in or out of class. The question to which students respond is generally "What does the passage or text mean to you?"
2. In pairs, students read and discuss, debate, or challenge each other's response and together write a new response that reflects their negotiated interpretation of given text.
3. Pairs pair, forming groups of four, and do as pairs did in stage 2 above: read and discuss, debate, or challenge each pair's response and collectively negotiate a new written response, reflecting their common interpretation of the given text.

Of course, we have also discovered that variations of these stages are appropriate and effective in given situations. Any of these variations involve students in four communicative processes: reading, writing, talking, and listening. Listening is one process that may require some discussion as a social skill.

The efficacy of the activity that I have described is best illustrated by an example. Shortly I presented the written response of four students from a class of 20 to whom, as a first review assignment in a precalculus class, I asked to read and respond to the passage in Figure 17.2, excerpted from the first chapter of their textbook. In the passage, the authors discuss the composition of the real number system.

Figure 17.2.

DECIMALS

$$8)\overline{7.000} \quad \frac{.875}{}$$
$$\underline{6\ 4}$$
$$\overline{60}$$
$$\underline{56}$$
$$\overline{40}$$
$$\underline{40}$$

Figure 5

$$11)\overline{2.00000} \quad \frac{.18181}{}$$
$$\underline{1\ 1}$$
$$\overline{90}$$
$$\underline{88}$$
$$\overline{20}$$
$$\underline{11}$$
$$\overline{90}$$
$$\underline{88}$$
$$\overline{20}$$
$$\underline{11}$$

Figure 6

There is another important way to describe the real numbers. We must first review a basic idea. Recall that

$$.4 = \frac{4}{10}$$

$$.42 = \frac{4}{10} + \frac{2}{100} = \frac{40}{100} + \frac{2}{100} = \frac{42}{100}$$

$$.731 = \frac{7}{10} + \frac{3}{100} + \frac{1}{1000} = \frac{700}{1000} + \frac{30}{1000} + \frac{1}{1000} = \frac{731}{1000}$$

Clearly, each of these decimals represents a rational number.

Conversely, if we are given a rational number, we can find its decimal expansion by long division. For example, the division in Figure 5 shows that $\frac{7}{8} = .875$. When we try the same procedure on $\frac{2}{11}$, something different happens (Figure 6). The decimal just keeps on going; it is a nonterminating decimal.

Actually, the decimal .875 can be thought of as nonterminating if we adjoin zeros. Thus

$$\frac{7}{8} = .8750000\ldots \quad = .875\overline{0}$$

$$\frac{2}{11} = .181818\ldots \quad = .\overline{18}$$

$$\frac{2}{7} = .285714285714\ldots = .\overline{285714}$$

Note that in each case, the decimal has a repeating pattern. This is indicated by putting a bar over the group of digits that repeat. Now we state a remarkable fact about the rational numbers (ratios of integers).

The rational numbers are precisely those numbers that can be represented as repeating nonterminating decimals.

What about nonrepeating decimals like

$$.12112111211112\ldots$$

They represent the irrational numbers, of which $\sqrt{2} = 1.4142135\ldots$ and $\pi = 3.1415926\ldots$ are the best-known examples. Together, the rational numbers and the irrational numbers make up the real numbers. Thus we may say that:

The real numbers are those numbers that can be represented as nonterminating decimals.

THE REAL NUMBERS

Rational numbers (the repeating decimals)	Irrational numbers (the nonrepeating decimals)

While it is true that the real numbers are the fundamental numbers of precalculus (and calculus), in practical situations we work with a very small subset of them. Who can calculate with nonterminating decimals? Neither humans nor electronic calculators. Calculators are, in fact, restricted to decimals of a certain length (perhaps 8 or 10 digits). Thus in practical calculations, most real numbers must be rounded. For example, π is often rounded to 3.141593, or perhaps to 3.14159. Our rule for rounding is to round down if the first discarded digit is 4 or less and round up if it is 5 or more. Thus π is 3.1416 rounded to four decimal places, 3.142 rounded to three decimal places, and 3.14 rounded to two decimal places.

C. Fleming, W., & Varberg, D. (1989), *Precalculus Mathematics: A Problem Solving Approach*, 2nd. ed., Englewood Cliffs, NJ: Prentice-Hall, pp. 3–4.

Students who responded to the above text, admitted to Rutgers' Newark College of Arts and Sciences through the auspices of the Educational Opportunity Fund program, are participants in a summer College Readiness Program. This course is one of a variety of others they take as a condition of their acceptance to the College. Before they began to read, to relieve writing anxieties I stated that I would not grade their writing and that they need not be concerned about errors in spelling, syntax, and grammar. However, I did explain that they would read their writing aloud to the class. Below are their individual responses to the text. Notice what information students include and exclude form their written responses.

Student A: This passage shows a mathematical deduction about decimals. Throughout our education we were taught to think of decimals as another way of writing fractions and percents, but here that is different. Sure that law still holds, they did use the example of $^4/_{10}$–0.4. But the passage gives a new definition.

  In this passage we are told that "real numbers are those that can be represented as nonterminating decimals." So, in other words, any number that can be written in a decimal is a real number. Some examples are: $^1/_{100}$ or $\div'2$. But number like $\div'-2'$ and $\div'-\ell$ are not real numbers, do the fact that they can not be written in decimal form, they are what is called imaginary number.

  So, the fact is all rational and irrational numbers are real numbers, for they can be written in decimal form.

Student B: To me this passage is also explaining how fractions and decimals are related. Also, it is explaining the types of decimals and how they work. This passage is giving a general background of decimals. The different types of decimals and rounding up of them.

Student C: This passage shows the difference in rational and irrational numbers and it lets you know that both are contained in the set of real numbers. It also shows you how decimals are rounded. In the beginning it showed you the broken down form of a decimal, what each number stands for. Also how to divide in order to get a fractions true decimal value.

Student D: To be honest this passage doesn't tell me anything I don't already know. I just learned a different way of saying that a rational number is one with a repeated decimal and an irrational number is a nonrepeating decimal.

I will not focus on the variety of styles and levels of abstraction in which they wrote; instead, I will point out information students include or exclude from their written interpretations. In an expressive, nonsummary style and in the space of three paragraphs, Student A compares his previous learning to information he perceived in the passage and uses his prior knowledge to demonstrate that there exists numbers, not expressible as decimals, other than the ones discussed by the authors. He concludes that rational and irrational numbers are real since they can be written in decimal form. This student's response contains information not literally contained in the passage and excludes some. For instance, seeming to claim that nothing in the passage is new for her, Student B does not report that the passage discusses the real number system but does state that it discusses rounding of decimals.

Like Student B, Students D and E also give no hint that the passage is about the real number system. And though Student C does, she interestingly summarizes in almost a reverse chronology.

These four students, after they paired and discussed their responses, wrote these new, negotiated responses:

Students A and B: The passage explains different types of decimals. It shows that decimals are another way of writing fractions and all other forms of real number—be it rational or irrational numbers.

It explains the definitions of the different terms used with decimals such as nonterminating decimals. It states all decimals are nonterminating because zeros can just be added on.

Students C and D: This passage explains that rational numbers which are repeating decimals and irrational numbers which are nonrepeating decimals are contained in the set of real numbers.

In the first response above, Students A and B dropped Student A's discussion of imaginary numbers and Student B's mention of rounding decimals. They included information that neither of them discussed in their first response: How all decimals can be termed non-terminating. The written response of the other pair of students displays a negotiated interpretation. In their collective response, Students C and D straighten the chronology of Student C's initial summary and omit Student C's discussion of rounding. In the new response, they include Student C's mention of the real number system and Student D's definition of rational and irrational numbers. From both of these paired responses, we have evidence of some aspects of the debate and negotiated interpretations. Moreover, each of the two responses is more concise than the longest response of students in the pair and direct than either of their initial responses.

Finally, the two pairs of students paired, discussed their interpretations of the textbook passage and negotiated the following statement to represent what the passage meant to them collectively.

Students A, B, C, and D: This passage explains the relation between decimals and fractions and how rational numbers, which are nonrepeating decimals are both contained in a set of real numbers. It also explains the rounding procedure for decimals.

This negotiated, collective response of the four students is clear, direct, and concise. The students report their interpretation without personal references. At this stage after discussion, debate, and challenges, in the context of socially constructing meanings, the above statement resembles the level of abstractness and precision that opinion would have us believe is the interpretive starting point of readers' response to transactional text.

The activity that I have described with the above example can be varied. Students could be asked to write with or without reference to the original text; they could be asked to write in response to other questions, such as ones that ask for paraphrasing or for analogies. Whichever activity is used, the point is that reader lean on their experiences, expectations, and knowledge to generate meanings and ideas and to generalize. Just as readers constantly make new meanings out of conversations or literary text based on personal associations, they do likewise when reading transactional texts, such as mathematics. As teachers, we can structure activities to support students exchanging their responses and analyzing the style and content of their responses so that they can integrate what they know with what they are learning.

Table 17.1   Matrix of Communication Skills in Mathematics

Reading and Listening

Student:

- reading for interpretation as a way of knowing
- listening to other students, as well as to the teacher, with comparisons interpretation, analysis as goals

Teacher:

- eliciting reflections
- helping to shape common understandings
- listening for divergent interpretations
- critical reading of text materials to anticipate divergent student interpretations, and for student misunderstandings

Writing and Speaking

Student:

- writing interpretations of text and problems
- making clarifying statements and convincing arguments
- using journals to show reflections
- taking part in mathematical investigations and recording progress
- representing mathematical situations through various models

Teacher:

- open questions that invite conjecture and reveal student thinking
- modeling problem-solving and other mathematical thinking
- modeling interpretation of mathematical writing

An Adventure in Brobdingnag

6

I became friends with a girl named Skliara. She was born on exactly the same day as me: the twenty-fifth of May in the year sixteen hundred and ninety-four. The first time she took me to visit her school I was amazed to see what at first appeared to be a fair-sized log lying on the floor of her classroom. It was about three inches thick and over six feet long. One end of it had been sharpened to a point, as if it were a fence post ready to be driven into the ground. Only slowly did I realize that... it was a pencil 10 times the size of one of mine. Then a brob picked it up with ease. I stood spellbound for several minutes when Skliara said "Let's see the rest of the school."

So we looked at the rest of the classrooms. The desk were huge and so were the chairs. If you looked at the school from outside you would faint. That's what happened to me. It was larger Then the Chicago Sears Tower

Page 4   Lesson 1: My First Days in Brobdingnag

Figure 17.2.

Changing Classrooms and Materials

It is evident from all of the preceding text that if reform of mathematics education is to proceed according to current recommendations, then communication in the mathematics classroom must look very different, involving both students and teachers in some unfamiliar behaviors. Table 17.1 represents several of the changes.

Evidently in order for mathematics classrooms to change so radically, the curriculum materials that are made available to teachers must change. In particular, there must be materials that incorporate the learning of mathematical concepts and skills in contexts where reading, writing, listening, and speaking are paramount.

The good news is that there are available models for such materials, which we can demonstrate with a recent example.

Example. In the past few years, the Journeys in Mathematics Project has produced a set of curriculum modules for upper-elementary grades, which are intended to demonstrate how the recent reform recommendations can be implemented in curriculum materials. Each of the modules is intended to be used by teachers over a period of several weeks. One, called "My Travels with Gulliver," uses reading, writing, and mathematical investigations to immerse children in a world of scale changes similar to the ones in Jonathan Swift's *Gulliver's Travels*. Figure 17.2 shows a student worksheet that is part of the module in which students are asked to complete a written passage concerning an object of different scale.

REFERENCES

Borasi, R., & Rose, B. (1989). Journal writing and mathematics instruction. *Educational Studies in Mathematics*, 20(4), 347–365.

Borasi, R., Sheedy, J.R., & Siegel, M. (1990). The power of stories in learning mathematics. *Language Arts*, 67, 174–189.

Countryman, J. (1992). *Writing to Learn Mathematics: Strategies that Work, K–12*. Portsmouth, NH: Heinemann.

Driscoll, M. (1984). *Research Within Reach: Secondary School Mathematics*. Reston, VA: National Council of Teachers of Mathematics.

Driscoll, M. (1986). *Stories of excellence: Ten case studies from a study of exemplary*.

Driscoll, M., & Confrey. (1986). *Teaching mathematics: Strategies that work*. Portsmouth, NH: Heinemann.

Hoffman, M.R., & Powell, A.B. (1989). Mathematical and commentary writing: Vehicles for student reflection and empowerment. *Mathematics Teaching* (126), 55–57.

Mathematical Sciences Education Board. (1990). *Reshaping school mathematics*. Washington, DC: National Academy of Sciences.

Peterson, B. (1982). In search of meaning: Readers and expressive language. In T. Fulwiler & A. Young (Eds.), *Language connections: Writing and reading across the curriculum* (pp. 107–122). Urbana, IL: National Council of Teacher of English.

Powell, A., with Frankenstein, M. (1989). Mathematics education and society: Empowering students. In C. Keitel, P. Dannerow, A. Bishop, & P. Gerdes (Eds.), *Mathematics education and society* (pp. 157–159). Paris: UNESCO

Powell, A.B., & López, J.A. (1989). Writing as a vehicle to learn mathematics: A case study. In P. Connolly & T. Vilardi (Eds.), *Writing to learn mathematics and science* (pp. 157–177). New York: Teachers College.

Siegel, M., Borasi, R., & Smith, C. (1989). A critical review of reading in mathematics instruction: The need for a new synthesis. In S. McCormick & J. Lutell (Eds.), *Cognitive and social perspectives for literacy research and instruction* (38th Yearbook of the National Reading Conference, pp. 269–277). Chicago: National Reading Conference.

Sterrett, A. (1990). *Using writing to teach mathematics.* Washington, DC: Mathematical Association of America.

Chapter 18

Conceptualizing in Science: Misconception Research Using a Contructivist Model

Edmund A. Marek

THE PARADIGM

Research examining how learners construct knowledge has provided the foundation to the research agenda at the University of Oklahoma's Science Education Center for the past 25 years. This knowledge construction is based upon a developmental model advanced by psychologist/epistemologist Jean Piaget (1963). Piaget's theory explains that the first overt act on the part of the learner is to *assimilate* data from the environment regarding the factor(s) under consideration. The results of assimilation cause the learner to raise doubts and questions. In other words, what the learner is experiencing from assimilation doesn't match with what he or she knows about an object, event, or situation and Piaget labeled that mental state *disequilibrium*. Disequilibrium should not be equated with frustration but if disequilibrium is allowed to persist, frustration may develop (Renner & Marek, 1988). In working out the doubts and questions produced from assimilation, the learner puts his or her thoughts (understandings) in accord with the things producing the assimilation; that act Piaget labeled *accommodation*. The learner next considers the new thought or understanding in terms of what is already known. Stated differently, the new concept is organized with prior knowledge and Piaget refers to this as *organization*.

The assimilation–disequilibration–accommodation–organization model advanced by Piaget is the theoretical basis for the teaching procedure known as the learning cycle. A learning cycle begins with *Exploration*, which means the learners are using specific materials and procedures provided by the teacher to gather data (i.e, record observations and measurements). Next, the learners, under the guidance of the teacher, combine their data and interpretations and then identify the concept(s) inherent in the data. This learning cycle phase is often referred to as *Conceptual Invention*. It is during this phase that the language or terminology associated with the concept is provided. Following conceptual invention the learners may use the newly invented concept in several different ways. They might engage in additional laboratory activities, work problems, answer questions, see films, and/or read about the uses and further descriptions of the concept. This phase has been labeled the *Expansion* and is structured to allow the learners to use and build upon the concept(s)—or ideas—they have just constructed. A thorough description of the learning cycle and its evolution can be found in "A Theory of Instruction: Using the Learning Cycle to Teach Science Concepts and Thinking Skills" (Lawson, Abraham, & Renner, 1989). Quite evidently, the exploration phase of the learning cycle produces assimilation, the conceptual invention leads to accommodation, and organization is provided by the expansion phase.

This mental functioning model advanced by Piaget and its inherent teaching procedure, the learning cycle, comprise the theory base of our research program. In recent efforts this research agenda has focused on what are often labeled in the literature as misconceptions of scientific phenomena. Research projects are presented in this chapter in an abbreviated form, often a modification of an abstract which has been published in the literature. Complete accounts of each study can be found in the articles cited in the References. The chronology of these studies is organized in this chapter as follows:

> Exploratory Studies
> Age/Developmental Studies
>> Elementary School
>> Middle/Junior High School
>> Cross-Age
> Small School/Large School Study
> Teaching Strategies and Misconceptions of Students
> Teaching Practices and Misconceptions of Teachers

THE DATA-GATHERING TOOLS

Measuring concept understanding has occurred in many forms: multiple-choice questions, essay questions, clinical interviews, and/or combinations of these forms. Each assessment type has inherent advantages and disadvan-

Figure 18.1. Concept Evaluation Statement for the Cell Concept
A sample of onion is examined with a microscope. The observer sees the onion skin divided into regularly shaped small compartments. A drop of pond water is examined with a microscope. The observer finds several very small creatures swimming and floating. A section of lung tissue is also examined with a microscope. Again the observer finds small compartments but this time the compartments are irregularly shaped. After examining the onion skin, the pond water organisms, and the lung tissue, the observer examines some sand, salt, and a piece of cloth. The observer again notices regularly shaped and irregularly shaped objects but the sand, salt, and cloth fibers do not have small structures within the compartments. The sand, salt, and cloth fibers appear to be much simpler objects when compared to the onion skin, pond water organisms, and lung tissue. Explain the differences in these living and nonliving specimens.

tages for gathering such data. In our research we have developed, tested, validated, and retested many essay-type CONCEPT EVALUATION STATE-MENTS (CES) designed to assess concept understanding. These CESs, which have been used with subjects from elementary school through graduate school and with students and teachers, represent an array of concepts from the life sciences, physical sciences, and social sciences. Two examples of CESs are displayed in Figures 18.1 and 18.2. From the subjects' responses to CESs, investigators in our research have discovered that these qualitative data can be readily and reliably grouped into "categories of understanding or misunderstanding" for a particular concept. Guidelines for categorizing degrees of understandings can be found in Figure 18.3. These or analogous instruments, similar procedures, and/or modified categories of understanding were used to assess science concept understandings and misconceptions in all of our research.

EXPLORATORY STUDIES

Do students learn the concepts their teachers want them to learn? Exploratory studies reported in two articles (Marek, 1986a, 1986b) examined student understandings and misunderstandings of four concepts fundamental to biology—a subject taken by more than 90% of high school students. The four concepts studied were: (a) the cell, (b) diffusion, (c) food chains, and (d) ecosystem. The students participating in these investigations attended a large urban high school in the Midwest and the mean age of these

Figure 18.2. Concept Evaluation Statement for the Diffusion Concept
A 10-gallon glass container setting on a table is full of clear water. Several drops of a dark blue dye are dropped on the surface of the water. In a paragraph, explain what will happen to the dye. Be sure to write down any specific details about the process you describe. Name the process.

Figure 18.3. A Generalized Format Used to Determine the Level of Student Understanding for Science Concepts

Scheme	Response
Complete Understanding	The student's response closely approximates the abstract, theoretical explanation found in a science textbook. The explanation has a molecular base.
Sound Understanding	The student's response indicates an understanding of the concept at a non-abstract, concrete level. Explanation at the molecular theoretical level is absent, but the answer given is scientifically accurate and complete at a concrete level.
Partial Understanding	The student's response contains part, but not all, of the information necessary to convey either a complete or sound understanding of the concept. No incorrect information occurs in the response.
Partial Understanding with Specific Misconception	The student's response contains correct information, but also indicates a misconception concerning some aspect of the concept.
Specific Misconception	The student's response indicates a complete misconception of the concept.
No Understanding	The student's response consist of "I don't know," the question repeated, or irrelevant remarks. There also may be no response.

10th graders was 16 years 2 months when the data were gathered late in the school year. Two classes of approximately 30 students each (30 females and 28 males total) were identified as representative and typical biology classes which met daily for 50-minute periods. The teacher, a male with 33 years teaching experience, used *Modern Biology*, published by Holt, Rinehart & Winston, as the primary curriculum for the course. Approximately 30% of class time was spent in laboratory work conducting experiments from a laboratory manual. During the remaining 70% of class time, students listened to lectures, read from the textbook, watched films, and completed written assignments.

Only 15.8% of the students demonstrated sound understanding of the cell; even fewer, 1.8% of the sample, demonstrated any sound understanding of the diffusion concept. Partial understanding of the cell and diffusion concepts was demonstrated by 28.1% and 35.7% of the students, respectively. Combining partial and sound understanding of each concept accounted for 43.9% (cell) and 37.5% (diffusion) of the students in the study. In other words, fewer than half of the students in this study demonstrated any degree of understanding of the cell or diffusion. The larger portion of the students had no response or held misconceptions of these two concepts (56.1% for the cell and 62.5% for diffusion).

Of the 58 students in the sample, only one student (2%) had a sound understanding of the concept of food chain. Only 34% demonstrated partial understanding of a food chain, while 57% showed specific misunderstanding and 7% had no response. For the ecosystem concept, 31% of the students demonstrated partial understanding and 33% showed specific misunderstanding. While only 4 students had no response to the food chain instrument, 21 students (36%) had no response to the ecosystem question. Furthermore, no student gave a response indicating sound understanding of an ecosystem.

The results of these exploratory studies were not unlike the results of the numerous other research efforts into misconceptions students hold of scientific phenomena. Students aren't "learning" the concepts their teachers are "teaching." The students in our exploratory studies had covered the test material and had completed objective examinations with the typical distribution of passing and failing. But *passing tests* and *recalling terminology* associated with scientific concepts does not mean the students *understand* the concepts.

AGE/DEVELOPMENTAL STUDIES

Elementary School

The study (Marek & Methven, 1990) abstracted here was part of a larger study which investigated the relationships among: (a) teacher's attitudes and implementation of inservice-workshop-developed science materials (learning cycles), and (b) elementary school student's language used to describe properties of objects and conservation reasoning. The following discussion focuses on the results associated with (b).

A set of data was gathered from over 100 students from grades K to 5 and their 16 teachers who had participated in an inservice program designed to examine laboratory-centered science curricula (learning cycles) and the educational and scientific theories upon which the curricula were based. Another set of data was gathered from a representative comparison group of students and teachers that generally matched the teachers participating in the inservice workshop except for one variable—the comparison group taught science traditionally, that is, by exposition. Over 220 student interviews were conducted and audiotaped in this quasiethnography to assess: (a) conservation reasoning as a measure of developmental level (Renner & Marek, 1988, pp. 3–27), and (b) descriptive language for the concept of property. Combined pre- and posttests of the student interviews produced 48 audiotapes which transcribed to over 300 pages of text.

Biographical data indicated that all of the participating teachers were females with 1 to 15 years of teaching experience and approximately ¼ of the participants had master's degrees. Teaching assignments of the teachers in the study ranged from kindergarten through fifth grade, excluding fourth grade, and the average class size was 25 students. All classrooms were within a 30-mile radius of a major midwestern metropolitan area.

Data from the research indicated that the teachers involved in the science inservice workshop implemented the workshop-developed materials into their science classes. Significantly greater gains in conservation reasoning and language usage occurred with the students (experimental group) of the teachers participating in the science inservice workshop as compared to the exposition classrooms (comparison group). The experimental group increased 44% in their conservation reasoning abilities during the school year, while the comparison group had an increase of only 17%. This difference in gains was significant and perhaps could be attributed to the numerous direct experiences with materials given to the experimental group. These experiences gave these students the opportunity to manipulate objects, observe and record data, interact with their peers and teacher, and construct concepts from their data. Such experiences were virtually absent in the comparison group. The experimental group demonstrated a higher quality of descriptive language when compared to the comparison group; in other words, the experimental students were better able to use property words and focus their attention on the object in question (see Tables 18.1 and 18.2).

In addition to this qualitative data of the student's language, a quantitative measure was made by calculating the average number of words used by each student per interview. A pretest (166.1 words) to posttest (175.3 words) *gain* of 9.2 words was demonstrated by the experimental group while a *decrease* of .6 words was demonstrated from pretests (134.4 words) to posttest (133.8 words) with the comparison group.

Middle/Junior High School

Two questions sharpened the focus of the physics concept research (Renner, Abraham, Grzybowski, & Marek, 1990) conducted with middle school students:

1. What were the degrees of understanding by eighth-grade students of the *Expansion Concept*—Expansion is the process in which the volume of a substance increases; *Doppler Effect Concept*—The Doppler effect is a change in a wave frequency caused by the motion of the wave source; *Floating Concept*—When the mass of the displaced liquid is equal to the mass of the object, the object floats; and *Kinetic Energy Concept*—

Table 18.1.   Interviews with Kindergarten Students

Interviewer (I)	Experimental: Kindergarten Student (EK)	Comparison: Kindergarten Student (CK)
I have a magnet that I would like to show you. I would like for you to look closely at both the magnet and these things that go on top of it. Pick them up and touch them with your fingers. If you would like to, you may put the things on top of the magnet. Tell me everything you can about all of the things.	One of these small ones are different than all these other small ones and more rounder. The big black magnet is bigger than the others, and it's also a different color.	My Dad has a lot of these, but this is about the biggest one. I think it is the biggest. I can tell that it's really big. My Dad has a lot of these in my garage. My Dad is a mechanic, and he's a policeman. My brother thinks he wants to be a policeman. He's good at making trouble. This is a towering building.

Notice how EK presented her data. She was very observant and well organized. She used many property words and did not add irrelevant information. Although CK did mention the sizes of the objects, his data were poorly organized and full of irrelevant information.

I have a marble that I would like to show you. Pick it up and feel it with your fingers. Look at it closely. Please tell me everything you can about the marble.	It's round. Right here it's darker, and here it's lighter than it is here. It looks like it's yellow on the outside, but it's really clear white.	It's yellow. It got a kind of a flower shape in it. It's round. Also it can spin and it won't go straight—it just goes wobbly. Looks like it goes that way. My brother's name is Robert. Also guess what I was this Halloween? Batman. Also my Mom said I didn't have one single thing missing from that thing.

CK began his description of the marble in much the same fashion as EK. However, he soon became unable to focus on the marble and began to talk about his past experiences or things that happened prior to the interview.

I have three bars that I would like to show you. I would like for you to pick them up and feel them with your fingers. Look at them closely. Tell me everything you can about these three bars.	Two of them are magnets, and one's plastic. They're all different colors. This one's lighter than this one. This one has a different color than both of these. These two are bigger than the green one.	One's lighter, and these two feel the same. They aren't magnetic. They don't stick. See.

Kinetic energy is energy of motion and kinetic energy can be changed to heat energy.

2. What was the relationship between the intellectual developmental levels of eighth-grade students and degrees of understanding developed of the four previously stated concepts?

Table 18.2.   Interviews with Third Grade Students

Interviewer (I)	Experimental: Third Grade Student (ET)	Comparison: Third Grade Student (CT)
I have a seashell to show you. I would like for you to pick it up and touch all of the parts of it with your fingers. Tell me everything you can about the seashell.	It has a hole in it. You can hear the ocean. It's white and brown. It can fit around your hand. A sea animal used to live in it. It can't roll. It sounds like a jar when you drop it. It has a line or seam. It's dirty inside. It makes a static sound.	Snails can live in it. You can hear the ocean. You can use these for many things. You can glue on them. You can make these out of horns.
I have a cotton ball that I would like to show you. Please pick it up and feel it with your fingers. Look at it closely. Please tell me everything you can about the cotton ball.	It's soft and white. You can pull it apart. It's furry. It's stringy when it's apart. It can't roll—no, it can. It's soft so it doesn't make noise when it falls.	It's rough. It's for your ears when you have an ear ache.
I would like for you to pick this up and feel it with your fingers. Look at it closely. Please tell me everything you can about this thing.	It's square. It's yellow. It's light. It can't roll. It's a square. It makes noise when you drop it. It's wood. It has scrapes and fingerprints on it. It's yellow. It has a grain. It has a white chip on it.	It's a square. You can use it for a house.
I would like for you to pick this up and feel it with your fingers. Look at it closely. Please tell me everything you can about this thing.	It's a triangle. It's red. It has a grain. It's light and wood. It's solid. It's red. It can't roll. It will stand up. It's like a ship's sail when it's on its side.	It's a triangle. You can use it for a house.

CT constantly draws on past experiences throughout his dialogues. For example, when describing the square and triangle, CT responded: "You can use it for a house." In addition, CT's usage of property words is very limited. ET rarely offers extraneous information.

Two measures of intellectual development and four physics CESs were completed by 257 students (133 females and 124 males) from 14 schools during the last month of the school year. The mean age was 14.2 years and, using both tasks, the mean intellectual development was 3.4 on a scale of 2–8. Standard scoring was used: early concrete (1) to fully formal (4) for each task. Complete descriptions of these scoring procedures and developmental stages can be found in Renner and Marek (1988, pp. 203–212). The responses to the intellectual development tasks and each of the four physics problems were read, discussed, and evaluated by two researchers simultaneously. The frequencies of the responses for each of the six categories that reflected a level of understanding were determined, and the percentage of the total sample each category represented was calculated. The data for this research were drawn from both urban and rural schools. Seven urban schools furnished 199 students from 29 classes, which were taught by nine teachers. Seven rural schools furnished 58 students from nine classes, which were taught by seven teachers; a rural school was defined in our research as having fewer than 50 students in Grade 8.

The research reported here was done to evaluate the understandings developed by middle school students who meet physics concepts through a textbook. According to the teachers of the 257-student sample, each of those students had studied each of the four concepts used in Grade 7 and/or Grade 8. All students had experienced science from the same textbooks.

In general, the students were intellectually operating at the concrete operational level, but 44 of the 257 were in transition between the concrete and formal levels or had entered the formal operational thought period. Although the data are not definitive, the transitional and formal students seemed to have developed better understandings of the concepts than had the concrete students. Those latter students achieved higher levels on the items that measured understanding of a concrete concept (Expansion Concept) than they did on the items that measured understandings of formal concepts (Doppler Effect, Floating, Kinetic Energy Concepts).

Perhaps the most telling conclusion that can be drawn regarding teaching science concepts by using a textbook is that 60.8% of the students in the research did not respond, developed no understandings, or developed specific misconceptions of the four concepts, while only 28.1% developed partial or sound understandings of those four concepts. Finally, in the judgment of these researchers, the writing ability demonstrated by the student responses to the four questions was poor. This raises questions concerning how much writing science teachers expect from their students. Of the 17 teachers whose classes participated in this study, only 5 indicated that they used short essay questions as part of their tests; the remaining teachers utilized objective questions to test their students.

In a related study (Marek & Bryant, 1990), five concepts common to middle/junior high school life science textbooks were examined: *Cell Concept*—A cell is the basic unit of structure in living things; *Diffusion Concept*—Diffusion is the movement of molecules of a material from regions of high concentrations to regions of lower concentrations of that material; *Classification Concept*—Organisms can be classified by observable similarities and differences into groups with standardized names; *Photosynthesis Concept*—Green plants absorb light energy, water and carbon dioxide to make food (glucose) and oxygen; and *Food Chain Concept*—A series of animals feeding on plants and/or other animals for food and the energy it contains makes a food chain. CESs for these five concepts were also completed by the sample of 257 eighth-grade students described previously in the physics concept research.

The concept of classification was partially understood by 43% of the eighth-grade students which was by far the greatest degree of understanding for any of the life science concepts. Although nearly one-fourth of the students had some understanding (partial) of the food chain concept, 24% held misconceptions—14% (misconceptions) plus 10% (partial understanding with specific misconceptions). Furthermore, there was no sound understanding of this concept, and over one-half (53%) had no understanding of the food chain. The concepts of diffusion and photosynthesis provided perhaps the best evidence that the junior high school students in the study knew very little about common, fundamental science concepts. Eighty-six percent of the students had no understanding or held misconceptions about diffusion, and 80% of these students had no understanding or demonstrated misconceptions about photosynthesis. Furthermore, only 27% had any understanding (sound and partial) of the concept of the cell with nearly two-thirds of this group of eighth graders having no understanding of the cell. And finally, the percentage average mean for no understanding for all five concepts was 53.2% and the mean for misconceptions was 16.8%. In other words, 70% of all responses of all eighth-grade students participating in this study represented misconceptions or no understanding of the cell, diffusion, classification, photosynthesis, and food chain.

Cross Age

Our cross-age studies (Westbrook & Marek, 1991, 1992) examined seventh-grade students in life science, tenth-grade students in biology, and college students in zoology for understanding of two concrete biology concepts—diffusion and the cell, and two formal or abstract biology concepts—homeostasis and gene function. Responses from 100 students from each grade level were selected for data analyses. Each student was asked to respond to a test packet consisting of a biographical questionnaire, two Piagetian-like developmental tasks, and four CESs. The seventh-grade sample consisted of 42 males and 58 females with a combined mean age of 13 years 1 month. The developmental tasks showed 89% of the sample to be either concrete operational or transitional; 11% were early formal and none were fully formal operational. The tenth-grade sample was composed of 53 males and 47 females, with a mean age of 16 years 2 months. Seventy-eight percent of the students were either concrete or transitional, 6% were early formal, and 16% were fully formal. The mean age of the college sample was

20 years 9 months and included 49 males and 51 females. Over half of the sample were freshmen, while the remaining 47% were sophomores, juniors, seniors, and graduate students. Thirty-four percent were concrete and transitional, 30% were early formal, and 36% were fully formal.

None of the 300 students across the three grade levels exhibited complete understanding of the diffusion concept, and there was no appreciable difference among the grade levels in regard to sound and partial understanding, misconceptions, or no understanding. You may wish to reexamine Figure 18.3 for an explanation of the categories of understanding, since "complete" understanding had not been used to this point in our research. An analysis of the misconceptions exhibited by the college sample showed that many of those misconceptions could be traced to a misapplication of scientific terminology. The college sample showed greater understanding of the cell concept than either the seventh- or tenth-grade samples. There was no apparent difference in the frequency of misconceptions among the three grade levels. The seventh grade sample exhibited a greater frequency of no understanding responses than the tenth-grade or college samples.

Although the college sample showed greater understanding than the precollege students of both the homeostasis and gene function concepts, the frequency of misconceptions among the college students of both concepts was also greater. The seventh-grade sample showed a greater level of no understanding for each concept than the tenth-grade and college samples. Ninety-five percent of the seventh-grade student responses to the gene function CES were evaluated as indicating no understanding of the concept (see Tables 18.3–18.5).

Chi-square analysis of the developmental levels versus the level of understanding indicated that, for both concrete concepts, the nonformal students showed less than expected "understanding." The formal students

Table 18.3.   Frequencies of Combined Levels of Understanding of the Diffusion and Cell Concepts Across the Three Grade Levels.

Grade Level	Diffusion				Cell			
	CU/SU	PU	PS/SM	N	CU/SU	PU	PS/SM	N
7	-	38	55	7	-	29	15	56
10	-	30	65	5	1	41	18	40
College	-	37	61	2	8	59	19	14

CU/SU = Complete or sound understanding
PU = partial understanding
PS/SM = partial understanding with specific misconception or specific misconception
N = no understanding
n = 100 for each grade

Table 18.4.   Combined Levels of Understanding of the Homeostasis Concept Across the Three Grade Levels

Grade Level	Combined Levels of Understanding		
	U	M	N
7	3[a]	46	51
10	12[a]	54	34
College	30	64	6

U = "Understanding" (complete or partial understanding—CU/PU)
M = "Misconception" (partial understanding with specific misconception or specific misconception—PS/SM)
N = "No understanding"
n = 100 for each grade level
[a]No responses exhibiting complete understanding

exhibited greater than expected "understanding" for both concepts. Misconceptions appeared to be independent of developmental level; the frequency of misconceptions was essentially the same for the two combined developmental levels. Chi-square analysis of the relationship between concept understanding of homeostasis and developmental level indicated that nonformal students showed a greater than expected level of "no understanding" and less than the expected degree of "understanding" of the homeostasis concept. The large number of "no understanding" responses to the gene function CES prevented chi-square analysis of those data. Responses of formal operational students to the homeostasis CES exhibited a greater than expected degree of "understanding" and less than expected "no understanding." Misconceptions existed regardless of developmental level.

Table 18.5.   Combined Levels of Understanding of the Gene Function Concept Across the Three Grade Levels

Grade Level	Combined Levels of Understanding		
	U	M	N
7	0	5	95
10	11[a]	13	76
College	12	20	68

U = "Understanding" (complete or partial understanding—CU/PU)
M = "Misconception" (partial understanding with specific misconception or specific misconception—PS/SM)
N = "No understanding"
n = 100 for each grade level
[a]No responses exhibiting complete understanding

SMALL SCHOOL/LARGE SCHOOL STUDY

Do students from small high schools show fewer understandings and more misconceptions of biology concepts than students attending large high schools? Fifty tenth-grade students from four different biology classes in large high schools (enrollments exceeding 900 students) and 50 tenth-grade students from four different biology classes in small high schools (enrollments with fewer than 150 students) were randomly selected and then evaluated on their understandings and misunderstandings of four biology concepts: diffusion, homeostasis, food production in plants, and classification of animals and plants. To control for the urban/rural factor, each school selected for this study was located in a rural area where agriculture was the predominant industry. The socioeconomic backgrounds of the students from all schools were similar, with the majority of students coming from white, low- to middle-class families; a small percentage of students were black or Hispanic. Seven different teachers taught the eight biology classes sampled in this study, and each of these teachers taught all four concepts listed above. Exposition was the primary teaching procedure with no teacher spending more than one day per week using laboratory activities.

Students attending small high schools showed fewer instances of understanding and more instances of misunderstanding the concepts of diffusion and homeostasis. These differences could be related to a higher percentage of students in large schools capable of formal operations (Simpson & Marek, 1985); sound understanding of diffusion and homeostasis as assessed in this study required students to use formal operations. No difference was observed between the large and small school samples for the concepts of food production in plants and classification of plants and animals. Perhaps this was due to the fact that the students in the small school sample *and* the large school sample lived in agricultural communities and their daily *experiences* allowed them to develop some understanding of plant growth (farming) and therefore may have prevented some instances of misunderstandings from being developed. Classification of animals and plants, as examined in this study, required only concrete operations to understand; therefore, students in the small schools, which consisted of more concrete and fewer formal operational students, were capable of developing sound understandings as well as students from the large schools in this study. As with the other studies summarized in this chapter, a complete data presentation, interpretation, and conclusions can be found in the original reports.

TEACHING STRATEGIES AND MISCONCEPTIONS
OF STUDENTS

The presence and persistence of misconceptions raises questions about the effectiveness of the extant teaching procedure common in science classrooms—namely, exposition, which could be described as chalk and talk, or tell 'em and test 'em! The hypothesis that the learning cycle teaching procedure might eliminate misconceptions guided the design for an experiment to test this question: Which teaching procedure, the learning cycle or exposition, leads to greater understanding of scientific concepts and fewer misconceptions (Cowan, 1989)?

Two biology classes totalling 35 students from a rural midwestern high school of approximately 400 students were used in this study. Eighteen of the students in the study were sophomores, and the remaining were from Grades 9, 11, and 12. One class (LC) experienced a learning cycle about the concept of diffusion while the other class (E) received instruction by exposition over the same concept.

Pretest evaluations demonstrated that 100% of the students (LC and E) in the study held some type of misunderstanding of the diffusion concept. The "misunderstanding" category in this study included the students with misconceptions, partial understandings with misconceptions, or no understandings. Posttests for class LC revealed 93.8% of the students demonstrated some degree of understanding (i.e., complete, sound, or partial understanding) of diffusion and 6.3% (one student) had a misunderstanding of diffusion. Posttests for class E revealed 57.8% of the students demonstrated some category of understanding of diffusion while 42.1% still held some type of misunderstanding. Although significantly more LC students replaced their misconceptions about diffusion with understandings compared to the E students, obviously some students have success with replacing misunderstanding with understanding in each "type of class" in this study.

When developmental level, as measured with the Test of Logical Thinking (Tobin & Capie, 1981), was considered, it was discovered that the formal reasoning ability or the lack of such reasoning was similar in the LC and E classes. Furthermore, the group who did not achieve understanding of diffusion during exposition may have been unsuccessful because of their inability to reason formally. Stated differently, while exposition appears effective in leading to an understanding of diffusion for those students who have some formal reasoning patters, the learning cycle appears to lead to understandings of diffusion for students who have formal reasoning patterns as well as those who do not.

The initial examination of science misconceptions and teaching methodology provided a foundation for such research. Much more research into the effects of teaching procedures on misconceptions is needed.

TEACHING PRACTICES AND MISCONCEPTIONS OF TEACHERS

The following study (Marek, Eubanks, & Gallaher, 1990) examined the relationships between high school science teachers' understanding of the

Piagetian developmental model of intelligence, its inherent teaching procedure—the learning cycle—and classroom teaching practices. The teachers observed in this study had expressed dissatisfaction with the teaching methods they used and, subsequently, attended a National Science Foundation-sponsored inservice program designed to examine laboratory-centered science curricula and the educational and scientific theories upon which the curricula were based. After the inservice program the teacher were asked to respond to the following:

1. Describe the relationships between the mental functioning model and the learning cycle teaching procedure.
2. How do your students' levels of cognitive development affect the kinds of concepts they are capable of learning? (Limit your discussion to concrete and formal operations.)

The data (teachers' responses to these questions) fell into one of four categories in this study: sound understanding (S), partial understanding (P), limited understanding (L), or misunderstanding (M). Two teachers from each of the four categories of understanding were chosen for observation. Subjects for the research sample were carefully selected to both (a) provide adequate data (observations) from each category of understanding and (b) accurately cross-section the type of schools represented in this project. Consequently, the teachers (five females and three males) observed in this study were secondary school science teachers; each taught in a public school with eight different school systems representing rural to urban, and small to large school districts. The average number of years of teaching experiences of these teachers was 8, and two of the teachers held master's degrees.

Two observational tools were combined and therefore used concomitantly in gathering data in the "learning cycle classrooms" of these teachers: The Learning Cycle Teaching Behaviors (LCTB) instrument and the Verbal Interaction Category System (VICS) instrument—Grzybowski (1991), and Amidon and Hough (1967), respectively (see Tables 18.6 and 18.7). In this study at least two complete learning cycles were observed for each teacher. In other words, each teacher was observed two or more times teaching each phase of the learning cycle. *Each* observation was done using the LCTB and VICS and lasted approximately 45 minutes.

The qualitative data gathered with the LCTB/VICS were also tape-recorded, yielding a voluminous amount of data. And although each phase of the learning cycle is thoroughly discussed in the original report (Marek Eubanks, & Gallaher, 1990), the results reported here are an abbreviated summary of that ethnography. The teachers who exhibited a sound understanding of the Piagetian model of intelligence and learning cycle were more likely to implement learning cycle curricula effectively. In other

Table 18.6.   The Learning Cycle Teaching Behaviors Instrument

Does the teacher: Yes/No	Behavior	VICS (See Table 7)
Exploration	provide materials from the environment of the classroom for the students to manipulate?	
	provide minimal guidelines such as how to use the equipment without telling the students the concept which they are supposed to learn?	
	move from one student group to the next and question the learners to give more direction as needed?	
	interact with students (individuals and laboratory groups) asking questions concerning the meaning of the data being gathered?	
Conceptual Invention	ask for qualitative reports of tests from each laboratory group?	
	ask for quantitative reports of tests from each laboratory group? assist students in summarizing information gained from their interaction with the materials used in the exploration?	
	use student data to develp the concept?	
	introduce the language of the concept?	
Expansion of the Idea	provide laboratory acitivites which allow the student to use the concept?	
	use demonstration laboratories to enable an entire class to observe an application of the concept?	
	provide readings and/or audio-visual aids which apply the concept to other situations without introducing new concepts?	
	provide questions and/or problem sets to reinforce the concept? continue to use the language of the concept as the concept is expanded and applied by the students?	
	assist students in summarizing information gained from their interaction with the materials (closure)?	

Table 18.7.   The Verbal Interaction Category System (VICS)

Teacher Initiated Talk	1.	*Gives information or opinion*: presents content or own ideas, explains, orients, asks rhetorical questions.
	2.	*Gives directions*: tells pupil to take some specific action; gives orders, commands.
	3.	*Asks narrow questions*: asks drill and factual questions, questions requiring one- or two-word replies or yes-or-no answers; questions to which the specific nature of the response can be predicted from previous instruction (convergent).
	4.	*Asks broad questions*: asks relatively open-ended questions, questions which are thought provoking. Apt to elicit a longer pupil response than 3 (divergent).
	4p.	*Asks probing questions*: asks questions of a convergent nature in response to a student's reply to a category 4 question.
Teacher Response	5.	*Accepts* (5a) Affective management—Teacher responses which stress the affective content or context of the occurrence. *Accepts* (5b) Behavior management—Teacher responses which stress the physical conduct or behavior fo the occurrence. *Accepts* (5c) Cognitive management—Teacher responses which stress the cognitive content or context of the occurence.
	6.	*Rejects* (6a) Affective management—Teacher responses which stress the affective content or context of the occurrence. *Rejects* (6b) Behavior management—Teacher responses which stress the physical conduct or behavior of the occurrence. *Rejects* (6c) Cognitive management—Teacher responses which stress the cognitive content or context of the occurrence.
Other	7.	*Silence*: pauses or short period of silence during a time of classroom conversation or a busy noise and return to topic.
	8.	*Confusion*: considerable noise which disrupts planned activities. This category may accompany other categories or may totally preclude the use of other categories.
	9.	*Withhold or ignore*: Teacher responses which neither accept nor reject the occurrence.

words, these teachers were successfully able to integrate their students' laboratory experiences with class discussions to construct science concepts. The teachers who exhibited misunderstandings of the Piagetian developmental model of intelligence and the learning cycle also engaged their students in laboratory activities, but these activities were weakly related to learning cycles. For example, the data gathered by their M students were typically not used in class discussions to construct science concepts. Therefore, these teachers (M) apparently did not discern the necessity of using the data and experiences from laboratory activities and the impetus for science concept attainment.

It was also discovered with the teachers in this study that relationships existed between teachers' questioning strategies and their degree of understanding of the Piagetian developmental model of intelligence and the learning cycle. Teachers who demonstrated a sound understanding (S) asked more questions, particularly divergent and probing questions, concerning the data gathered by their students than did any of the other teachers in this study. The *quality* and *quantity* of the questions asked by the teacher may indicate a teacher's degree of understanding of the necessity of student involvement when constructing knowledge.

YOU ARE INVITED...

Misunderstandings about natural phenomena pervaded our research results regardless of the ages, environments, developmental levels, or experimental treatments of the students. Below is a list of 15 common misconceptions we gathered. You are invited to study this list and identify the concept(s) associated with each misconception.

- Something living is made of cells.
- A cell has life in it, and things that are not cells do not have life... Onion cells have no life.
- Diffusion is where a chemical change takes place and changes water to blue dye.
- The molecules in the water accept the blue dye, so then, as the molecules in the water move, so does the dye.
- To classify something, try feeding it people food. If it eats it, then he is an animal; if he doesn't, then it's a plant.
- If it gives birth to live young or eggs, it is an animal. If it makes seeds, it is a plant.
- Plants gain weight by eating the soil and drinking the water.
- Plants grab moisture from the air and make food (chlorophyll) for itself.
- Proteins, sugar, carbohydrates, and fats are only found in living organisms.
- Organisms in an ecosystem will have to learn to compromise in order to survive.
- Animals look for the same food. They breathe the same air; they help each other out when they are in trouble.
- Sweat is just a fat being removed from the body.
- The eye pigment gene has enzymes. Different enzymes make different eyes. When you're missing a specific enzyme, your eyes will be blue or green. When you have all the enzymes, you will have brown eyes.
- Eye color genes in cells that are used in the eye of a person are started in

the womb of the mother, where the eyes start to develop. It matures and grows until the genes are the color of the eyes.

As the title of this chapter connotes, our social-scientific interpretations of how concepts were learned were based upon developmental models. Through a process called *mental functioning*, it is theorized that learners construct knowledge (Piaget, 1966). This knowledge and the *quality of thought* the learner uses has been classified into stages or developmental levels (Piaget, 1963). The Quality of Thought and Mental Functioning models served us well as we labored to make sense out of our many observations of students' and teachers' understandings and misconceptions. You are invited to examine these abstracted studies in their entirety and offer alternative interpretations based upon other extant models of learning.

REFERENCES

Amidon, E., & Hough, J. (1967). *Interaction analysis: Theory, research and application.* Reading, MA; Addison-Wesley.

Cowan, C.C. (1989). *The effects of two teaching procedures on concept understanding.* Unpublished master's thesis, University of Oklahoma.

Grzybowski, E.B. (1991). *A qualitative study of concrete and formal teaching.* Doctoral research in progress, University of Oklahoma.

Lawson, A.E., Abraham, M.R., & Renner, J.W. (1989). A theory of instruction: Using the learning cycle to teach science concepts and thinking skills. *NARST Monograph*, No. 1.

Marek, E.A. (1986a). They'll misunderstand but they'll pass. *The Science Teacher, 53,* 32–35.

Marek, E.A. (1986b). Understandings and misunderstandings of biology concepts. *American Biology Teachers, 48,* 37–40.

Marek, E.A., & Bryant, R.J. (1990). I don't know. I don't understand! *Science Scope, 14*(4), 44–45, 60.

Marek, E.A., Eubanks, C., & Gallaher, T.H. (1990). Teachers' understanding and the use of the learning cycle. *Journal of Research in Science Teaching, 27* (9), 821–834.

Marek, E.A., & Methven, S. (1990). Effects of the learning cycle upon student and classroom teacher performance. *Journal of Research in Science Teaching, 28* (1), 41–53.

Piaget, J. (1963). *The origins of intelligence in children.* New York: W.W. Norton.

Piaget, J. (1966). *Psychology of intelligence.* Totowa, NJ: Littlefield Adams.

Renner, J.W., Abraham, M.R., Gryzbowski, E.B., & Marek, E.A. (1990). Understandings and minsunderstandings of eighth graders of four physics concepts found in textbooks. *Journal of Research in Science Teaching, 27* (1), 35–54.

Renner, J.W., & Marek, E.A. (1988). *The learning cycle and elementary school science teaching.* Portsmouth, NH: Heinemann Educational Books, Inc.

Simpson, W.D., & Marek, E.A. (1985). Cognitive development of students in small rural schools. *The Small School Forum, 6* (2), 1–4.

Simpson, W.D., & Marek, E.A. (1988). Understandings and misconceptions of biology concepts held by students attending small high schools and students attending large high schools. *Journal of Research in Science Teaching, 25* (5), 361–374.

Tobin, K., & Capie, W. (1981). Development and validation of a group test of logical thinking. *Educational Psychological Measurement, 41,* 413–424.

Westbrook, S.L. & Marek, E.A. (1991). A cross-age study of student understanding of the concept of diffusion. *Journal of Research in Science Teaching, 28* (8), 649–660.

Westbrook, S.L., & Marek, E.A. (1992). A cross-age study of student understanding of the concept of homeostasis. *Journal of Research in Science Teaching, 29* (1), 51–61.

Chapter 19

Literature for the Special Learner: The Urban, At-Risk Student

Nancy J. Ellsworth

"Why do we have to read this stuff, Mrs. Jordan? This is dumb!" James just can't get started with his reading. As he frets, he distracts Maria, his Puerto Rican friend who sits next to him; soon James isn't even pretending to read today's story. Since many others in his class will have read it, James will be odd man out once again when the discussion begins. What a way to start the school day!

Why doesn't James want to read the story? Like many urban children, James's reading skills are significantly below grade level. Rarely has anyone read to him, his labored decoding is inaccurate, and he lacks effective comprehension strategies and vocabulary. In addition, he has had little exposure to literature he likes. Why should we expect James to want to tackle another sixth-grade story?

LITERACY IN THE UNITED STATES: NEW DIMENSIONS

In recent years there has been a growing consensus that at-risk and learning disabled (LD) students lack competence in reading (Williams & Ellsworth, 1990). Because of its impact on academic and employment success, insufficient mastery of reading skills is of particular concern, nationwide as well as in urban areas. Speaking of the broad population of students, the NAEP (National Assessment of Educational Progress, 1990) reported that most students read for surface understanding, to identify specific information, and to gain a general grasp of the material; however, they do not read analytically and they have difficulty synthesizing what they have read.

What is the impact of this low achievement in reading? According to the National Alliance of Business (1987), large numbers of high school graduates lack the skills needed in the workplace. For urban students, the discrepancy between basic skills learned and those needed for employment or further schooling is even greater. In New York City, drop-out rates escalated to the point where 11 "alternative" high schools were established for students at risk of dropping out of school (Harrington, 1987). Efforts have also been mounted on broader fronts in response to these concerns, such as the September 1988 Education Summit in Charlottesville, Virginia.

One of the most striking forces currently affecting education is demography (Yates, 1988). Rapid population changes exert powerful impact on educational outcomes, yet educators have no control over these changes. Today Hispanics are the fastest growing minority group; according to the census Bureau, the Hispanic population in the United States has increased by 30% since the 1990 census, almost 10 times the growth rate of the general population ("Hispanic Population Found to Be Growing Rapidly," 1986; Ortiz & Yates, 1988). Longitudinal studies suggest that language minority children such as those of Hispanic origin are often so deficient in reading skills that they are placed inappropriately in special education classes because of their limited English proficiency, rather than as a result of a handicapping condition (Benavides, 1988).

While some students like these may be incorrectly classified as handicapped, many others are truly learning disabled and are classified as such. We now know that LD students perform poorly in reading comprehension in comparison with nondisabled students (Ellsworth, 1989; Larson & Gerber, 1987; Warner, Schumaker, Alley, & Deshler, 1980). This is indeed cause for concern, for in the 1988–1989 school year, just under 2,000,000 children in the United States were classified and receiving services because of learning disabilities (U.S. Office of Education, 1990), a marked increase from the approximately 800,000 students identified as LD in 1976–1977 (Jordan, 1989).

The special needs of at-risk and LD students for improved reading and comprehension skills have been cited frequently. But how can we address these needs as we plan our teaching of literature? One way is by structuring the curriculum so that students are reading widely in literature they enjoy, for through copious reading coupled with direct instruction in skills comes increased competence.

LITERATURE FOR STUDENTS AT RISK: A RATIONALE

Literature is especially important in the lives of urban children such as James and Maria. For them, life may be slimmer and more tentative than for those children who are developing in the mainstream. Consider Helen Keller's (1902) view.

> Literature is my Utopia. Here I am not disfranchised. No barrier of the senses shuts me out from the sweet, gracious discourse of my book friends. They talk to me without embarrassment or awkwardness. (p. 100)

The vicarious experiences available through reading can stimulate the imagination and provide fun of the highest order. Have you ever known a child who did not like to be read to? The chance to share the Grinch's Christmas spirit or Paul Bunyan's footprint creation of the geography of America is special to us all. But how can James and Maria participate?

Among the problems as well as the riches of the cities is the insularity of many children's lives within their own ethnic or cultural groups. Tensions and conflicts result from a lack of understanding of the heritage of others, as well as from sparse knowledge of the legacy of mainstream America. Reading is one way for students to gain insights into themselves and the broader worlds which surround them. They are prime candidates for participation, for surely James would be the richer for sharing Maria's adventures of Juan Bobo (Ramirez, 1979), as would be Maria could she partake of James's family traditions. Within their school experiences, students will read the various literatures of the predominant culture, as well as of their own subcultures.

A TEACHING CHALLENGE

The skills and resources needed to teach such children effectively are considerable. The focus for the teacher is twofold: first, devising a teaching methodology that encompasses the multiple needs of the children in the class; and second, selecting the literature to be read. The traditional approach of having everyone engaged in a lock-step program of readings, often selected from an all-purpose basal, is insufficient. While James and Maria are poor readers, there are probably some like Edith in the class who are learning well. The story which may be exciting, readable, and appropriate for one child may be equally inappropriate for others. Beginning with the needs of the child is an important key to an effective literature program.

The literature program presented here incorporates: (a) interactive teaching, (b) motivating students, (c) setting priorities, (d) individualizing instruction with a wide range of literature, and (e) providing direct instruction in basic skills.

Interactive Teaching

One type of interactive teaching has been investigated by Palincsar and Brown (1988). They reported that reciprocal teaching, an instructional method which promotes directly the interaction between teachers and students, as well as among peers, has been found to be particularly effective in the teaching of reading. In reciprocal teaching, the teacher and a group of students take turns leading discussions for the purpose of discovering the meaning of the text. After extensive participation in these dialogues, poor readers improved their independent reading comprehension, both in the classroom and on standardized tests (Brown & Palincsar, 1985).

Another example of the active involvement of students in the learning process is reported by Giles (1989). Literature study groups are described in which adolescents select the books they wish to read from sets of several copies of a variety of books. As they read, students record their thoughts and questions in journals and share them in ongoing discussion groups both with peers reading the same book and with the teacher. These shared interpretations contribute to new perceptions, perhaps more meaningful than students' reactions written alone. This account is typical of a number of examples of interactive teaching reported in the literature in the last few years.

Motivating Students

In urban schools one frequently hears, "These children come to school unmotivated!" but when James lacks interest in attempting today's story, indeed it must be the teacher who steps up to the challenge. Is James unwilling to try because of past failures? Is the reading level too easy or too hard? Does the subject matter interest him? The necessity for teachers to assume the responsibility to motivate students to read has been difficult for some to accept; yet we know that teachers' motivational strategies are critical in enlisting students' active involvement (Bos & Vaughn, 1988).

In interviews, Roettger (1978) asked children how reading and school could be made more enjoyable. Students' answers provide guidelines to teachers for interesting students in a literature program: (a) know students' interests and help them locate books they would enjoy, (b) talk with students about books that might interest them, (c) give students time to read books every day, and (d) give children time to talk with each other and with the teacher about the books they are reading. Why should it be surprising that reading and interacting about topics that interest us are inherently motivating?

If students are confident that the literature program is one in which they will succeed, their full participation is more likely. As they build comprehension skills, such as mastery of various genre of text, their increasing competence becomes stimulating in itself.

Setting Priorities

For students at risk, the decision of which skills and content are given precedence in the focus of instruction evolves from an ongoing assessment of student progress and needs, as well as from the basis of traditional literature curricula. At times the purpose may be student enjoyment. At others, it may be to build basic decoding and comprehension skills or to increase fluency. Within the framework of group instruction, specific objectives may be individualized to meet the differing needs of students. One student may be reading to build fluency, another to create a bridge to the writing he will do in conjunction with the reading, and yet another to enrich the background knowledge needed in order to function better in school or in the transition to higher education or adult employment.

For example, in social studies, Maria is expected to learn about the growth of America. While Maria has revisited Puerto Rico, that is not the topic being studied. How can she begin to catch up? How can she, with her limited vocabulary, fathom the heritage of the American political system, the protections of the Constitution, the heroes of the past and the plans for the future that have been transmitted to many children over the breakfast table? Experiencing these things through literature is one way in which Maria can begin to discern more of this culture that will become hers, too. Without guidance from a teacher who has established this as a high priority for Maria, however, it is unlikely that she will locate and select relevant literature on her own. Her lack of understanding that reading will provide pride and self-esteem also stands in her way.

Helping students learn to work together by using literature to create cooperative learning experiences can also be an important priority guiding the teacher's decisions. When several students have read stories of fantasy, discussion and collaborative process writing in which the output of the group is published as a thematic unit can be an exciting achievement. The group support provided in activities with this type of structure encourages some children to participate who may feel unable to do so otherwise. When based on an assessment of student needs, important learning can result from awarding a high priority to shared experiences as an objective for a literature unit.

Individualizing Instruction with a Wide Range of Literature

How, then, can we meet the needs of this diverse, heterogeneous group? How can James and Maria, and also Edith find enjoyment and challenge in reading with the same classroom group? Their differences in interests, prior knowledge, cultural background, and reading skills create a major challenge for the best of teachers. And yet, to provide this opportunity is obviously possible, for many good teachers do so.

The teacher can plan readings and activities that both individualize the work and unify the class. When all students are reading the same literature, the teacher provides sufficient help that the poor reader can still succeed. On the other hand, when students read different literature, it can be sufficiently related for the teacher to synthesize a meaningful unity from the diversity. Each student needs to find his or her own niche within the program while also feeling an integral part of the whole.

Reading the Same Literature as a Group. For students of widely varying reading skills to read the same selections successfully require adaptations of the instructional methods used. One way for students to share the same literature is for the teacher to read it aloud. An ongoing story, be it fact or fiction, which compels the attention of adult and students alike, can open each class session with a shared experience and provides a positive beginning for whatever is to follow. This stimulus can be used to generate discussion, statements of opinion and fact, and writing. It can provide a forum in which all can participate—a forum in which the teacher may not need to predominate.

For students of varying skills to read the same literature themselves is a greater challenge. The selection of the reading is important, because some stories and books are of sufficient interest to hold the attention of all the students, even though the reading level is above or below that usually appropriate for a particular student. The inherent motivation of the reading will be increased if the teacher focuses on the rewards to be gained through the experience. For instance, if an objective is to kindle the imagination, the teacher might ask students to produce something imaginative based on the reading. Well-chosen literature can stimulate student participation in the reading experience to be shared by the class.

Given a complex mix of students, the teacher's instructional methods become even more pivotal. Students can be primed for the reading they are about to do in ways that will optimize their chances for a good experience. Like adults, students' experience is more limited than they wish. Prior knowledge of a subject areas enhances our understanding of what we read, so enriching the knowledge base on which the literature rests before beginning to read can influence comprehension directly. For example, in a high school English class, a piece of classical literature may be introduced by viewing a videotape. To watch Marlon Brando as Julius Caesar, to partake of the excitement of Zeffirelli's (1968) production of *Romeo and Juliet*, or even to view an episode of TV's portrayal of *Little House on the Prairie* (Wilder, 1933) prior to reading can increase a student's likelihood of achieving a meaningful understanding of a new piece of literature. While skeptics may fear that knowing how the story ends may lessen willingness to read, this is probably not so. Mature readers often enjoy a piece of literature more the second or third time they read it.

Some students' reading skills are so far below expectation that specific interventions will be needed if the students are to be able to "read" on their own, and the teacher must acknowledge and provide for this limitation. Hedley (1987) has noted that, if a child is unwilling to read, the task may be too hard. In order to gain such a student's active participation, he or she must feel confident of reasonable success. For students with major reading deficits, one way to accomplish this is for another person to read aloud while the student follows in the text. Another is for the student to listen to an audiotape of the literature borrowed from the Library of Congress, the state, or other sources of recordings available for the visually impaired (for which a student who is functionally unable to read qualifies). A volunteer reader may be enlisted to tape a selection for fellow students. Technological aids such as these can allow a diverse group of students to share some reading experiences as a group.

Reading Different Literature Together. A second component of the teacher's planning is to structure the unit so that students read different, but related, literature. The teacher must know the students' interests, backgrounds, and skills; this personal involvement, including the diagnostic inquiry that yields this information, is critical. One way to integrate students' reading experiences is to focus on a theme which furnishes the opportunity to share their thoughts through discussion and through group projects such as dramatization, debate, writing, and illustration. To guide in the selection of their literature, the teacher can give brief book talks which contain a hint of the difficulty of the reading; students will usually make appropriate choices given the opportunity to look through the book.

For instance, in a traditional literature program for middle school students the focus might be the theme of growing up. One student might choose to read *Sweetgrass*, Jan Hudson's (1984) story of an Indian girl growing up during the smallpox epidemic of 1837 (interest level; 10+; reading level: 4). Another may prefer *Sea Glass*, Lawrence Yep's (1979) tale of an Asian boy's struggle to make his father understand his desires (interest level: 10+; reading level: 6). A more accomplished reader may opt for Louisa Alcott's (1868) *Little Women* or Mark Twain's (1885) *Huck Finn*, which also address the theme of growing up. The point is that these varied pieces of literature cover a wide range of maturity, interests, and reading levels, but they are all focused on a topic which seems to be of universal interest to students at this stage of development. Purchasing only a few copies of a selection of related readings can build the resources needed to teach in this way.

Beginning with a base of reading about other people's problems in growing up, students may move naturally to consider the challenges that their friends (and, of course, they themselves) may face. In one of the most interesting sessions that I had with a ninth-grade class in New York City the students shifted, in a matter of seconds, from Huck Finn's temptations and need for personal strength to those of adolescents growing up in cities today, and then to these students' personal struggles with the proliferation of drugs and school drop-outs. They directed this shift of focus, for I had not anticipated the connection. The interactive method of teaching appeared to have allowed them to invest themselves in the discussion to the extent that they exerted control and moved the focus to one that was more important to them. We concluded this discussion with writing, some done individually and some done cooperatively, but all of which related to maturing. This was published as one project and kept in our classroom, a good reminder of what we could accomplish together.

The answer, then, seems to lie in individualizing the learning while, at the same time, unifying the class. Sometimes this can be achieved by having students read the same literature, despite their varied reading skills, but with specific instructional provisions designed to build motivation and ensure understanding. At other times, they may be reading different selections, but with planned themes, discussions, and activities that create a group experience. Whatever the mix, at-risk, urban students are unlikely to make good progress if specific conditions are not created that accommodate their diverse reading levels and interests.

Direct Instruction in Basic Skills

If reading is to be a useful tool for James and Maria, they must learn to interact with text in such a way as to construct meaning; but James and Maria lack this skill, and they are in trouble. Many other students who read poorly do so not because of problems of motivation, cultural deprivation, or learning English as a second language, but because they are learning disabled. These students' reading skills are at a significantly lower level than we would expect based on their aptitude, even if we cannot identify an obvious cause of their difficulties. They will need direct instruction leading to a practical understanding of the subjects they are reading about, and competence in predicting and questioning while reading in order to improve their comprehension.

While we know that students profit from direct instruction (Hare & Borchardt, 1984; Schumaker, Deshler, & Ellis, 1986), in complex curricular areas like comprehending narrative and expository text, this instruction is seldom provided. Although LD students are able to learn comprehension strategies, they are often unable to generalize them to other content areas and settings (Bransford, Arbitman-Smith, Stein, & Vye, 1985). This difficulty in applying appropriately the knowledge or skills learned in one part of the curriculum to another is one of the most debilitating learning problems for which LD students must compensate. These difficulties suggest the need for direct instruction in the broader application of the strategies being taught, for if students cannot effectively read social studies, science, and the newspaper, as well as the fiction on which schools spend so much instructional time, their functional ability to read will remain severely impaired.

Usually efforts to improve reading comprehension have focused on either the text or the reader. Textual manipulations such as using advance organizers (Harley & Davis, 1976), adjunct questions (Anderson & Biddle, 1975), and graphic representations (Schallert, 1980) have sometimes produced increased comprehension of that specific text; however, they have seldom shown positive effects on understanding new texts (Tierney & Cunningham, 1980).

More promising are the instructional methods focused on the reader, with the purpose being to teach students specific ways to understand and find meaning in whatever text they are reading. One way is through understanding the various schemata, or structures, that characterize different types of text, for recent research has suggested that the structure of the text and the expectations in the reader's mind are important in facilitating comprehension (Kintsch & van Dijk, 1978). If you teach the reader the elements that are specific to a genre and have him or her read and interpret using these elements as the schema, or framework, the reader should be able to comprehend better (Rumelhart, 1980).

The effectiveness of questioning strategies incorporated into instruction to prompt readers to become more cognitively active in the comprehension process has been well documented (Dyck & Sundbye, 1988). These procedures include such things as generating questions for future investigation, retelling the content for the purpose of helping to summarize and organize what has been read, and identifying the relationship between postreading comprehension questions and the sources of information used to answer the questions (Raphael & Gavelek, 1984; Raphael & Wonnacott, 1985). Writing and publishing one's own literature, with the endless quest for structure and vocabulary that is inherent in the writing process, builds comprehensions when the student is functioning as a reader (Graves, 1983). The problem is not that we don't know how to improve comprehension skills; it is that we seldom devote the instructional time to do so.

A number of reports of direct instruction in reading comprehension skills have now been published. An interesting first-hand account of a high school literature teacher's shift from concentrating solely on the content of literature to focusing on teaching students how to read literature independently is given by Metzger (1988). She views these learned reading skills, taught through specific instruction, as "tools in a hardware store," tools that will be available to students when they need them.

With elementary school children, Perretti (1989) describes a literature-based process approach which incorporates skills instruction into a remedial reading program. Minilessons are focused on a specific aspect of the reading/writing process such as word attack skills and comprehension. The minilesson is followed by a time for silent reading, journal writing, and discussion with four or five peers. Part of the discussion is based on the agenda created by students' journals, and part is structured by a written question posed by the teacher. Finally, interaction involving the entire class concludes the period.

Instruction which includes basic skills as an essential part of a literature program need not be obtrusive or burdensome; it simply helps students build the competencies they need in order to understand and enjoy what they are reading. Because students want to learn and to succeed, cooperation is usually forthcoming when they realize that they will indeed become more proficient through their participation in the literature and skills program.

CONCLUSION

The teacher's power to influence the learning, taste, and cultural values of generations of students poses an invitation to the profession to excel. The body of research which documents the effectiveness of teaching heterogeneous groups of students how to read while, at the same time, having them read good literature is changing instruction in schools today. The growth of this knowledge base is critical, for teaching urban students with cultural, language, and learning differences requires considerable skill and preparation on the part of the teacher. The first criterion for an effective program is an instructional methodology that evolves from the requirements of individual students, rather than from the tradition of proceeding through the curriculum together; otherwise, the needs of only a few will be met. Second, instructional methods that incorporate teaching interactively, motivating students, setting priorities for individual students as well as for the group, individualizing instruction, and providing direct instruction in basic skills are needed if these at-risk students are to make good progress.

The recent proliferation of inexpensive, printed material has created a veritable feast of literature from which teachers may choose alternatives to offer their students. Fortunately, the days of being bound to a hardback anthology are past. Given the diversity of interest and reading skills of urban students today, the use of a broad selection of reading is essential. Teachers must require students to read challenging books and stories, but they must also provide help with their selection so that those chosen meet students' needs. James and Maria, and also Edith must find literature that they like and from which they will learn, yet they must also be welded into a collaborative group.

Why should these at-risk students make the investment of time and energy in extensive reading in addition to learning their other subjects? For the same reason given in the mid-19th century:

> How many a man has dated a new era in his life from the reading of a book.
> (Thoreau, *Walden*, p. 97)

REFERENCES

Anderson, R.C., & Biddle, B.W. (1975). On asking people questions about what they read. *The Psychology of Learning and Motivation, 9,* 89-132.

Benavides, A. (1988). High risk predictors and preferral screening for language minority students. In A.A. Ortiz & B.A. Ramirez (Eds.), *Schools and the culturally diverse exceptional student: Promising practices and future directions* (pp. 19-31). Reston, VA: Council for Exceptional Children.

Black progress. (1988, January 16). *Wall Street Journal,* p. 14.

Bos, C.S., & Vaughn, S. (1988). *Strategies for teaching students with learning and behavior problems.* Boston: Allyn & Bacon.

Bransford, J.D., Arbitman-Smith, R., Stein, B.S., & Vye, N.J. (1985). Improving thinking and learning skills: An analysis of three approaches. In J.W. Segal, S.F. Chipman, & R. Glaser (Eds.), *Thinking and learning skills* (Vol. 1, pp. 133-206). Hillsdale, NJ: Erlbaum.

Brown, A.L, & Palincsar, A.S. (1985). *Reciprocal teaching of comprehension strategies: A natural history of one program for enhancing learning* (Tech. Rep. No. 334). Urbana, IL: Illinois University, Center for the Study of Reading.

Dyck, N., & Sundbye, N. (1988). The effects of text explicitness on story understanding and recall of learning disabled children. *Learning Disabilities Research, 3*(2), 68-77.

Ellsworth, N.J. (1989). *Using a cognitive schema to teach problem-solving skills to urban, learning-disabled adolescents.* Unpublished doctoral dissertation, Columbia University, Teachers College, New York.

Giles, C. (1989). Reading, writing, and talking: Using literature study groups. *English Journal, 78*(1), 38-41.

Graves, D.H. (1983). *Writing: Teachers and children at work.* Exeter, NH: Heinemann Educational Books.

Hare, V.C., & Borchardt, K.M. (1984). Direct instruction of summarization skills. *Reading Research Quarterly, 20*(1), 62-78.

Harley, J., & Davis, I.K. (1976). Preinstructional strategies: The role of pretests, behavioral objectives, and advance organizers. *Review of Educational Research, 46,* 239-265.

Harrington, D. (1987). *Beyond the four walls: Teacher professionalism in action.* New York; United Federation of Teachers.

Hedley, C.N. (1987). Early reading. In B. Fillion, C.N. Hedley, & E.C. DiMartino (Eds.)., *Home and school: Early language and reading* (pp. 65-79). Norwood, NJ: Ablex Publishing Corp.

Hispanic population found to be growing rapidly. (1986, January 29). *Austin American Statesman,* p. A-11.

Jordan, J.B. (Ed.). (1989). *1988 special education yearbook.* Reston, VA: Council for Exceptional Children.

Kintsch, W., & van Dijk, T. (1978). Toward a model of text comprehension and production. *Psychological Review, 85,* 334-394.

Larson, K.A., & Gerber, M.M. (1987). Effects of social metacognitive training for enhancing overt behavior in learning disabled and low achieving delinquents. *Exceptional Children, 54*(3), 201-211.

National Alliance of Business. (1987). *The fourth R: Workforce readiness.* New York: Author.

National Assessment of Educational Progress. (1990, September). *Accelerating academic achievement: A summary of findings from 20 years of NAEP* (Report No. 19-ov-ol). Princeton, NJ: Educational Testing Service.

Ortiz, A.A., & Yates, J.R. (1988). Characteristics of learning disabled, mentally retarded, and speech-language handicapped Hispanic students at initial evaluation and reevaluation. In A.A. Ortiz & B.A. Ramirez (Eds.), *Schools and the culturally diverse exceptional student: Promising practices and future direction* (pp. 51-62). Reston, VA: Council for Exceptional Children.

Palincsar, A.S., & Brown, A.L. (1988). Teaching and practicing thinking skills to promote comprehension in the context of group problem solving. *Remedial and Special Education (RASE), 9*(1), 53-59.

Perretti, R.T. (1989). Reading improvement groups read novels. *Teaching Teacher, 42*(6), 447-448.

Roettge, D. (1978, May). *Reading attitudes and the Estes scale.* Paper presented at the twenty-third annual convention of the International Reading Association, Houston, TX.

Rumelhart, D.E. (1980). Schemata: The building blocks of cognition. In R.J. Spiro, B.C. Bruce, & W.F. Brewer (Eds.), *Theoretical issues in reading comprehension* (pp. 33-58). Hillsdale, NJ: Erlbaum.

Schallert, D.L. (1980). The role of illustrations in reading comprehension. In R.J. Spiro, B.C. Bruce, & W.F. Brewer (Eds.), *Theoretical issues in reading comprehension* (pp. 503-524). Hillsdale, NJ: Erlbaum.

Schumaker, J.B., Deshler, D.D., & Ellis, E.S. (1986). Intervention issues related to the education of LD adolescents. In J.K. Torgesen & B.Y.L. Wong (Eds.), *Psychological and educational perspectives on learning disabilities* (pp. 329-365). New York: Academic Press.

Tierney, R.J., & Cunningham, J.W. (1980). *Research on teaching reading comprehension* (Tech. Rep. No. 187). Urbana, IL: Center for the Study of Reading, University of Illinois.

U.S. Office of Education. (1990). *Twelfth annual report to Congress on the implementation of the Education of the Handicapped Act.* Washington, DC: Author.

Williams, J.P., & Ellsworth, N.J. (1990). Teaching learning disabled adolescents to think critically using a problem-solving schema. *Exceptionality, 1*(2), 135-146.

Yates, J.R. (1988). Demography as it affects special education. In A.A. Ortiz & B.A Ramirez (Eds.), *Schools and the culturally diverse exceptional student: Promising practices and future directions* (pp. 1-5). Reston, VA: Council for Exceptional Children.
Zeffirelli, F. (Director and Producer). (1968). *Romeo and Juliet* by William Shakespeare. (Videotape reissued by Paramount Pictures, 1988.)

LITERATURE CITED

Alcott, L.M. (1868). *Little women.* Boston: Roberts Brothers.
Hudson, J. (1984). *Sweetgrass.* Alberta, Canada: Tree Frog Press.
Keller, H. (1902). *The story of my life.* Garden City, NY: Doubleday.
Ramirez, J. (1979). *Adventures de Juan Bobo.* Mayaguez, PR: Ediciones Libero.
Thoreau, H.D. (1937). Walden. In B. Atkinson (Ed.), *Walden and other writings of Henry David Thoreau* (pp. 3-297). New York: Random House. (Original work published 1854).
Twain, M. (1885). *The adventure of Huckleberry Finn.* New York: Charles L. Webster.
Wilder, L.I. (1933). *Little house on the prairie.* New York: Harper & Row.
Yep, L. (1979). *Sea glass.* New York: Harper & Row.

RESOURCES FOR THE TEACHER

Books

Adventuring with books: A booklist for pre-k-grade 6. (1985). Ed. by Diane L. Monson and the Committee on the Elementary School Booklist of the National Council of Teachers of English. Urbana, IL: NCTE.
American Indian stereotypes in the world of children: A reader and bibliography. (1982). By Arlene B. Hirschfelder. Metuchen, NJ: Scarecrow Press.
Best books for children: Preschool through the middle grades. (1985, 3rd ed.). Ed. by John T. Gillespie & Christine B. Gilbert. New York: Bowker.
The best in children's books: The University of Chicago guide to children's literature 1966-1972. (1973). Ed. by Zena Sutherland. Chicago: The University of Chicago Press.
The best in children's books: The University of Chicago guide to children's literature 1973-1978. (1980). Ed. by Zena Sutherland. Chicago: The University of Chicago Press.
The best of children's books: 1964-1978: with 1979 addenda. (1980). Ed. by Virginia Haviland. Washington, DC: Library of Congress.
The black experience in children's books. (1984). By Barbara Rollock. New York: New York Public Library.
The bookfinder: A guide to children's literature about the needs and problems of youth aged 2-15. (1981). By Sharon Spredemann Dreyer. Circle Pines, MN: American Guidance Service.

Books and the teenage reader: A guide for teachers, librarians and parents (2nd rev. ed., 1980). G. Robert Carlsen. New York: Harper & Row.

Books for the teen age. (1985 annual). New York: New York Public Library.

Books in American history: A basic list for high school and junior colleges. (2nd ed.). (1981). Ed. By John E. Wiltz and Nancy C. Cridland. IN: Indiana University Press.

Children's books: Awards and prizes. (Revised periodically). Comp. by the Children's Book Council. New York: Children's Book Council.

Children's books in print. (Annual). New York: Bowker.

A comprehensive guide to children's literature with a Jewish theme. (1981). By Enid Davis. New York: Schocken.

Easy reading: Books series and periodicals for less able readers. (1979). By Michael F. Graves, Judith A. Boettcher, & Randall A. Ryder. Newark, DE: International Reading Association.

The Great Lakes region in children's books: A selected annotated bibliography. (1980). Ed. by Donna Taylor. Brighton, MI: Green Oak Press.

A Hispanic heritage: A guide to juvenile books about Hispanic people and cultures. (1980). By Isabel Schon. Metuchen, NJ: Scarecrow Press.

Hispanic heritage: Series II. (1980). By Isabel Schon. Metuchen, NJ: Scarecrow Press.

Index to fairy tales, 1949-1972, including folklore, legends and myths in collections. (1973). Comp. by Normal Olen Irland. Ann Arbor, MI: Faxon.

Indian children's books. (1980). By Hap Gilliland. Billings, MT: Montana Council for Indian Education.

Let's read together: Books for family enjoyment. (4th ed.). (1981). Comp. by Association for Library Service to Children, Let's Read Together Revision Committee. Chicago: American Library Association.

Literature by and about the American Indian: An annotated bibliography. (2nd ed.) (1979). By Anna Lee Stensland. Urbana, IL: National Council of Teachers of English.

More juniorplots: A guide for teachers and librarians. (1977). Ed. by John T. Gillespie. New York: Bowker.

A multimedia approach to children's literature: A selective list of films, filmstrips, and recordings based on children's books. (3rd ed.). (1983). Ed. by Mary Alice Hunt. Chicago: American Library Association.

Newbery medal books: 1922-1955. (1955). Ed. by Bertha Mahony Miller and Elinor Whitney Field. Boston: The Horn Book, Inc.

Newbery and Caldecott medal books: 1956-1965. (1965). Ed. by Lee Kingman. Boston: The Horn Book, Inc.

Newbery and Caldicott medal books: 1966-1975. (1975). Ed. by Lee Kingman. Boston: The Horn Book, Inc.

Notable children's books, 1940-1970. (1977). Comp. by Children's Service Division. Chicago: American Library Association.

Notable children's books, 1971-1975. (1981). Comp. by 1971-1975 Notable Children's Books Re-evaluation Committee, Association for Library Service to Children. Chicago: American Library Association.

Notes from a different drummer: A guide to juvenile fiction portraying the handicapped. (1977). Comp. by Barbara Baskin and Karen Haris. Boston: Bowker.

A parent's guide to children's reading. (5th ed.). (1982). By Nancy Larrick. Louisville, KY: Westminster Press.

Periodicals for school media programs: A guide to magazines, newspapers, periodical indexes (rev. ed.). (1978). Comp. by Selma Richardson. Chicago: American Library Association.

Reading for young people: The great plains. (1979). Ed. by Mildred Laughlin. Chicago: American Library Association.

Reading for young people: Kentucky, Tennessee, West Virginia. (1985). Ed. by Barbara Mertins. Chicago: American Library Association.

Reading for young people: The middle Atlantic. (1980). Ed. by Arabelle Pennypacker. Chicago: American Library Association.

Reading for young people: The Mississippi Delta. (1984). Ed. by Cora Matheny Dorsett. Chicago: American Library Association.

Reading for young people: The Northwest. (1981). Ed. by Mary Meacham. Chicago: American Library Association.

Reading for young people: The Rocky Mountains. (1980). Ed. by Dorothy Heald. Chicago: American Library Association.

Reading for young people: The Southeast. (1980). Ed. by Dorothy Heald. Chicago: American Library Association.

Reading for young people: The Southwest. (1980). Ed. by Elva Harmon and Anna L. Milligan. Chicago: American Library Association.

Reading for young people: The Upper Midwest. (1981). Ed. by Marion F. Archer. Chicago: American Library Association.

A reference guide to modern fantasy for children. (1984). By Pat Pflieger. Westport, CT: Greenwood Press.

Science books for children: Selections from booklists, 1976-1983. (1983). Selected by Denise M. Wilms. Chicago: American Library Association.

Special collections in children's literature. (1982). Ed. by Carolyn W. Field. Chicago: American Library Association.

Periodicals

Appraisal: Science Books for Young People. Boston: Boston University School of Education.

The Booklist. Chicago: American Library Association.

The Bulletin of the Center for Children's Books. Chicago: Graduate Library School, University of Chicago Press.

The Horn Book Magazine. Boston: Horn Book.

Interracial Books for Children. New York: Council on Interracial Books for Children.

Journal of Reading. Newark, DE: International Reading Association.

Science Books and Films. San Francisco: American Association for the Advancement of Science.

Author Index

Subject Index